THE TRUMAN AND EISENHOWER BLUES

THE TRUMAN AND EISENHOWER BLUES

African-American Blues and Gospel Songs, 1945–1960

Guido van Rijn

continuum
LONDON • NEW YORK

Continuum

The Tower Building
11 York Road
London SE1 7NX

15 East 26th Street
New York
NY 10010

First published 2004

For further copyright information see p. xiv.

British Library Cataloguing-in-Publication Data

A catalogue record for this book is available from the British Library.

ISBN 0-8264-5657-X (hardback)
    0-8264-5658-8 (paperback)

Library of Congress Cataloging-in-Publication Data

Rijn, Guido van, 1950–
        The Truman and Eisenhower blues : African-American blues and gospel songs, 1945–1960 / Guido van Rijn.
            p. cm. –
        Includes bibliographical references and index.
        ISBN 0-8264-5657-X – ISBN 0-8264-5658-8 (pb.)
            1. Blues (Music) – Political aspects. 2. Gospel music – Political aspects 3. African Americans – Music – Political aspects. 4. Truman, Harry S., 1884–1972 – Songs and music – History and criticism. 5. Eisenhower, Dwight D. (Dwight David), 1890–1969 – Songs and music – History and criticism. I. Title. II. Series.

        ML3521.R56 2003
        782.421643´1599—dc21

                                                                                                2003043560

Typeset by Kenneth Burnley, Wirral, Cheshire
Printed and bound in Great Britain

CONTENTS

FOREWORD

Ever since the Negro spirituals first reached a broader public consciousness in the years during and immediately following the Civil War, African-American folk-songs and their popular extensions in blues and gospel song have been viewed by listeners, critics, collectors, and scholars as expressions of an entire race within America, or at least of a vast portion of that race, one that had few other outlets of expression that left any lasting record. With few exceptions, the singers and composers of these songs were not the writers of poems, books, articles, and letters to the editors of newspapers. They were not leaders in politics, the church, and business. Many, particularly those involved mainly in secular music, were not even members of churches, labor unions, or other organizations. Yet they had opinions about the world around them, they served as organizers of the opinions of others and, with the help of mass media such as phonograph records, as spokespersons for millions of people from similar back-grounds. While their songs were created and intended almost entirely for hearing and circulation within their own social group, many curious and sym-pathetic listeners of a more formally educated and literate class have found these songs to be an invaluable key to understanding this group which otherwise often seems inarticulate, inscrutable, or threatening. These songs not only provide insight into another social world, but they entertain and please the ear with their artistry. Unintentionally perhaps, they bridge some of the great social and racial divides that America has created, as well as providing spiritual and artistic nourishment for the victims of these divides.

Writers and scholars have concentrated on three major domains in the study of the lyrics of African-American folk, blues, and gospel songs. They have seen them as examples of literary expression, as reflections of daily life and living conditions, and as expressions of opinion and psychological states. Even when

concentrating on one of these domains, most writers have shown some awareness of the others. In searching for literary expression, one can hardly avoid the
social content of these songs, and with opinion and description of daily life often
comes great artistry.

Early-twentieth-century writers and collectors, such as Howard Odum, Guy
Johnson, Newman White, Dorothy Scarborough and John A. Lomax, saw the
song lyrics as examples of the "folk poetry" or "folk psychology" of "the Negro."
Although some indicated that they were struck by the power and artistry of particular performances and the personalities of some of their informants, for the
most part they treated the songs as anonymous collective expression. Odum,
however, felt compelled to create a composite character, a Black Ulysses, to be
the voice for many of the songs he had collected in the South, and Scarborough
consulted black songwriter W. C. Handy as an expert on the meaning of the
blues. Lomax did provide the names of his informants along with occasional bits
of biographical information. In 1934 he displayed his star informant, Huddie Ledbetter ("Leadbelly"), an ex-convict no less, as a living representative of the black
folksong tradition, taking him around to concerts at universities. Little did Lomax
realize at the time that he had unleashed a creative musical force with a mind of
his own and a desire to build a professional career as a performing artist, a man
who would, in fact, become an important voice on a variety of political and social
issues, including the fight against Jim Crow.

It was the twin forces of musical professionalism and commercialism that
forced writers and scholars away from the simplistic interpretation of these
songs as expressions of "the Negro" and toward a more multi-faceted approach
that would take into consideration the personalities and varieties of life experience and opinion of individual singers and composers. W. C. Handy himself
served as a bridge to this new understanding. In his 1926 collection *Blues: An
Anthology* and his 1941 autobiography *Father of the Blues*, Handy discussed the
specific circumstances of his encounters with folksongs and his transformations
of this material into his own popular compositions. In the former book he also
included the works of several other blues songwriters. Handy viewed his source
material as exploitable common property for musically literate composers like
himself and his own compositions as works deserving the protection of copyright. Nevertheless, in dipping so deeply into the common well of
African-American folksong, he set himself up as a spokesperson for his entire
race and his life as an example of progress from the status of anonymous
"Negro" to that of an American household name.

Concerts by performers like Leadbelly, compositions by songwriters like Handy, and especially phonograph records by countless blues and gospel artists brought these songs to the attention of millions of Americans and interested listeners overseas. By 1960 enough records had been issued and enough large private collections built that a British record collector and scholar, Paul Oliver, could publish a book called *The Meaning of the Blues*. In this and several subsequent publications, Oliver examined the variety of themes and opinion in a large sampling of commercial recordings made between 1920 and 1943, showing how these songs reflected a black American working-class culture with rural and urban, sacred and secular, dimensions, exhibiting change and variety over space and time, and studded with individual personalities.

The early folksong scholars and collectors had not ignored songs that dealt with themes of politics, economic conditions, wars, and race relations. Particularly noteworthy were John J. Niles' *Singing Soldiers* (1927) and Howard W. Odum's *Wings on My Feet* (1929), both of which discussed the songs and experiences of black American soldiers during World War I. But all of these studies were weakened by their authors' insistence on revealing the mood and expression of "the Negro." By the 1940s and 1950s the overwhelming number of blues songs on themes of love, romance, and sex, and gospel songs on themes of sin and salvation made it appear that there were few, if any, African-American songs on these broader sociopolitical topics. To remedy this apparent lack, left-wing ideologues encouraged singers like Josh White and Leadbelly to create and record new "folksongs" of protest against fascism, racism, and economic exploitation. Some scholars, like Miles Mark Fisher in his *Negro Slave Songs in the United States* (1953), examined folksongs of earlier eras, claiming to detect coded references to historical events and messages of black resistance. While Fisher could not substantiate most of his interpretations with clear evidence and while Josh White and Leadbelly sometimes seemed like isolated voices of protest directed at sympathetic ears mostly outside their own communities, the need for new sociopolitical songs was eventually met in the early 1960s by the civil rights movement's adaptation of spiritual and gospel songs in support of its cause. In the arena of scholarship Paul Oliver's *The Meaning of the Blues* revealed a rich vein of sociopolitical commentary, including protest, in blues on "race records" that had been recorded and intended for sale almost entirely within the American black community.

Oliver and other scholars who examined these records in the 1960s and following years were hampered somewhat by an inability to acquire and listen to all of the known and possibly relevant recordings and by fragmentary background information on the singers and the historical events and social conditions underlying the songs. Not until the mid-1990s were all of the factors in place that would allow a more sophisticated and detailed analysis of the lyric content of this material. These factors were the reissue on LPs and CDs of virtually all of the African-American blues, gospel, and folk material recorded up to 1943 and a great amount recorded after that date; a worldwide network of research-oriented record collectors ready and willing to fill in gaps where reissue albums were lacking; comprehensive blues and gospel discographies running up to 1970; and an enormous new body of literature about singers, composers, and record companies and about African-American history and culture.

Exploiting these resources (and having helped to build many of them over the years), Guido van Rijn undertook to examine *all* of the recorded African-American songs containing overt commentary on political events and issues during the years 1933–1945. His *Roosevelt's Blues: African-American Blues and Gospel Songs on FDR* (1997), with a foreword by Paul Oliver, arranges these songs thematically and chronologically, relating them to specific historical events, personalities, issues, and programs. Information about individual singers, songwriters, record companies, and recording sessions is all brought to bear, when appropriate, to explain particular song texts, and the latter are transcribed with great accuracy. Only a very small percentage of the total number of songs recorded during this period dealt with political topics, but van Rijn shows that such songs were recorded by a representative range of blues and gospel singers. Although they often mixed political opinion with humor, sexual themes, religious doctrine, and other highly personal concerns, and tended to view President Roosevelt as a benevolent and powerful patron or "bossman" able to protect and intervene directly in their lives, the singers nevertheless displayed an incipient political consciousness. That is impressive when one considers that these singers were almost totally shut out from the political process during this period except as recipients of government relief during the Depression and soldiers during World War II. Roosevelt's willingness to listen to African-American voices and to take action on their behalf led singer Otis Jackson to memorialize him with the following lines:

> *Only two presidents that I ever felt:*
> *Abraham Lincoln and Roosevelt.*

In the present study Guido van Rijn has tackled the somewhat more problematical task of examining the blues and gospel songs dealing with political topics during the presidencies of Harry S. Truman and Dwight D. Eisenhower (1945–1960). Once again attempting to survey all of the known material, the author shows that these songs do not present a view of nearly total approbation as they did for President Roosevelt. Truman was seen as a sometimes fallible leader who, despite his actions and directives in support of equal rights, was not able to control fluctuations in the economy, could not hasten racial progress fast enough, and got America into an unwinnable war in Korea. Eisenhower, after an initial burst of enthusiasm for his arranging of the Korean armistice, came to be seen as unresponsive to the economic plight of black people as well as their growing demands for equal rights. By the time of his second term of office, singers were virtually ignoring him and his administration altogether, just as they had ignored the unresponsive Presidents before Roosevelt. Having gained a hold on the development of political thought and an incipient sense of involvement during the Roosevelt era, blues and gospel singers, as van Rijn shows, displayed a greater awareness of abstract political issues during the Truman and Eisenhower years and less concentration on the personalities and deeds of the Presidents themselves. His masterful study is one of the few lengthy examinations of any body of commercially recorded blues and gospel lyrics after World War II. It prepares us for the momentous era of the 1960s. Let us hope that Guido van Rijn will examine the songs of that period with the same thoroughness that he displays here and in his previous work.

David Evans
The University of Memphis

ACKNOWLEDGMENTS

My lifelong involvement with the blues began in 1962 in the first form of Pius X Lyceum in Amsterdam, when my music teacher, Nico Hermans, played a record of "Pinetop's Boogie Woogie" to the class. A few years later Arend Jan Heerma van Voss led me to the Dutch magazine *Jazz Wereld* (1965–1973) and later to the British journal *Blues Unlimited* (1963–1987).

In 1970, the late Martin van Olderen and I founded the Dutch Blues and Boogie Organization, and together we organized the first concerts by American blues artists. My thinking on blues in those early years was greatly influenced by Leo Bruin, Herman Engelbart, Rob Hoeke, and Wim Verbei. In 1978 I started the Agram Blues reissue label, and have since produced eighteen albums. My friends Hans Vergeer and Cor van Sliedregt have been closely associated with this project. I am indebted to the editors of specialist periodicals such as *Blues Unlimited*, *Blues & Rhythm*, *Juke Blues* and *Living Blues* for publishing articles that I have written.

The late Max Vreede (1927–1991) became a respected friend, and many evenings spent discovering treasure trove in his collection of 78-rpm records did much to deepen my understanding of the blues.

When an opportunity to embark upon a thesis arose, I took as my subject blues and gospel songs about American Presidents. I decided to concentrate on President Franklin Roosevelt and make a deeper analysis of songs specifically relating to him and his presidency. The progress of the Roosevelt manuscript was supervised by Alfons Lammers, Professor of American History at Leiden University, and David Evans, Professor of Music at the University of Memphis. The Ph.D. ceremony took place at Leiden University on 19 October 1995, with Chris Smith and Jan Spoelder as my "paranimfs".

As was the case with *Roosevelt's Blues*, the influence of both Chris Smith and

David Evans is felt throughout the present work, both in the analysis of the songs and in the accuracy of their transcription. Brian Ward, Professor of History at the University of Florida, urged me to publish the present book, generously lent me his massive knowledge of American civil rights history, and made useful suggestions about the structure of this book. Caroline Wintersgill, Alexandra Webster, Janet Joyce and David Barker, my editors at Continuum, have supported the project from the start with wise advice and gentle encouragement.

A number of other people contributed ideas, support and information, and I extend my thanks to Ray Astbury, Eric Bentley, Alasdair Blaazer, John Broven, Leo Bruin, Tony Burke, Sandranette Chenet-Hairston, John Cowley, Bob Eagle, Simon Evans, Byron Foulger, Peter Goldsmith, Daniel Gugolz, Cedric Hayes, Jaap Hindriks, Robert Javors, Tom Kelly, Klaus Kilian, Dan Kochakian, Mike Kredinac, Alfons Lammers, Robert Laughton, Kip Lornell, Dave Moore, John Newman, Tom Neylon, Paul Oliver, Johnny Parth, George Paulus, Victor Pearlin, Gerard Robs, Mike Rowe, Tony Russell, Howard Rye, Robert Sacré, Richard Shurman, Neil Slaven, Jan Spoelder, Robert Springer, Bob Stone, Steve Tracy, Billy Vera, Wim Verbei, Hans Vergeer, Tony Watson, Hans Westerduijn, George White and Rien Wisse.

Much research was conducted in libraries and/or by librarians at my request, and I would especially like to thank the Kennedy Institute of Freie Universität in Berlin; the library of Vrije Universiteit, Amsterdam; Leiden University Library; the Koninklijke Bibliotheek, The Hague; Rob Kroes of the Amerika Instituut of the Universiteit van Amsterdam; Hans Krabbendam of the Roosevelt Study Center, Middelburg; Bill Fischer, Reference Technician of the Center for Electronic Records; and Robert L. Stone, Outreach Coordinator of the Florida Folklife Program.

Finally, I must thank my wife, Nelleke, and my children, Paul and Emily, for their continued and unstinting support. With their backing, *Kennedy's Blues* should become a reality as well.

Copyright

ABBREVIATIONS

AAA	Agricultural Adjustment Administration/Agency (1933–1945)
AFM	American Federation of Musicians
AME	African Methodist Episcopal Church
CIO	Congress of Industrial Organization
COD	cash on delivery
CWA	Civil Works Administration (1933–1934)
FDR	Franklin Delano Roosevelt
FEPC	Fair Employment Practices Committee
GE	General Electric
GI	Government Issue
NAACP	National Association for the Advancement of Colored People
NATO	North Atlantic Treaty Organization
NRA	National Recovery Administration (1933–1935)
OPA	Office of Price Administrations (1941–1946)
PDQ	pretty damn quick
PWA	Public Works Administration (1933–1941)
RCA	Recording Company of America
ROK	Republic of Korea
UAW	United Automobile Workers of America
VJ	Victory over Japan (2 September 1945)
WPA	Works Progress Administration (1933–1943)

For Nelleke, Paul and Emily

INTRODUCTION

Despite the growing literature on the black experience during the twentieth century, there are still many important and under-appreciated elements of African-American history and culture that can be usefully illuminated by close analysis of black musical forms. This is no simple task, however. It is only by dogged perseverance and openness to the diverse signals and shades of meaning imbedded in black music that a more comprehensive view of the black experience in the United States can emerge. Yet, the call of this music demands to be heard and responded to; historians of blues and gospel must learn how "to signify," to borrow the verb from the black idiom that Henry Louis Gates Jr. uses to characterize the process of establishing complex, mutually dependent intertextual relationships in black culture.[1] In other words, in order to hear, understand and interpret blues and gospel songs accurately, the musicologist needs to consider their connections, not just to other songs in the black repertoire, but also to a whole range of black and white cultural creations and historical circumstances that help to determine their meanings and significances. This book pursues that goal by examining those blues and gospel songs from the period 1945 to 1960 which dealt explicitly with the great social and economic concerns of the day.

For outsiders, the blues is often merely entertainment. But for the African-American working class in particular, the music is also a social ritual that "reinforces a sense of order in life and preserves the shared wisdom of the group."[2] Literary theory may help to crack the encodings of black music, but the ways in which it has reflected the social life of a people has often been obscured by what Gates calls a "lack of sophisticated scholarly attention" to its historical context.[3] Since the early 1920s, thousands of blues and gospel songs have been recorded, but these important resources have seldom been used by historians in any systematic manner. Charles Wolfe, who has written extensively on American music, believes that listening to the blues is the best way to get at "the thought, spirit and history of the very segment of the Negro community that historians have rendered inarticulate through their neglect."[4] As Lawrence Levine has observed, "By largely ignoring this tradition, much of which has been preserved, historians have rendered an articulate people historically inarticulate, and have allowed the record of their consciousness to go unexplored."[5] This book represents an attempt to revisit the lost consciousness and restore the silenced voices of many African Americans by revisiting the blues and gospel songs of the Truman and Eisenhower years.

Blues lyrics usually deal with experiences common to the singer and his or her audience. Although the lyrics are frequently imaginative – allusive or allegorical – they are usually based on personal experience and thus invoke or even imitate a tangible reality. Many songs allow the artists and their audiences to escape temporarily from hardship by a celebration of "the joys and frustrations of love," as David Evans has argued in an analysis of blues lyricism. In particular, the blues is rich in sexual imagery. Evans explains the emphasis on the man–woman relationship in two ways: "It is the area most subject to daily change and fluctuation in people's lives, and it is closely related to the dancing and partying context in which blues are most often performed." Ultimately, most blues revolved around the success or failure, anticipation or loss, of romance and sex. Meanwhile, most gospel music revolved around either the sweet anticipation of a just and humane Promised Land somewhere in the future or the invocation of the Lord's help to survive the hardships of the here and now. By contrast with these themes, overt political commentary in recorded blues and gospel songs was very rare until the late 1960s. This may have been because of the fear of dire consequences for any artist or label seen to be challenging the racial status quo in song. But it was also a function of the way in which the politics of the blues worked. Blues is not usually directly about racial discrimination; rather, racism is considered implicitly, in terms of its consequences. However, as Evans observes, the singers may unconsciously have channeled "the problem of discrimination into less controversial areas."[6]

The primary aim of my first book, *Roosevelt's Blues* (1997), was to shed some light on why FDR became so popular among African Americans in the 1930s by analyzing those blues and gospel lyrics of his era that featured explicit social and political comment. Hidden in the grooves of the old 78-rpm recordings, the black voices of the period could still be heard. A painstaking transcription of the lyrics revealed the emotional coordinates as well as the more pragmatic rationale for black attachment to Roosevelt in ways that few other sources could match. The sheer frequency of songs about FDR spoke volumes about his significance in black lives and consciousness. Only four of the seven Presidents from the period 1901–1945 are mentioned in known blues and gospel lyrics, and those only in isolated examples. Theodore Roosevelt, Wilson and Hoover hardly received any attention from the blues and gospel singers. Taft, Harding and Coolidge were ignored altogether. In contrast, after 1933 no fewer than 40 songs were directly devoted to Franklin Delano Roosevelt. The vast majority, if by no means all, of these songs were highly favorable in content.

In February 1997 the commercial edition of my thesis was published by the University Press of Mississippi under the title: *Roosevelt's Blues: African-American Blues and Gospel Songs on FDR*. The accompanying CD (Agram Blues ABCD 2017) is still available from the author.

Since then my research into the Presidents after Roosevelt has continued. *The Truman and Eisenhower Blues* continues the analysis into the Cold War years from 1945 to 1960. An advantage of the coupling of the two Presidents has been that reactions to the whole of the Korean War can be discussed without interruption. Single chapters have been devoted to Truman and Eisenhower's varying responses to economic and civil rights issues and the way in which they were perceived by the African-American community. Truman's decision to use the atomic bomb yielded enough material for a further chapter on that issue alone; and another technological development with major political implications, the space race under Eisenhower, forms a major part of a subsequent chapter.

When FDR died in 1945, World War II was still in progress and African Americans were still working for a "Double V": a victory over Fascism abroad, and a concomitant victory over discrimination at home. Black servicemen and women had again proved their fighting spirit, democratic idealism, and basic patriotism when the nation called, and the hope was that after the war, both the armed forces and civilian society would accept black Americans on a basis of equality. As the long-lost blues and gospel songs analyzed in this book so vividly reveal, during the fifteen years that followed the end of the war, those dreams and aspirations were only partially fulfilled. Certainly, the songs reflect a very different, generally more hostile, black response to the Truman and Eisenhower administrations than was the case during the Roosevelt presidency. At the same time, however, alongside the obvious black frustration with continued racism and discrimination, one can also detect a rising tide of militancy, determination, and urgency in some of the songs, reflecting the new black consciousness that would find political expression in the civil rights movement of the late 1950s and 1960s. The songs analyzed in this book thus illuminate black consciousness at a crucial, transitional moment in the black experience, just as a new era of mass activism and protest was emerging.

A Technical Note

The majority of recordings had always been issued on brittle ten-inch 78-rpm records, but in 1949 RCA Victor introduced the "unbreakable" seven-inch 45-rpm record. The 1950s were a transition period and consequently many of the records discussed in this book were issued in both formats.

Accurate discographical details about post-war records are much harder to obtain than for those recorded before the war, because of the change from a limited number of big companies to a host of obscure, independent post-war labels. The latter often operated erratic book-keeping systems, the data of which can now only be gleaned from the labels of the rare 78s and 45s. Consequently we are often at a loss about precise recording dates and sometimes locations. This makes the present research more difficult than the study on the Roosevelt era. Fortunately in most cases, the recording locations are known, and the origins of most singers can be established by biographical research.

Lyrics are always presented in their complete form, although repetitions of lines have been omitted for reasons of space. The utmost attention has been given to accurate transcription, but the songs should preferably be heard for the full emotional impact of their messages to be communicated, and accordingly a CD (Agram Blues ABCD 2018) is available with the book. Full discographical details are given in the notes in order that the songs quoted, but not included on the CD, may be followed up for listening purposes.

PACIFIC

BERKELEY   CALIFORNIA

601 B

RECONVERSION BLUES

(HUNTER)

IVORY JOE HUNTER
AND HIS BAND

1036

I THOSE RECONVERSION BLUES

In Delmer Daves's film *Hollywood Canteen* from 1944, the Golden Gate Quartet, the popularizers of the rhythmic spiritual, sang a song entitled "The General Jumped at Dawn," which stressed the multi-ethnic nature of the army and looked back at the Normandy invasion. In order to "have a barbecue in Berlin" the general needed every available soldier, irrespective of his origins. Although the fully mobilized American army was segregated during World War II, the song expressed hope for an end to discrimination after victory. In the March 1945 studio recording of the James R. Mundy and Larry Orenstein composition, "The General Jumped at Dawn," the word "jump" is used as a pun on "parachute drop" and "dance."

> Says the captain to the General: "Pops, we're gonna cause a commotion,"
> Then one early morn they up and gone, the general jumped, he jumped at dawn.
> Says the general to the captain: "Man, we're gonna battle the Channel,"
> Then one early morn they up and gone, the general jumped, he jumped at dawn.
>
> Bye bye, bye bye,
> I'll see you in the sky at Versailles,
> Drop in, drop in,
> We'll have a barbecue in Berlin.

chorus: *Says the private to the general: "Jack, my jeep is ready and steady,"*
Then one early morn they up and gone, the general jumped, he jumped at dawn.

Well, the general had a groovy crew,
A million lads and I'm telling you,
There were white men, red men on the beam,
A real, solid all American team,
He had tall men, small men, fat and lean,
The fightingest crew that you've ever seen,
Every creed, every color and every belief,
From an Eskimo to an Indian Chief.

He had a sergeant Swenson, a corporal Kelly,
Rosenberg and a cook Morelli,
Lieutenant Jackson and a Private Joe,
When the general said: "Let's hit the road."

Well, jump, two, three, four,
Remember, boys, we gotta win the war![1]

All the blues and gospel songs analyzed in *Roosevelt's Blues* show strong support for the President. Criticism of FDR by black singers is very rare indeed. A noteworthy exception is "The Induction Blues" by the Lorenzo Flennoy Trio. More than ten million men entered the armed forces through the Selective Service System from 1940 to 1946, including 945,862 in 1945, when this song was recorded.[2] Vocalist Jimmie Edwards is war-weary and blames Roosevelt personally for his induction, albeit with a degree of humor when he describes his vain attempt to find a job at the shipyard in order to escape the draft and basic training in the notoriously inhospitable camps of Texas. The lyrics of this uncharacteristically critical song make it clear that it was recorded in Roosevelt's final hundred days, since the singer reveals that he has already voted for FDR on four occasions.

Yes, I got my greetings this mornin', cool chills ran up and down my spine,
Yes, I got 'em from the President, and I voted for him four times.

Said, I ran down to the shipyard, they said, "Boy, you can't come in,
We ain't hirin' nothin' here, but chicks and one-legged men."

Now, I'm standin' at the induction station, standin' in that great, great, great, long line,
Whoever started all this mess, sure ain't no friend of mine.

Western Union, Western Union, please write down me a telegram,
I want to send it to the President and charge it to my Uncle Sam.

Dear, dear, dear Mr. President, twelve long years we've been good friends,
Now, if you send me down in Texas, that's where our friendship ends, friendship ends.[3]

During the three months of his fourth term (from 20 January 1945 to 12 April 1945) President Roosevelt was a very sick man, but his death still sent a shockwave through the nation. In the many *in memoriam* blues and gospel songs the late President was virtually sanctified. Josh White (1914–1969), probably the only blues singer that Roosevelt knew personally, recorded a eulogy entitled "The Man Who Couldn't Walk Around." Given the efforts to hide FDR's disability from the general public, this was a pretty bold title for the song. By emphasizing the President's achievements despite a handicap, White may have been encouraging blacks to strive to achieve despite the "handicap" of color in US society. White must have been grief-stricken when his President died, but the mood of this dignified song is resolutely optimistic: White insists that FDR's legacy must not be wasted.

Little boy, oh sober face,
Oh, crutch that lies beside you,
Rubber wheels to ride you.

Little boy, let your fairest fancies wander,
With the great commander,
One who had to sit as still as you.

I'm dreaming of a man we knew,
Who loved us all, we loved him too,
I mean a man, who couldn't walk around.

He wore a cloak of navy blue,
We made him captain of our crew,
I mean a man who couldn't walk around.

My friends, United Nations, Lend Lease, the March of Dimes,
We trusted him in trouble,
We cheered his name four times.

We served the guns he manned for us,
We'll do the things he planned for us,
That certain man, who couldn't walk around.

Little boy, look up and smile,
And grasp the chance he gave you,
Let his courage save you.

Little boy, though your world is full of sorrow,
There is still tomorrow,
Even though one sits as still as you.

I'm dreaming of a laugh we heard,
The broadest smile, the bravest words,
I mean a man who couldn't walk around.

He shook the earth, the sky and seas,
And couldn't even move his knees,
That certain man who couldn't walk around.

One afternoon in Georgia, he slept away, they say,
But people across the oceans,
Still praise his name today.

He's watching from the highest hill,
His nerve is in this nation still,
That certain man who couldn't walk around.[4]

"The Man Who Couldn't Walk Around" was written by MacKinlay Kantor and all royalties went to the Infantile Paralysis Foundation. Josh White sang it at the President's birthday ball in 1947. He later said that this occasion was the only time he ever saw Mrs. Roosevelt cry, and he made the song a regular part of his concert programs.[5] *Variety* magazine commented in 1947: "Its message is to polio victims to take heart from the example of the late President Roosevelt and it makes a perfect addition to the White House repertoire of folk and pseudo-folk tunes."[6]

Roosevelt's successor Harry S. Truman was born in Lamar, Missouri, on 8 May 1884, the son of a livestock farmer and trader. During World War I he served in France as an artillery battery commander. After the war he opened a men's clothing store in Kansas City, which he had to close in the Depression. In 1924 he became judge in the Eastern District of Jackson County. It took him only one year to become presiding judge. As a protégé of Thomas J. Pendergast, the "big boss" politician of Kansas City, he became junior senator from Missouri for the Democratic Party in 1935.

As a senator, Truman supported Roosevelt's New Deal measures and made his reputation by his efficient leadership of the Senate Special Committee to Investigate the Defense Program in 1943. On 20 January 1945 he became Roosevelt's Vice President in succession to Henry Wallace, who had lost the support of both the President and the Democratic Convention. Only a few days after Truman was sworn in following Roosevelt's fatal cerebral hemorrhage,[7] a topical salute entitled "God Bless Our New President!" was recorded by blues piano player "Champion" Jack Dupree (1909–1992). It was issued as the flipside of the eulogy "F.D.R. Blues."[8] On 28 April, only ten days after the session, the record was advertised in *Billboard* as a "new sensational timely 'blues' record," but only 420 copies were sold. In contrast two of the non-political 78s by Dupree from this session sold around 5000 copies each.[9] The reason for the discrepancy is unknown.

> *May God bless our new President!*
> *Because I believe he was heavenly sent.*
>
> *He sure got a tough job, and it is on his hands,*
> *To try to bring peace, brotherly love to our land.*

Stand behind our President Truman, each and every one of you,
For you know that's what FDR would want us to do.

It is our duty, put our shoulders to the wheel,
Harry Truman would be our friend just as I feel.

Oh, it's a hard thing, to fill FDR's shoes,
But if we all would help, ooh, well, well, I swear we cannot lose.[10]

After the Germans and the Japanese had surrendered American soldiers could return home. Blues singer Walter Brown (1917–1956) recorded "I'm Glad to Be Back" as the flipside of a 1945 remake of his hit song "Confessin' the Blues." Brown sang that he had been a soldier for three years and saw his friends lying dead at his feet. He has learned how to put life into perspective, and developed a pragmatic outlook. He realizes that his girlfriend has not been faithful to him, but is resigned to the fact that she had been "used but not bruised."

Advertisement for Champion Jack Dupree, "God Bless Our New President!," Joe Davis 5102, *Billboard*, 28 April 1945.

(I wanna) call my babe, but she has no telephone,
I wanna call and tell her that her G.I.'s come back home.

I've been gone three years, but it seems like five or six,
I wanna find my baby and get some fine old kicks.

I've been everywhere, seen everything,
I missed my baby and her wild little swing.
That's why I'm glad to be back, yes, I'm glad to be back,
Things may not be like they used to, boys, but I'm glad to be back.

I gave up all my pleasures, had nothing to eat,
Even saw my best friends, laying dead at my feet.
That's why I'm glad to be back, yes, I'm glad to be back,
It was a tough pill to swallow, boys, but I'm glad to be back.

So when I run across my baby, made my own post-war plan,
I've been away, but I'm still her best man.
That's why I'm glad to be back, yes, I'm glad to be back,
She's been used but not bruised, boy, and I'm glad to be back.[11]

On 2 September 1945 the war ended in victory over Japan. The following month New Orleans piano player Cousin Joe (1907–1989) sang "My post-war future has been planned since V-J Day." The lyrics voiced a common sentiment among soldiers, and *Modern Screen Magazine* declared the song "record of the month."[12]

My post-war future, has been planned since V-J Day,
Now that it's all over, I'm going back to the USA.

We've been fightin' in the east, we've been fightin' in the west,
Now I'm going back home, to take my proper rest.

chorus: *That's my post-war future, when I get back home,*
Now that it's all over, no more battlefields will I roam.

I'm gonna buy that little cottage, I'm gonna build it on my farm,
So me and my baby, can call it our happy home.

We gonna raise some chickens, we gonna raise some ducks,
We gonna raise some children, if we have any luck.
We gonna raise two little boys, and we gonna raise a little girl,
So we can live our happy lives, in this free and peaceful world.[13]

Joseph Pleasant (Cousin Joe), NBBO Blues Festival, Amstelveen, The Netherlands, 2 March 1974. Photo by Hans ten Have.

The week after the Japanese surrender the *Chicago Defender* announced that in Chicago alone, 50,000 African Americans would be laid off by Christmas: 5000 at Dodge Chicago Plant, 2000 at Buick Motors, 900 at Pressed Steel and no fewer than 15,000 at US War Agencies.[14] Seven hundred thousand GIs were expected back home in a year and the United States economy had to be "reconverted" to peaceful purposes. Expectations were high; after rationing and price control, Americans wanted to be able to buy whatever they liked at reasonable prices. Louis Jordan (1908–1975) was a saxophone player, bandleader and songwriter, who recorded prolifically from 1937 to 1974. One of the most popular rhythm and blues artists in his day, he was billed as "King of the Jukeboxes." Jordan articulated public opinion when he sang his "Reconversion Blues" in October 1945.

I got those re-, reconversion blues,

Can't wait to buy a new automobile and a pair of two-tone shoes.

I can walk right past my draft board, and I won't get no dirty looks,

I can go down to see my grocer, without taking my ration books,

I got those re-, reconversion blues,

I can drive in a gas station and get most anything I choose.

I forgot the taste of bacon and of butter and whipped cream cake,

At night I wake up screaming: "Bring me a nice, fat, juicy steak,"

I got those re-, reconversion blues,

I'm gonna buy my baby nylons, gonna buy her all that she can use.

No more fish on Tuesdays, I get plenty meat in my stews,

There's plenty of cigarettes and chewing gum and nuts and bolts and screws,

Got those re-, reconversion blues,

If someone say: "For the duration," brother, I'm gonna blow my fuse.

I'm gonna reconvert my baby with a house and a diamond ring,

We're gonna lock our doors this winter and we won't come out till spring,

I got those re-, reconversion blues,

I'm gonna buy a brand new radio, that don't know how to get the latest news.[15]

"When A Feller Needs Friends," cartoon by Melvin Yapley, *New York Amsterdam News*, 29 September 1945.

By 1946 people were tired of wartime limitations and finally wanted to live life to the full again. In its ingenious last line, which expresses a wish to retreat from the affairs of the world, "Reconversion Blues" articulates the fear of another war and its accompanying restrictions.

Plans for the post-war welfare of the nation were outlined in a 21-point reconversion program, which included an extension of the Fair Employment Practices Committee (FEPC), increased unemployment benefits, full employment, raising the minimum wage, increased housing, public works development, maintenance of U.S. Employment Offices under federal auspices, agricultural aid to the small farmer, aid to small business, and eleven other ambitious economic and political controls. The African-American *New York Amsterdam News* opined that this was no time for fights between Republicans and Democrats, writing in its 29 September 1945 editorial that the problems of reconversion called for a sense of national unity: "Any politician who puts party or personality before these bread-and-butter issues has betrayed the welfare of the nation."

After the war, overtime opportunities lessened and in spite of regulation prices started to rise. In October 1945 blues pianist Roosevelt Sykes (1906–1983) alluded to the problem in an amusing sexual metaphor entitled "High Price Blues."

> I got a gal, she got a bakershop,
> Her jellyroll is the highest thing she's got.

chorus: *Everything's gone higher, way up higher,*
> *It's giving us so much trouble, I wonder what shall we do?*

> *I walked in her shop this morning, 'bout half past four,*
> *I said: "You're doing all right, baby, go ahead and sell some more."*

spoken: *Johnny Walker,*[16] *ride, ride! Talk to me a while!*

> *I know you gonna be bothered, with beggars and bums,*
> *But don't worry, baby, just don't give 'way a crumb.*

> *I'm laying here, baby, lonesome as I can be,*
> *If you have any trouble, just contact me.*[17]

Wartime employment had resulted in a period of relative economic independence for many women. Men who expected women to keep house may have felt threatened. These fears are echoed by several blues compositions of the period,

Roosevelt Sykes, NBBO Blues Festival, Amstelveen, The Netherlands, 18 May 1974. Photo by Hans ten Have.

all by male singers. Blues singer Leadbelly (= Huddie Ledbetter; 1888–1949) recorded no fewer than three versions of his "National Defense Blues," a song about a woman whose pay from her wartime factory work equaled that of her boyfriend. Now those days are over and she is independent no longer. Here is the first version from early 1946:

spoken: *Yes, Defense!*

> *I had a little woman, working on that National Defense,*
> *That woman got to the place, act like she did not have no sense.*

> *Just because she was working, making so much dough,*
> *That woman got to the place, Fred,[18] she did not love me no more.*

> *Every payday come, her check was big as mine,*
> *That woman thought that Defense was gonna last all the time.*

Now, the Defense is gone, listen to my song,
Since that Defense been gone, that woman done lose her home.

spoken:　*Yes, she is! Yeah!*

I will tell you the truth, and it's got to be the fact,
Since that Defense been gone, that woman lose her Cadillac.

I'm gonna tell you people, tell you as a friend,
I don't believe that Defense will ever be back again.[19]

Jimmy Witherspoon (1923–1997), singing with the Jay McShann band, was more outspoken. The shipyard is closing and the women have to "give us men our privilege back," Witherspoon sang in his July 1945 "Shipyard Woman." Surveys revealed that of the six million women who had been employed during the war, 75 per cent wanted to remain employed, but it was argued that traditional family life would be disrupted as a result. Veterans returned to their jobs under the Selective Service Act and 75 per cent more female workers than male were dismissed.[20] However, many more women remained in the workforce than after the demobilization of World War I.

Well, all the defense workin' women, they have turned in their bag of tools,
But as long as they were workin', well, they played all of us men for fools.

Some women are all right, but they're not all the same,
Well, the way they treat us poor men, it's a lowdown, lowdown, dirty shame.

Well, a woman sure is ornery, when she's makin' more money than a man,
Well, you take my advice and keep her in the kitchen, yes, where she can
wash those pots and pans.

Well, they say the war is over, and peace is here again,
Every time they want some new shoes, they will have to come and see us men.
Yes, shipyard woman, hang your slacks upon the rack,
You had better put on some of those fine dresses, and give us men our privilege back.[21]

The "shipyard women" theme was evidently quite popular. Wynonie Harris and Frankie Ervin also recorded songs about the shipyards and in late 1945 or early 1946 Pee Wee Wiley, vocalist for "Big" Jim Wynn (1912–1977), an influential bandleader and saxophonist from El Paso, Texas, recorded a "Shipyard Woman."

Well, they've said the war is over, and peace is here again to stay,
You shipyard workin' women sure did have your way,
But it's all over, baby, now you girls have got to pay.

A woman sure can act hinkty,[22] she's makin' money like a man,
Yes, you girls all get hinkty, when you're workin' like a man,
If you don't buy what she ask you, she'll tell you quick: "Don't you know I can?"

Throw your lunch pail in the closet, hang your slacks back on the rack,
Get right back into your dresses, give us men our privilege back.
Shipyard woman, girl, I know you hate to go,
But it's all over, baby, you can't have your way no more.

Since the war is over, baby, you so lovin' all the time,
But that stuff you puttin' down, you can throw it out o' your mind.
Shipyard woman, girl, I know you hate to go,
But it's all over, baby, you can't have your way no more.

Yards all closed – no more![23]

Many of the women who were laid off after the war were subsequently rehired, not least because they were cheaper: on average earning only 53 per cent of men's wages. By 1950 32 per cent of the workforce was female, against 27 per cent at the outbreak of World War II.[24]

Another recurrent theme for the male blues singers in the aftermath of World War II was the woman who has been unfaithful while her man was fighting overseas: *Daddy, daddy, yes, you been gone too long, Yes, I tried hard, daddy, to keep from doing wrong,*[25] or *Now, this war is over, I want my baby by myself, You know, I'm sorry, my boy friend, you'll have to get you someone else.*[26]

The soldiers often noted that they were fighting for the women they had left behind as well as for the nation: *Nineteen and forty-three, I went to the Philippines, came back in nineteen and forty-five, I only live for that woman, that's why I'm still alive,*[27] or *Now, when I started fighting, I was fighting and didn't give a damn, Long as I was fighting for the woman I love, and my dear old Uncle Sam.*[28]

The women, however, were lonesome and some found themselves a "Jody Man." *When I got back to the USA, I found her Jody on my pillow where I used to lay,*[29] or *Uncle Sam, Uncle Sam, please find something for Jody to do, Why don't you send him over there, to dodge them bullets too?*[30] "Jody" has been the proverbial civilian lover of the soldier's wife since World War II. In an article about the legend of Jody in blues and soul recordings made during the Vietnam War, Jeff

Hannusch described how the drill sergeants in World War II called out: "Ain't no sense in getting home," to which the black soldiers answered: "Jody's got your girl and gone."[31]

Domestic strife was often increased by the fact that the allotment a soldier's wife received out of his pay was spent by the time the war drew to a close: *Yes, I loved my baby, better than I did myself, But she spent all of my allotment, and then she run off with somebody else,*[32] or *When she was gettin' that allotment, everything was really vout,*[33] *She's been capitalizin' on you, Jack, and you sure better watch out.*[34] or *When I was in the army, you had a war plant job, You even got my allotment, now you're hollerin' 'bout the times is hard.*[35]

In some songs the lovers are very much afraid of the returning soldiers: *Now your man been to the army, I know that's awful tough, I don't know how many men he done killed, but I think he done killed enough.*[36] One returnee threatens to kill the man who stole his girl with a souvenir weapon: *My baby, my baby, she's been runnin' 'round, I'm gonna take my German Luger and blow their playhouse down.*[37]

These examples indicate an increasing inde-
pendence of women, and emphasize the social tensions that were the inevitable result of the return of the soldiers after the end of the war.

Reconversion was no easy task. In 1946 millions of people were laid off and wages fell so low that fears of a second Depression loomed large. The dilemma is best summarized in blues piano player Ivory Joe Hunter's (1914–1974) "Reconver-sion Blues." Hunter's new poverty damages his luck with the ladies:

The war is over, now, baby, what are you goin' to do?
I used to give you twenty, but now one or two will have to do.

I bought you a mink coat, baby, and I bought you a diamond ring,
I even bought you a Packard, I tried to buy you everything,
But now, woman, my bankroll is gone,
I'll have to get a COD[38] *ticket, baby, to ship you back to your home.*

In '32 you said: "Daddy, beer or wine will do,"
In '45 I bought you zombies[39] and I bought some champagne too,
But so, baby, let's go back where we started from,
Because if you were lovin' me for my money, no, no, baby, I'm not the one.

We used to ride in taxis, we couldn't even walk a block,
But since the Japs surrendered, that jive will have to stop,
Because, hey, hey, hey, hey, hey, I haven't got a lousy dime,
So start your reconversion, let's go back to the smaller times.

spoken: *I'm broke, I lost my job, so, baby, goodbye![40]*

The same sentiments were expressed in the 1946 "I'm a Bum Again" by Charles Gray (a pseudonym for soprano saxophonist Buster Bennett): *I used to eat fried chicken, and steaks big enough for two, But now I'm lucky, if I can buy some groundhog stew.*[41]

In February 1946 Roosevelt Sykes advised the nation to get used to austerity and a buyer's market for labor in his "Living in a Different World."

Jobs gonna be scarce, and that's gonna be bad,
You gonna need that money that you once have had.

chorus: *'Cause this country's in a whirl,*
So you see we're living in a different world.

Now, you gotta change your ways, boys, through and through,
If you don't, you ain't gonna get very much work to do.

I can remember, the times right around here,
I could take me a big fat nickel, get me a big bucket of beer.

Looka here, Jack, don't be no fool,
We all gotta get used to these new rules.[42]

In his 1947 "Unemployment Blues" Texas blues guitarist Smokey Hogg (1914–1960) painted a dismal picture of women who spent their allotments on partying and cashed in their war bonds. There are so many people after jobs, the police can demand bribes not to run them off in front of the unemployment office. War bonds[43] could now be redeemed. The cashing-in is an attempt to maintain the lifestyle the allotments had paid for in wartime.

You don't believe peoples livin' hard, go to the unemployment office every day,
When a man come around for some work to do, they run over you if you don't
                                                              get out of the way.
When the war was going on, they was letting the good times roll,
Now the police is charging ten dollars, for standing in front of the unemployment door.

Yeah, women throwed parties, all over town,
Yeah, when they got their allotment, they throwed parties all over town,
Swear they wouldn't work no more, but be runnin' the dark down.[44]

They done cashed their bonds, most done throwed their dough away,
Yeah, they done cashed their bonds, and near 'bout all have throwed their dough away,
Yeah, in a few more days, they'll be hustlin' that unemployment office the same old way.[45]

Meanwhile attacks were being launched on the OPA (Office of Price Administrations) that recall those made on the National Recovery Administration in 1933–1935.[46] The OPA had been set up by Roosevelt in 1941 and as a result prices had been frozen since March 1942.[47] Blues artists had always been critical of the OPA blaming it for the scarcity of life's necessities, and vocalist Dossie "Georgia Boy" Terry, who recorded "The OPA Blues" in 1946, was no exception. Invoking the Serviceman's Readjustment Act of 1944, known as the GI Bill of Rights, which helped ease military personnel back into civilian life by providing veterans with loans, educational subsidies, and other benefits, Terry bitterly proclaims that GIs have a better time of it than civilians.

The OPA has stopped my car from runnin', got to walk everywhere I go,
Trolleys don't hardly run, ooh Lord, they can't hop no stops no more.

chorus: *Ah, GI Joe, boy, you living that life I choose,*
I'd rather be in Uncle Sam's army, than to have these OPA blues.

I work fourteen hours each day, come home to eat,
My wife tells me she's sorry, but she just couldn't get no meat.

I work seven days each week, never do relax,
Make a dollar overtime, oh Lord, they take it out in tax.

They got poor Jody on a wonder, just don't understand,
Why all the womens go and get a soldier man.

And when GI Joe come home, turn on all the lights,
Joe gonna be happy under that GI Bill of Rights.[48]

Truman, whose knowledge of economics was limited, was baffled by the complexities of Reconversion.[49] Congress wanted to continue the OPA to facilitate Reconversion, but the President decided to veto the OPA renewal bill on 30 June 1946. On 6 July South Center, a Chicago department store on 47th Street, advertised in the *Chicago Defender*: "We have not changed our policy. For over 18 years, Before OPA – South Center's Policy has been keeping quality up and prices down. OPA or no OPA . . . we shall adhere to this policy as in the past and shall continue to sell present stocks at the same prices existing during the time of OPA."[50] Evidently stocks were soon exhausted, however, and prices began to soar. These

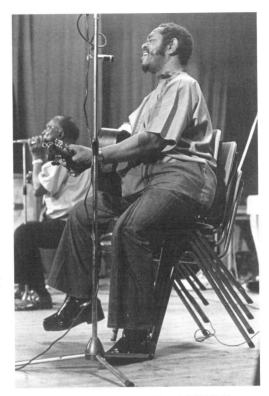

Brownie McGhee (with Sonny Terry), NBBO Blues Festival, Amstelveen, The Netherlands, 18 May 1974. Photo by Hans ten Have.

consequences of Truman's decision were criticized by guitarist Brownie McGhee (1915–1996) in his late 1947 "High Price Blues."

> *I'll tell you something, ain't no joke,*
> *High cost of living, is keeping me broke.*

chorus: *Prices going higher, yes, way up higher,*
> *Prices going so high, what more can we do?*

> *Walked in a meat market, just about noon,*
> *Meat is higher now, (than) when the cow jumped over the moon.*

> *Lame is going to walk, blind is going to see,*
> *But I say these high prices, (is) killing me.*

Meat, butter and eggs, getting higher still,
You don't even get no change, out of a five-dollar bill.

Prices going higher, yes, way up higher,
Well, it's no disgrace to be poor, but it's a little unhandy for me.

The horses and the numbers, odds are still the same,
Look like the bankers would raise ten per cent on the game.

Prices going higher, yes, way up higher,
Prices gone so high, I don't think I will work no more.[51]

Prices went sky high: a pound of veal cutlets went from 50 to 95 cents, milk from 16 to 20 cents a quart. Vocalist George "Blues Man" Vann "couldn't stretch it no more" in his 1946 "Inflation Blues." His job as a fireman on the Frisco line does not pay enough to pay the rent and to keep the car running. There is only one way out for the blues man (who is simultaneously deploying some sexual imagery):

Pork chops cost a dollar, corn meal's fifty-nine,
I can't stretch it no more, baby, workin' on that Frisco line.

Rent went up to fifty, then your mama came,
Can't stretch it no more, baby, it comes out just the same.

Piston's went kerflooie, my axle's bust in two,
Can't stretch it no more, baby, oil job I got to do.

Can't get no more credit, someone stole my booze,
Can't stretch it no more, baby, each time I win I lose.

Yes, I asked that Frisco fireman/foreman, when I'd get a raise,
Can't stretch it no more, baby, can't make that hustlin' pay.

Tried to be a fireman, stoke that box all day,
Can't stretch it no more, baby, hustlin's gotta stay.[52]

From June 1946 to December 1948 prices rose by 38 per cent.[53] Unemployment would have been even worse if prices had stayed frozen. No wonder Ivory Joe Hunter had the "High Cost, Low Pay Blues" in February 1947.

I've got the high cost and low pay blues,
What I'm gonna tell you, people, every word of it is true.

When I go down to the store and try to buy at pre-war price,
The man behind the counter look at me and say: "Brother, no dice."
I've got the high cost and low pay blues,
If I don't make more money, I don't know what I'm gonna do.

I make out a big long list of the stuff I wanna buy,
Go down town and count my money, shake my head and only sigh.
I get the high cost and low salary blues,
I'd like to ask my grocer: "How come you do me like you do?"

Prices rising in the east, prices rising in the west,
Oh, my bank account is flatter than a undertaker's chest.
I've got the high cost and low salary blues,
Oh, the times are getting terrible and my dollars are so few.

Oh well, oh well, I wonder what the end is going to be,
I would like to know who cut down that doggone money tree.
I've got the high cost, low salary blues,
Oh, the bossman has got to raise me, as sure as one and one is two.[54]

In April 1947 alto saxophonist Eddie "Cleanhead" Vinson (1917–1988) recorded "Luxury Tax Blues," also recorded in 1953 by Herbert Beard.[55] The luxury tax was a levy on goods or services considered to be luxuries rather than necessities. Vinson jokingly complains that he has to pay $10 luxury tax for sexual intercourse, and this is yet another example of a blues song that combines comment on contemporary economic circumstances with inventive sexual imagery.

No, I don't wanna buy it, that meat's too high for me,
I used to get it for two dollars, way back in nineteen forty-three.

Well, I went to see my baby, she said: "Daddy, just relax,"
But that night as I was leaving, I paid ten dollars luxury tax.

Now, you know this here inflation, is kinda hard on a man,
It's causing me such aggravation, but I do the best I can,
I'm gonna take a little vacation, going from east to west,
Make a survey of this nation, see who's causing all this mess.

No, I don't wanna buy it, I know where I can get it free,
But I'll never name the city, 'cause it might start a big stampede.[56]

In a draft speech that he did not deliver a frustrated Truman had railed against "greedy industrialists and labor leaders who are now crying beef bacon. . . . You've deserted your President for a mess of pottage, a piece of beef – a side of bacon."[57] For the man in the street meat was becoming "too high to buy." In his October 1947 "High Priced Meat" Smokey Hogg even considered a return to the South where you could still get "good old hog meat." He recalls the small farmer's life, less dependent on shopkeepers, and dreams nostalgically of rural self-sufficiency versus urban dependence. In so doing, Hogg was ignoring the harsh conditions that were often the reality of sharecropping. At the same time "hog meat" is also a sexual pun on the singer's surname, implying that willing women will not be in short supply back home.

You know, it's mighty bad, that meat goin' higher every day,
And we ain't got the job, the price they have we can't pay.

Oh, we can't go to the meat window, select anything we need,
If we do, pork chops and steak would put us in misery.

I'm goin' home in the morning, yeah, I'm gonna ride that cotton patch train,
Where I can get good old hog meat, and never be in a strain.

Yeah, blues fell on me when the war was over, when all war plant jobs went down,
I know I gotta go back to the country, people, I can't live in town.[58]

In 1947 or 1948 blues guitarist Floyd Jones (1917–1989), who had just come to Chicago from Arkansas, recorded his classic "Stockyard Blues" about the Union Stockyards in Chicago. In 1983 he explained the circumstances: "I worked there for a little while, not long. They went on a strike. That's what made me leave there. All them things (in the lyrics) is true. At the time, that's when all that was happenin'. The strike was on: the streetcar fare was raised and the meat and everything – everything I was sayin', it was true. I got on the streetcar and I give the guy 11 cents. He says, 'Hold it, hold it, fella! You owe me two cents more, man!' And I went to the Stockyard market on Maxwell Street and the meat had gone up. And so all them things happened."[59]

Well, I left home this morning, boy, you know, 'bout half past nine,
I passed the stockyard, you know, the boys were still on the picket line.

chorus: You know, I need to earn a dollar, you know, I need to earn a dollar,
But the cost of living have gone so high, darling, I don't know what to do.

Well, now, I went down to the butcher man, you know, in his showcase I give a peek:
He said: "I got a four cent raise, man, on all of my meat."

spoken: Man, I need to earn a bunch of dollars!
Your time, Snooks![60]

Well, I caught the street car this morning, boys, you know, 'bout half past four,
I give the man eleven cents, he said: "Son, it's two cents more."

spoken: All right, Buddy![61]

Jones's second 78, from 1948, included another eloquent social document, which he called "Hard Times." It provided further details about the strike at the stockyards. The efforts of the trade union apparently failed to produce the desired "raise on the hour," and unemployment had taken its toll.

The CIO Packinghouse Workers Union had asked for an increase of 29 cents an hour. Production had dropped 47 per cent because of the strike in the big Chicago meat-packing plants. Three members of President

Advertisement for Floyd Jones, "Ain't Times Hard," Vee-Jay 111. *First Pressings*, July 1954.

Truman's fact-finding board toured the Chicago Union stockyard as part of their study of the case that had to be completed by 1 April 1948.[62]

chorus: Hard times, hard times is carrying me down,
If it don't get no better, I believe I will leave this town.

Said, you know, the company and the union men, began to meet:
Say: "Slow production: we'll give you, four days a week."

I left home this morning, you know, right early soon,
I met my best friend-girl, she said: "Meet me in the afternoon."

spoken: *Take it away, Sunny!*[63]

Well, the men began to talk, boys, and they wanted a raise on the hour:
"It's a bad time, we're laying 'em off by the thousands."[64]

Another blues song about a 1948 strike was recorded by Texas vocalist L. C. Williams (1924–1960). Accompanied on guitar by Lightnin' Hopkins, Williams complains that hard times are getting the best of him:

Hard times, hard times, hard times is going around,
Well, you know the strike is on, baby, I believe it's trying to keep me down.

No more joy, no more joy, baby, no more fun for me,
Well, you know, my strike is on, and it's trying to get the best of me.

Well, I'm going back home, see if I can meet some of my old friends,
Well, you know the strike is on down here, I ain't got no money to spend.[65]

Inflation was one of the major reasons why Truman's popularity in the Gallup Polls dropped from 87 per cent when he took office after Roosevelt's death, to a mere 32 per cent in November 1948 when he was standing for election. The people did not understand why the President was so powerless in this issue. In "Money Getting Cheaper" from November 1947, Jimmy Witherspoon looks to the politicians for decisive action, perhaps recalling FDR's New Deal. The song is also a further example of the "romance without finance is a nuisance" theme that intersects with these "poverty" blues. The song was written by Dootsie Williams and Jessie Mae Robinson and had first been recorded by Charles Brown earlier that year.[66]

Money's getting cheaper, prices getting steeper,
Found myself a woman, but I just couldn't keep her.

chorus: *Well, times getting tougher than tough,*
Yes, things getting rougher than rough,
Well, I make a lot of money, but I just keep spending the stuff.

Porkchops on the market, asked the butcher for a pound,
Couldn't buy a porkchop when I laid my money down.

> *Politicians tellin' folks, to cut down on their meat,*
> *Why don't they cut down on the prices and let the people eat?*
>
> *I can't afford to live, but I guess I'll have to try,*
> *The undertakers got a union and it costs too much to die.*[67]

The progress of inflation in the Truman era can be seen in the annual consumer price index percentages for the period: 1945 (2.3); 1946 (8.3); 1947 (14.4); 1948 (8.1); 1949 (–1.2); 1950 (1.3); 1951 (7.9); 1952 (1.9).[68] From 1946 to 1948, the gap really was widening between the President and "Average Joe," as Louis Jordan called himself in his December 1947 "Inflation Blues." Truman acted well when he stopped rationing, Jordan argues, but he does not seem to know how to fight inflation. It is also quite remarkable to hear a blues singer address the President as "Hey, Prez."

> *Now, listen, Mr. President, all you Congressmen too,*
> *You got me all frustrated and I don't know what to do.*
> *I'm tryin' to make a dollar, can't even save a cent,*
> *It takes all my money, just to eat and pay my rent.*

chorus: *That's why I got the blues, got those inflation blues.*

> *I'm not one of those highbrows, I'm Average Joe to you,*
> *I came up eatin' cornbread, candied yams and chicken stew.*
> *Now, you take that paper dollar, it's only that in name,*
> *The way that paper buck has shrunk, it's a lowdown dirty shame.*
>
> *Hey, Prez, please cut the price of sugar, so I can make my coffee sweet,*
> *I like to smear some butter on my bread, and you know I gotta have my meat.*
> *When you stopped rationing, you really played the game,*
> *But things are going up, and up, and up, and up, and up*
> *and my check remains the same.*[69]

That same month in 1947 a second version of "Inflation Blues" was recorded by Rabon Tarrant (1909–1975), vocalist and percussionist for Jack McVea & His Orchestra. It shows that there was some hostility towards the Marshall Plan that had been announced on 5 June 1947. At Harvard University, Secretary of State General George C. Marshall had called for American assistance in restoring the infrastructure of Europe to prevent famine and political chaos. The result was the Economic Cooperation Act of 1948, which aimed at the restoration of agricultural and industrial productivity.[70] "Inflation Blues" suggested that as long as the US has the inflation blues, no money should be sent to Europe: "Ain't we done enough?"

> Now, listen, Mr. President, Congressmen too,
> You got me all frustrated and I don't know what to do.
> I'm tryin' to make a dollar, I can't even save a cent,
> It takes all of my money, just to eat and pay my rent.

chorus: *I've got those inflation blues, blue as I can be,*
> *I've got those inflation blues, blue as I can be.*

> Now, that almighty dollar, why, it's that just in name,
> No longer is it worth a buck, its power ain't the same.
> I'm not one of the wealthy, I can't afford the things I need,
> I have a lot of meatless days,[71] which have not been decreed.

> About this aid to Europe, food and all that stuff,
> Don't think that I'm a-fussin', but ain't we done enough?
> I wanna be a citizen, who can shoulder his share,
> But till you stop inflation, all US won't give a care.

spoken: *Watch that inflation!*[72]

A 23 August cartoon in the *Afro-American* criticized the plan to lend nine billion dollars to Europe for economic relief by referring to "slum areas in southern states," "broken promises to colored citizens," "high rents" and "no constructive program for minority groups."[73] However, the implementation of the Marshall Plan may have helped to stimulate employment in the US and this probably mitigated the initial hostility.

Some veterans saw a possible way out of economic disasters by re-enlistment. For vocalist Turner Willis in his "Re-enlisted Blues," this strategy is a disappointment because he misses the woman he had fallen in love with when he came back from the war.[74] However, in his February 1947 "Things Ain't Like They Use to Be" [sic] Walter Davis (1912–1963) definitely wants to escape the States, where he does not feel at home any more. It is better anywhere else, even on the Burma Road!

"A Penny for Your Thoughts,"
cartoon by E. Simms Campbell,
Afro-American, 23 August 1947.

I spent two years in the European country, way out across the deep blue sea,
And since I've been round here, don't seem like home to me.

All the friends I used to have, wonder where could they be?
Lord, I see strange faces, every time I walk down the street.

If I would enlist back in the army, wonder could I go back across the European Sea?
I don't like here no more, things ain't like they used to be.

Gonna get up early in the morning, goin' down to my local Board,
Just anywhere away from here, if it's out on the Burma Road.[75]

Post-war expectations of material prosperity were very high indeed. The complicated process of Reconversion made demands on President Truman. He could not fathom why wartime solidarity had disappeared and he felt "betrayed" by both consumers and producers. When prices soared, the common people could no longer afford to put meat on the table. In contemporary blues lyrics the President was personally called to account. There are practically no blues lyrics personally critical of Franklin Roosevelt, and his predecessors were virtually ignored by blues singers, so we are here confronted with a nearly unprecedented phenomenon in blues and gospel music, explicit criticism of a (white) politician. The songs depict a President who was unable to fight inflation and had become unpopular as a result, at the very moment when he was running for election.

In 1948 the Sons of Heaven, a pseudonym for the Selah Jubilee Singers, a famous gospel quartet that would also acquire pop fame as "The Larks" in the 1950s, recorded "The World Is in a Bad Condition," in which they criticize President Truman. The Democrats, who abolished Prohibition, have been in power since 1933, but as Truman does not understand the condition of ordinary people, there is "trouble in the land." The song is also important because it is one of the first to offer a general critique of politics, seeing both parties as making empty promises to win votes.

chorus: *I declare this old world is in a bad condition, (3×)*
           And the people ought to serve the Lord.

           Well, some said we need a new President,
           Repeal that 18th Amend-ament,[76]
           They brought back liquor and they brought back beer,
           Said that times would be better in the coming year.

           Well, the Democrats had their new government, so
           Republicans promise to do much more;
           But there's trouble that is in the land,
           They tell me the President don't understand.

           Well, Lord,
           My Lord,
           Oh Lord, I can't stand these hard times,
           Father, I can't stand so.[77]

2 ATOM AND EVIL

Relying on his memoirs, historians used to claim that Truman knew nothing of US nuclear experiments until Secretary of War Henry Stimson informed him after his inauguration. More recent research has shown that Truman had known about the development of the atomic bomb since July 1943.[1]

In 1943 Senator Harry S. Truman was president of a Senate Special Committee to Investigate the National Defense Program. In the course of the investigations, information about a mysterious "Manhattan Project" began to surface. On 17 June Truman called Henry Stimson about the issue, and was told that the project served a unique purpose that needed to remain secret.[2] Although Truman assured Stimson that there was no need to provide further details, within a month he had acquired enough information to write to a friend, mentioning "the construction of a plant to make a terrific explosion for a secret weapon that will be a wonder."[3] In the latter half of July 1945, while the new President attended the Potsdam Conference with Stalin and Churchill, he was informed of a successful atomic test at Alamogordo, New Mexico, which unexpectedly produced energy equivalent to 20,000 tons of TNT.[4]

On 24 July 1945 President Truman authorized the dropping of an atomic bomb on any one of four Japanese cities as soon after 3 August as the weather permitted. It was decided not to warn the Japanese because of the potential consequences to Allied prisoners held in Japan. Some historians have argued that Truman gave orders for the bombs to be dropped in order to intimidate the Soviet leaders, "forcing them to accept an American-imposed world order."[5] Most agree, however, that his principal objective was "to shorten the agony of war, in order to save the lives of thousands of young Americans," as he himself phrased it.[6] The worst scenario for a Japanese defeat without using the atomic bomb indicated an additional 46,000 American casualties.[7] To a President who had seen the horrors of World War I, this prospect was unacceptable.

On 6 August 1945 the "Enola Gay," a B-29 commanded by Colonel Paul Tibbets, dropped "Little Boy" on Hiroshima, killing some 80,000 people. The event prompted Percy Wilborn, a convict at Retrieve State Farm in Snipe, Texas, to add a few original lines to the spiritual "Oh, What a Time."[8] Wilborn and his Friendly Five Gospel Singers had begun to perform this song immediately after the war. Some of the performances were broadcast over local radio in Gladewater, Texas.

> Well, the story I'm a-telling it may not rhyme,
> But uh, "Hush!" one day I heard a B-29.
> Coming through the air, Lord, big and bold,
> She had a one little bomb way back in the hold.
> Well, the pilot called the bombardier,
> And said: "Jack, this is it and you can drop it right here!"[9]

Blues singer "Memphis" Willie Borum (1912–1993) went into the service in January 1942. He took part in the first North African invasion in December 1942 and in the landings in Sicily and on the mainland of Italy under the command of General Eisenhower. By the end of the war he was serving with a Quartermaster Unit in the Italian mountains, where he worked as a colonel's driver and sang at parties when off duty.[10] Looking back at the closing days of World War II from the heat of the Cold War in 1961 when the world hovered at the brink of nuclear war during the Cuban missile crisis, Borum recorded an "Overseas Blues."

> I was way overseas; I was way over in New Jerusalem,
> General Eisenhower said:
> "You soldiers got to go in Tokyo," say: "And do the best you can."

chorus: *But I told him: "No, Little Willie don't wanna go,"*
Say: "I had so much trouble with them Germans, don't send me over in Tokyo."

He said: "Germany done fell now," say: "You soldier boys know what it's all about,"
Say: "You gotta go way over in them islands, and help General MacArthur out."

You know, General Eisenhower and General MacArthur had a conference, they
                                                    were talking about that atomic bomb,
He said: "If it do what I think, Ikey Boy," say: "Your mens won't have to come."

We was sittin' in the stationary, waitin' on the results of that atomic bomb,
Finally MacArthur sent Eisenhower a letter saying: "Your boys don't have to come."

I told him I had a sweet thing in the U.S.A., she is sweet as she can be,
She got a lot of work she want did and she saved the job for me.[11]

Borum describes wartime Italy as "New Jerusalem," a biblical term for an ideal world.[12] Despite his experience of combat, the privations and discomfort, he evidently held cherished memories of his overseas service, in a country relatively free of racial discrimination. In a 1969 interview he remembered Italy as "a land of lovely signorinas."[13] The scene in which the soldiers "in the stationary" (apparently coined by analogy with "commissary") were waiting for MacArthur's decision is imagined, but the atomic explosion was indeed the reason why Private Willie Borum could return home to his girl after V-J Day (2 September 1945).

Another song devoted to the bombing of Hiroshima is the September 1946 "Atomic Bomb Blues" by Mississippi-born singer Homer Harris (1916–2000). The recording has subsequently reached a wider audience because of the presence of guitarist Muddy Waters on one of his first commercial recordings.

It was early one morning, when all the good work was done,
And that big bird was loaded, with that awful atomic bomb.

Wrote my baby, I was behind the risin' sun,
I told her: "Don't be uneasy, because I'm behind the atomic bomb."

Nation after nation, was near and far away,
Well, they soon got the news, and there where they would stay.

Over in east Japan, you know, they let down and cried,
And poor Tojo, had to find a place to hide.[14]

Mushroom cloud 60,000 feet over Nagasaki, 9 August 1945. US National Archives 1242.

When he sings "I'm behind the atomic bomb" Harris appears to imagine the dropping of the bomb as a shield he can hide behind so that he will not have to fight. "Poor Tojo" was Baron Hideki Tojo (1884–1948), the hawkish Japanese general who served as Prime Minister from 1941 to 1944. He was sentenced to death by an international court and subsequently hanged. Tojo personified the Japanese foe for the blues singers and there are many blues recordings referring to him, but very few which mention Emperor Hirohito.[15]

On 9 August 1945 the second American atomic bomb was released over Nagasaki, killing another 40,000 people. On 14 August the Japanese finally surrendered after a conventional bombing raid that devastated Tokyo.

On 11 August the Chicago Defender proudly headlined: "Negro scientists help produce 1st atom bomb." According to this source, the University of Chicago estimated that at one point no fewer than 15 per cent of the key scientific workers were African Americans. It then lists the African-American scientists from Chicago and singles out J. Ernest Wilkins as the most outstanding of them. Wilkins, who had been brought to the university from Tuskegee, Alabama, was a brilliant mathematician who had earned a degree of celebrity two years earlier, when he became the youngest Doctor of Philosophy in the nation at the age of eighteen.[16]

At the atomic bomb plant in Oak Ridge, the 7000 colored workers from the southern states had no school facilities for their children, and had to use Jim Crow wards in the hospital and the dental clinic. For three years the workers had been kept in the dark about the true nature of their job. They began to question whether anything was being produced at all, since they could see huge quantities of material coming in, but nothing going out.[17]

The nuclear explosions in Japan were seen as having great moral implications. Many people believed that mankind was on the verge of total destruction. Gospel artists uttered apocalyptic warnings. The first of these to be recorded was a Zaret–Singer composition entitled "Atom and Evil," sung by the Golden Gate Quartet in June 1946. Evil is courting innocent Atom, but the singer warns us of the dreadful dangers of a union between the two. There appear to be two takes of the song. On the original 78-rpm record line 18 is: *Lord, if Atom plays with Evil*. The CD version, which claims to be a reissue of the 78, is clearly an alternative, possibly previously unissued, take. That version is transcribed here:

> *Now, brothers and sisters, I'm troubled to say,*
> *Brother Atom is gone astray.*
>
> *Listen, listen, listen, listen, listen!*
>
> *This is a story of Atom and Evil,*
> *Their courtship is causing a great upheaval.*
> *Now, Atom was a sweet, young, innocent thing,*
> *Until the night that Miss Evil took him under her wing.*
>
> *Now, Atom was an honest, hard-working man,*
> *He wanted to help out the human clan.*
> *But Miss Evil got him drunk on prejudice and hate,*
> *And she taught him how to gamble with humanity's fate.*
>
> chorus: *So, true! I'm talking 'bout Atom and Evil, Atom and Evil,*
> *If you don't break up that romance soon,*
> *We'll all fall down and go: "Boom, boom, boom!"*[18]
>
> *Now, if Evil gets Atom, it will be such a shame,*
> *Because plenty of big shots are playing that dame.*

Now, his sleep will be troubled and his life will be cursed,
Now, if Atom sleeps with Evil, Jack, he won't be the first.

Now, Atom is a youngster and pretty hard to handle,
But we'd better step in and stop that scandal.
Because if Atom and Evil should ever be wed,
Lord, then darn near all of us are going to be dead.

We're sitting on the edge of doom, doom, doom, doom, doom![19]

Charles Wolfe's article on the atomic bomb in country music also lists some atomic jazz recordings from 1946: "Atom Buster" (Barney Kessel), "Atomic Boogie" (Pete Johnson), "Atomic Cocktail" (Slim Gaillard), "Atomic Did It" (Maylon Clark) and "Atomic Polka" (Brunon Kryger).[20] To this list might be added the blues instrumentals "Atom Boogie" (Sammy Franklin) from 1945, "The Atom Leaps" (Saunders King) from 1946 and "Atomic Energy" (Clarence "Gatemouth" Brown) from 1949. Later instrumentals are "Atomic Rocket" (Joe Morris) from 1951, "Atom Bomb" (Joe Houston) from 1952 and "Atomic Blues" (Joe Richardson) from 1960. In January 1946 Lyle Griffin started his Atomic label for jazz, rhythm and blues, pop, and country and western in Hollywood, CA.

For four years there was an American monopoly on the possession of the atomic bomb. As the "iron curtain" descended and the Soviet Union showed an openly expansionist face, a wave of anti-Communism spread through the United States. The question foremost in everybody's mind was how long it would take the Russians to develop their own nuclear weapons. This fear was well expressed by the Strangers Quartet, who recorded "This Atomic Age" in June 1949:

chorus: *There's only one hope for this atomic age:*
           That's God's way,
               Hallelujah!
           God's mercy,
               Hallelujah!
           God's peace,
               Hallelujah!
           Good will to all men.

           We have won World War Number Two,
               Yet we don't know what to do,
           We have now reached the place,
               Where man's plan has fallen through,
           If we would only return to God,
               He will teach us what to do,
           God has helped us to come through,
               We have won World War Number Two,
           When we sit down to make peace,
               We told God that he may see,
           But remember in his words,
               He says: "I am the Prince of Peace."

           Nations of the world are so disturbed,
           Wonderin' what will become of this world?

           Mussolini, Hitler and Tojo,
               They were knocking at Democracy's door,
           They had declared unto the world,
               That Democracy must go,
           God revealed the atomic to man,
               And we destroyed a part of Japan,
           God declared dictators shall not stand,
               That brought peace to troubled land(s),
           If we would only hold God's hand,
               He will lead us to the Promised Land.

           Nations of the world are so disturbed,
           Wonderin' what will become of this world?[21]

When on 19 September 1949 a reconnaissance plane discovered an area of intense radioactivity in the USSR, physicist J. Robert Oppenheimer, who had been director of the atomic bomb project at Los Alamos, New Mexico, knew that the Russians had exploded their first atomic bomb. Four days later the President issued a statement to the press that an atomic explosion had occurred in the USSR.[22]

In January 1950 the Pilgrim Travelers had a very influential hit with their "Jesus Hits Like the Atom Bomb." Basing themselves on Genesis 9, verses 11–17, they assumed that the covenant God made with Noah provided that God would send fire from the sky when man had sinned again. In reality the Bible says only that God promised "by the rainbow sign" that he would not send the rains down any more. James Baldwin based the title of his collection of essays *The Fire Next Time* (1963) on this theme in gospel music and even President Truman asked himself if the bomb "might be 'the fire of destruction' prophesied in the Bible."[23]

chorus: *You know, now everybody's worried, well, about that atom bomb,*
          And no one seems worried about the day my Lord shall come.
          You'd better set your house in order, well, he may be coming soon,
          Well, and he'll hit like an atom bomb,
          When he comes, when he comes.

          In nineteen hundred and forty-five,
          The atom bomb became alive.
          Nineteen hundred and forty-nine,
          The USA got very wise,
          They found that a country across the line,
          Had an atom bomb of the very same kind.
          People got worried over the land,
          Just like the people in Japan.
          God told Elijah he'd send down fire,
          Send down fire from the sky.
          Showed old Noah by the rainbow sign,
          Won't be water, but fire next time.

          Now, don't you get worried, bear in mind,
          Trust King Jesus and you shall find,
          Peace, happiness, joy divine,
          With my savior on the line.

God told Elijah he'd send down fire,
Send down fire from the sky.
He said he would, and I believe he will,
He'll fight your battle if you'll keep still.[24]

There is an implied warning in this song that America should not be lulled into a sense of false security. "Jesus Hits Like the Atom Bomb" was so successful that no fewer than six other gospel groups recorded versions of it in 1949 and 1950.[25] The chorus lines surface again in a 1969 gospel song about the Vietnam War[26] and there is even a version that was recorded as late as 1993.[27] The song was also recorded by a number of white groups.[28]

The notion that Jesus will hit like an atomic bomb was also incorporated by the Swan Silvertone Singers from the "clay hills of Alabama" into their June 1950 "Jesus Is God's Atomic Bomb." The atomic bomb can kill your body, but the even greater power of Jesus can kill your soul.

Have you heard about the blast in Japan?
How it killed so many people and scorched the land? Oh, yes.
Oh, it can kill your natural body,
But the Lord can kill your soul,
That's why, I know Jesus, oh,
Jesus is God's, I declare, atomic bomb.
Oh, oh, yes.

Oh, Jesus is God's atomic bomb,
Greatest power, that ever was.
Jesus is God's, His atomic bomb,
Shook the grave, causing death to run.
Yes, God shook the grave, child,
Put old death on a run,
Through trials and tribulations,
God's work was done,
That's why I know Jesus, yes, He's my God's, His atomic bomb.[29]

Atomic energy was also employed as a sexual metaphor. In January 1950 Texas blues and boogie-woogie pianist Amos Milburn (1927–1980) called his "Atomic Baby" U 92, the number of uranium in the periodic table, also freely mixing his metaphors with comparisons from electronics, engineering and rocketry.

> *I love my baby, she makes me, oh, so blue,*
> *She keeps me so worried, that I call her U 92.*
>
> *She's got a high potential and a low resistance point,*
> *I have to be so careful, that gal might blow up the joint.*
>
> *Yes, she heats my room, she lights my light,*
> *She starts my motor and it runs all night.*
>
> chorus: *She's my atomic baby, yes, she's my atomic baby,*
> *She's my atomic baby, and I have to handle her with care.*
>
> *They can build them small, they can build them large,*
> *But they can't build a motor that will stand the charge.*
>
> *Yes, she's a little bitty mama, who needs a whole lots of room,*
> *She can ignite your rockets and lead you on to the moon.*[30]

In January 1950 President Truman gave permission for the further development of the hydrogen bomb. Although the first American test of this "H-bomb" did not take place until 1 November 1951, the first song to mention its development actually dates from January 1951. This was another topical composition by the Pilgrim Travelers, who see the atomic bomb as an effective deterrent against the Korean and Chinese Communists in their "Jesus Is the First Line of Defense."

> chorus: *Well, my Jesus is the first line of defense, of defense,*
> *Well, my Jesus is the first line of defense, of defense,*
> *He's shelter in a mighty storm, well, a battle-ax in the time of war,*
> *Well, my Jesus is the first line of defense, of defense.*
>
> *We're gonna build big armies and arm to the teeth,*
> *Tell the other nations that we want peace,*
> *Even build big ships and airplanes too,*
> *If you haven't got God, won't any of this do.*

We ought to watch, pray as well as fight,
Because the Bible says that right be might.
Joshua fit the battle of Jericho,
He marched round seven times,
Had a sword in his hand and God on his side,
And the walls come tumblin' down.

Now, it was just nine years ago,
About Pearl Harbor we all know,
It's a good thing to have allies as friends,
God is your best friend in the end.
If all the people every day,
Would get down on their knees and pray,
Then make the H-bomb and Atom too,
Tell the Reds we'll turn them loose.
Our boys will stop dying, the land will stay free,
'Cause God said: "I'm the Prince of Peace."[31]

The lesson of the song is that God is firmly on the side of the USA. To reinforce his argument, James W. Alexander, the song's composer and one of the two tenors of the group, quotes the gospel classic "Joshua Fit the Battle of Jericho," a song that refers to the story in Joshua 6 in which Joshua "had God on his side."[32]

Most Americans assumed that any nuclear strike against America would be directed at the major urban centers of population. Consequently, California blues vocalist Frankie Ervin (b. 1926) advised his listeners to seek refuge in the forest. In "I'd Rather Live Like a Hermit" from January 1951 there is a symbolic contrast between the "jive cats standing on the (city) corner" in urban idleness and the "hermit in the (pastoral) forest" in rugged rural self-sufficiency. The song expresses common cold war disillusionment with both modern civilization and the science that created the A-bomb – a science that seemed to place the world permanently on the verge of apocalyptic disaster. Ervin wishes that it were possible to escape by going back to an Arcadian state of "natural" innocence.

I'd rather live like a hermit in the forest,
With Mother Nature on my side.
I'd rather live like a hermit in the forest,
Because then I might survive.

You better get way out of that city.
You gonna look just like a clown.
You better be way out of that city,
When the bombs come tumbling down.

Now you jive cats standing on the corner,
You better find some place to hide,
Because when those bombs start falling,
You gonna jump right out o' your hide.

You better wake up, wake up, brother.
You better dig just what I say,
Because when those bombs start falling,
It might be too late.

So I'm going way down to the forest.
You better fall down on your knees,
And ask the Lord up above for shelter,
That will save you in the time of need.[33]

In August 1951 the most famous gospel group from Memphis, the Spirit of Memphis Quartet, recorded a topical update of the classic gospel song "The Royal Telephone."[34] If you don't know what to do, you can always talk to Jesus on "The Atomic Telephone." The song, which was also recorded by the white Harlan County Four,[35] makes a plea for the peaceful use of atomic energy and is probably the only song of its kind to mention the medical uses of radioactivity.

spoken: *God have given us a great new power,*
          Want us to use it for the good of all
                                    mankind.
          Some people wanna use it to destroy everything,
          Oh, oh, God didn't mean it like that,
          He wants it used for the good of all mankind.

chorus: *I just talked to Jesus, on the atomic telephone,*

Lord, and no man knows its power, oh, oh, only God alone.

Lord, and it can cure the sick, or destroy the evil,

With one sweep of power, known by God alone.

Oh, God is not too busy, to know the sins of man,

You may hear from heaven, you may feel his hand.

If you are in trouble, and afraid of all mankind,

Hey, pick up the atomic telephone, and get him on the line.

Oh, for this call to heaven, there will be no charge,

Just like old man Noah, who prayed from an ark,

You can ask your God, just what to do,

He'll lead you from the wilderness, and out of the dark.[36]

It was extremely difficult to deal with the devastating consequences of the atomic bomb, so people evaded them by applying "atomic" as a generalized term of approval or a signifier of great energy. There is much evidence of this phenomenon in the blues and gospel world of the 1950s. From 1954 to 1960 the Rev. H. H. Harrington operated a record label called Atomic-H. Pianist Bob Ferguson, who made recordings for a variety of labels from 1951 to 1960, was given the nickname "H-Bomb" Ferguson by his record company in 1951. When he objected to being nicknamed after a bomb, complaining "that doesn't sound human," Ferguson was told that it referred to the way his voice broke out in an explosion each time he started to sing.[37] Count Basie recorded a famous album for Roulette in 1957 under the title "The Atomic Mr. Basie," the front cover of which depicted an atomic explosion. In a song called "Atomic Love"[38] Little Caesar felt explosions inside and sparks before his eyes and concluded that this must be atomic love for his beloved. In "You Hit Me Baby Like an Atomic Bomb"[39] blues singer Fay Simmons surrendered to her honey for that very reason in 1954. After the 1950s the atomic craze died down and there is only the occasional reference in later recordings.[40]

When Truman left the White House in January 1953 the United States possessed almost 1000 atomic bombs.[41] Three-quarters of the American people had supported the President in his decision to proceed with the development of the "H-bomb," viewing it as a necessary step to counter the threat of Soviet expansion.[42]

In blues, atomic energy appears mainly as a sexual metaphor, but in gospel music it was used as a metaphor for God's power. The message is as often religious (repent or else!) as political. The blues and gospel songs which mention the atomic bomb provide clear evidence of the way in which the black population judged their President's atomic policies. There is relief that the lives of thousands of American soldiers were spared as a result of the bombing of Hiroshima and Nagasaki. A sense of wonder instilled by the awesome atomic power possessed by the United States is mingled with feelings of apprehension when it is learned that the Russians have acquired their own version. Fear of the Communists dominates, but the gospel singers are convinced that God is on the side of America and that, if necessary, He will send down fire to annihilate the Soviet enemy.

3 THE FREEDOM CHOO CHOO

The African-American community was profoundly affected by the death of its beloved President Roosevelt. In its obituary editorial the *Chicago Defender* mentioned that discrimination had been discarded in the setting-up of the Works Progress Administration, that Negro leaders were given positions of responsibility, that Mary McLeod Bethune and Walter White were respected advisors of the President, that the Committee on Fair Employment Practices ended discrimination in defense factories and war plants and that the President had visited Liberia and Haiti, two black republics. In contrast, mention was also made of rumors circulated by the Hearst press to the effect that the newly sworn-in President Truman had once been a Ku Klux Klan member. "Truman denied the story," the African-American weekly added.[1]

A week later a White House correspondent of the *New York Amsterdam News* asked the new President the "$64,000 question" about his attitude toward the African-American population. Truman replied that by looking up his record the correspondent would find how he stood and that he would be pleased with what he found. The correspondent did just that and was reassured.[2] On 8 September 1945 the *Afro-American* had learned from a high administrative source that Truman would call for legislation establishing a permanent Fair Employment Practices Committee (FEPC).[3]

One of the conclusions in my *Roosevelt's Blues* is that few recorded blues and gospel songs, whether from the Roosevelt era or the years before 1933, contained explicit social protest. With rare exceptions, outspoken criticism of racial discrimination could not be recorded commercially, and the singers cloaked their messages in veiled metaphors if protest was uttered at all. After World War II a very gradual change took place in this respect.

With his outspoken lyrics during the early 1940s, Josh White was an early exception to the general rule of caution and avoidance. His audience increasingly consisted of white, educated people on the left of the political spectrum. White's May 1946 recording of the Harburg–Robinson composition "Free and Equal Blues" with its confrontational lyrics was a daring enterprise although part of his live repertoire remained unissued at the time. Before White's scheduled appearance at a Winnetka, Illinois, high school his booking agent advised him to omit the song from his program. White refused. "Kids are no dummies," he later commented, and the principal asked him to sing the song twice because he considered it good education.[4]

> I went down to that St. James Infirmary, and I saw some plasma there,
> I ups and asked the doctor man, now was the donor dark or fair?
>
> The doctor laughed a great big laugh, and he puffed it right in my face:
> He said: "A molecule is a molecule, son, and the damn thing has no race."
>
chorus: And that was news, (sing it) yes, that was news,
> That was very, very, very special news,
> 'Cause ever since that day, we've had those free and equal blues.
>
> You mean, you heard that doc declare,
> That the plasma in that test tube there,
> Could be white man, black man, yellow man, red?
> That's just what that doctor said,
> The doc put down his doctor book,
> And gave me a very scientific look,
> And he spoke out plainly and clear and rational,
> He said: "Metabolism is international."
>
> Then the doc rigged up his microscope with some Berlin blue blood,
> And by gosh it was the same as Chungking, Québecois, Chattanooga, Timbuktu blood.[5]
> Why, those men who think they're noble,
> Don't even know that the corpuscle is global.

Try and disunite us with their racial supremacy,
And flyin' in the face of old man chemistry.
And takin' all the facts and tryin' to twist them,
But you can't overthrow the circulatory system (get it?).

So I stayed at that St. James Infirmary,
(Ha, ha, ha, ha, I couldn't leave that place, it was too interesting),
And I said to the doctor: "Give me some more of that scientific talk talk," and he did,
He said: "Melt yourself down into a crucible,
Pour yourself out into a test tube and what have you got?
Thirty-five hundred cubic feet of gas,
That's the same for the upper and lower class,"
(Well, I let that pass.)
"Carbon, twenty-two pounds, ten ounces,"
"You mean that goes for princes, dukeses and countses?"
"Whatever you are, that's what the amounts is.
Carbon, twenty-two pounds, ten ounces,
Iron, fifty-seven grains,
Not enough to keep a man in chains.

Five hundred ounces of phosphorus,
That's whether you're poor or prosperous,"
(Hey buddy, can you spare a match?)
"Sugar, sixty ordinary lumps.
Free and equal rations for all nations,
When you take twenty-two teaspoons of sodium chloride (that's salt),
And you add thirty-eight quarts of H_2O (that's water),
Mix two ounces of lime, and a pinch of chloride of potash, a drop of magnesium,
A bit a sulphur and a soupçon of hydrochloric acid,
And you stir it all up and what are you?
You're a walking drugstore. It's an international metabolistic cartel."

And that was news, yes, that was news (now you change it),
So listen, you African and Indian, and Mexican, Mongolian, Tyrolean and Tartar,
The doctor's right behind the Atlantic Charter,[6]
The doc's behind the new Brotherhood of Man,
As prescribed in San Francisco[7] and Yalta,[8] Dumbarton Oaks[9] and at Potsdam,[10]
Every man, everywhere, is the same, when he's got his skin off.[11]

In the early 1950s White was often interrogated by the FBI about his supposed Communist sympathies. The reports confirm that during World War II, although he was asked not to sing "Free and Equal Blues" because it "might cause dissension among Negroes in the armed forces," he insisted on playing whatever songs he chose.[12]

The civil rights situation in the Truman era is exemplified by the song "Black, Brown and White." In his autobiography *Big Bill Blues* Big Bill Broonzy tells how he had written the song in 1945 and had offered it to RCA Victor, Columbia, Decca and several of the newly formed independent record companies, but none of them wanted to record it. Broonzy had written the song to show how black workers were treated in the United States. When he asked the record companies the reasons for the rejection, he was told: "You see, Bill, when you write a song and want to record it with any company, it must keep the people guessing what the song means. Don't you say what it means when you're singing. And that song comes right to the point and the public won't like that."[13] As a result Big Bill had to wait until 1951 before he could record the song commercially in Europe for a white and overseas audience.[14]

In the meantime Broonzy was singing the song in public so that other artists were able to learn it. Indeed the first American recording of Broonzy's famous protest song was made, not by the composer himself, but by Brownie McGhee, who cut it in late 1947 for Encore, the small record company he briefly co-owned with Irwin Silber, editor of the folksong magazine *Sing Out!* Encore managed only two releases, and with its slogan "People's Songs" was clearly aimed at the sort of leftist audiences associated with *Sing Out!* At Encore, the combination of a black blues singer and a white radical with progressive racial views as co-owners seems to have created a rare opportunity to record and release such forthright material.

This little song I'm singing, brother, know that it's true,
If you're black and got to work for a living, here's what people will say:

chorus: *If you're white,*
You alright,
If you're brown,
Stick around,
If you're black,
Oh, brother: Get back, get back, get back!

I was in a place the other night, they were having fun,
They were drinking beer and wine, and me I couldn't buy none.

I was in an employment office, got my number and I fell in line,
They called everybody's number, but they never did call mine.

Me and a man workin' side by side, this is what it meant:
He was making a dollar an hour, and I was only getting fifty cents.

I helped to build this country, I fought for it too,
Now I guess you can see, what a black man's got to do!

Helped to win this victory, with my plow and hoe,
Now I just want to know: What you gonna do about the Jim Crow?[15]

"Jim Crow," the personification of American segregation politics, was statutory in the South from the late nineteenth century onwards and customary in many other parts of the United States as well. Leadbelly recorded two songs entitled "Jim Crow Blues." Although it is not known when they were recorded, their lyrics contain indications of a date around 1946 or 1947.

Confirming the conclusions of the President's Committee on Civil Rights in "To Secure These Rights," Leadbelly reported that "Jim Crow" was not just a southern phenomenon, but was to be found in examples of racial prejudice and discrimination all over the United States. His frustration over his abortive attempts to become a movie actor in Hollywood was clearly in evidence here. In 1944 Leadbelly had hoped to get the part of "De Lawd" in *Green Pastures* and 1945 plans for a Paramount film *Adventures of a Ballad Hunter* about John Lomax failed to materialize.[16] The song "Jim Crow" was issued to a sympathetic audience, but the fact that Leadbelly felt it safe to record is still remarkable.

spoken: *And I feel a little sorry for the people, when you walk in a place and this is one world, we're in the same boat, brother. Why don't we be kind to each other? What difference do it make? But it's some places you go, and you can't find — when I was coming on the train I stopped in Las Vegas, went around there and I walked in, the white fellow was with me, and went and sat down, I thought everything was all right. Man touched me on the shoulder and said: "I'm sorry, we don't serve colored." And I said: "Say you don't?" He said: "No." The white fellow got right up to him, and went on and said: "I declare this . . ." We didn't get nothing to eat in Las Vegas. We come on down further.*

So many places are like that. Course it's done . . . , I don't . . . , I just feel sorry for the people, 'cause they ain't woke up yet. As long as you fight, you gonna keep on, it's gonna be war, but if you quit fightin' you got peace. You can't never get peace in fightin'. Got to get together and let it don't be no stormy weather, and we'll all be in the same boat, brother.

OK, now you gonna want this "Jim Crow Blues," huh? That bring news and makes a man wear out his shoes, when he get in a Jim Crow place.

Bunk Johnson[17] told me too,
This old Jim Crowism's dead bad luck to me and you.

I been travelin', I been travelin' from shore to shore,
Everywhere I have been, I find some old Jim Crow.

One thing, people, I want everybody to know,
You gonna find some Jim Crow every place you go.

Down in Louisiana, Tennessee, Georgia is a mighty good place to go,
And get together, break up this old Jim Crow.

spoken: *Break it up now!*

I told everybody, over the radio,
Make up their mind and get together, break up this Old Jim Crow.

I wanna tell you people something that you don't know:
It's a lotta Jim Crow in a movin' picture show.

I'm gonna sing this verse, I ain't gonna sing no more,
Please get together, break up this old Jim Crow.[18]

"Jim Crow Blues #2," which remained unissued until a 1997 CD release, presents a list of all the places where "Jim Crow" still reigned supreme. Again Leadbelly's anger about Hollywood's reluctance to use black actors is ventilated. This is not a second version of the above, but a different song with the same title. In contrast to the issued song it just states the situation, without calling for action, which may be the reason why producer Moses Asch did not issue it.

> If you drop down in Alabama, you gonna find Jim Crow,
> If I didn't know what I'm talking about, people, I would not have told you so.
> Drop down in old Alabama, you gonna find Jim Crow,
> If I didn't know what I'm talking about, people, I never would have told you so.
>
> Drop down in old Richmond, Virginia, you gonna find plenty Jim Crow,
> If I didn't know what I'm talking 'bout people, you would not hear me say so.
> Drop down in Richmond, Virginia, you gonna find Jim Crow,
> If I didn't know what I'm talking about, people, I never would have told you so.
>
> If you drop down in old Tennessee, you gonna find Jim Crow,
> They will not take your money, if you walk into the grocery store.
> Drop down in old Tennessee, you gonna find Jim Crow,
> They won't take your money, if you walk into the grocery store.
>
> Look out for old Louisiana, you gonna find Jim Crow,
> If I didn't know what I'm talking about, people, never would have told you so.
> Drop down in old Louisiana, you gonna find Jim Crow,
> If I didn't know what I'm talking about, peoples, I never would have told you so.
>
> You can get out in old California, you gonna find Jim Crow,
> That's the reason there ain't no more Negroes today, in a movin' picture show.
> Drop down in old California, you gonna find Jim Crow,
> That's the reason there ain't no more Negroes today, baby, in a movin' picture show.[19]

On 21 November 1948 Leadbelly sang a second version of "Jim Crow Blues" at a private party in Minneapolis. In those circumstances he even felt able to mention the name of singer/actor Paul Robeson, then under fire because of his Communist sympathies.

> Paul Robeson, Paul Robeson, Paul Robeson told me too,
> This old Jim Crowism's dead bad luck to me and you.
>
> One thing, I want everybody to know:
> Why don't you get together, break up this old Jim Crow?
>
> It's Jim Crow, everywhere I go,
> It is Jim Crow, everywhere I go.

Down in Georgia and Tennessee, Alabama is a good place to go,
And get together, break up this old Jim Crow.

spoken: *Yes!*

You can go to Alabama, I want you to know,
When you get in Alabama, you gonna meet this old Jim Crow.

Come on up to California, I want you to know,
Some places you can go in California, you'll find some old Jim Crow.

In New York City, I want you to know,
In them China restaurants, boy, it's a plenty Jim Crow.

I find Jim Crow, everywhere I go,
I find Jim Crow, everywhere I go.

Local Number 6, in San Francisco,
It wasn't nothing but, eh, that old Jim Crow.

spoken: *That's right too. You'll find Jim Crow everywhere you go.*[20]

Leadbelly had joined Local #802 on 20 June 1940 and he was a member in good standing until his death. In 1946, Leadbelly had been prevented from recording with white musicians Ellis Horne, Squire Girsbach and Paul Lingle by the white San Francisco Local #6 of the American Federation of Musicians. When Leadbelly had earlier recorded with Paul Mason Howard, they were both "associated" with the black Los Angeles Local #747 by Capitol for accounting purposes. Local #6 wouldn't allow a similar subterfuge. It was alleged at the time that the matter had unsuccessfully been appealed to James Petrillo, president of the American Federation of Musicians (AFM) from 1940 to 1958. The suggested arrangement was said to have been denied by one of Petrillo's vice-presidents.[21]

Traditionally, many African Americans derived strength from their Christian faith. There are "No Restricted Signs (Up in Heaven)," the Golden Gate Quartet proclaimed in June 1946. At the "Pearly Gates" St. Peter does not put up "No Colored" signs, and everybody is welcome, irrespective of race or religion. This call for inter-racial and inter-religious solidarity against Jim Crow contains a rare example of an allusion to a non-Christian spiritual leader. Obliquely the song may also refer to the shortage of decent and affordable housing available to African Americans in the United States.

Knocka, knocka, knock, knock. Knock, knock.

Folks were knockin' at the Pearly Gates,

    Oh, knock, knock. Knock, knock.

Askin' 'bout the rooms, about the rates.

Old St. Peter was the official greeter, he was present to let them in,

Some looked down because their skins were brown, but Pete hollered with a great big grin:

chorus: *"You're welcome, welcome!*

    There are no restricted signs in heaven, there's no selected clientele,

    There are no restricted signs in heaven, brother, brother, that goes double, oh, hallelujah."[22]

    Oh, knock, knock, knock, knock.

Pete he said: *"Now, won't you follow me?"*

    Oh, knock, knock, knock, knock.

They looked around and what did they see?

Snow white angels, colored angels, sons of David and Chinese:

"You don't have to look swell, not for this hotel, you can even check in, in your dungarees."

    Knocka, knocka, knock, knock. Knock, knock.

Pete he knocked upon a door of stone,

    Oh, knock, knock, knock.

And, lo, there was the Lord upon a simple throne,

And he looked like Moses and he looked like Buddha, and he looked like the Savior so good

                and kind,

And he spoke to the young in their native tongue: *"You are all my guests, if you keep in*

                mind:"[23]

On 21 August 1947, Senator and former Governor Theodore "The Man" Bilbo, died in New Orleans. Bilbo had been an outspoken supporter of white supremacy and the Ku Klux Klan. In a speech in Greenville, Mississippi, delivered during his 1946 campaign, Bilbo had said: "I'm the best friend the nigger's got in the State of Mississippi. I'm trying to do something for 'em. I want to send 'em back to Africa where they belong."[24] In this context, the irony of the first stanza of Andrew Tibbs's "Bilbo Is Dead" from September 1947 is obvious. Tibbs (1929–1991) waited until his final verse to indicate his true feelings, concluding that the death of the vile Bilbo might make Mississippi a fit place to live again for the thousands of African Americans who had migrated to the cities of the North. The deeper meanings of Tibbs's song apparently did not escape the

"C'mon In. The Water's Fine," cartoon by E. Simms Campbell, *Afro-American*, 13 July 1946.

notice of southern authorities: according to Muddy Waters, the record was widely banned in the region.[25]

> Well, I've been down to Dallas, Texas, even went to San Antone,
> But when I got to Mississippi, my best friend was dead and gone.

chorus: Yes, Bilbo is gone, well, he had to put it down,
> Well, I feel like a lonesome stranger, yes, a stranger in my own hometown.

> I was a playboy and a devil, I had times that was really wild,
> Since Mr. Bilbo is dead, it makes me feel like a fatherless child.

> Well, you've been livin' in the big city, broke and had to get a loan,
> But you can hurry back to Mississippi, 'cause Bilbo is dead and gone.[26]

"Though a minor hit among blacks, 'Bilbo Is Dead' was too inflammatory to be put in jukeboxes in the South and to get what little airplay was available for black music," Nadine Cohodas concludes in her history of the Chess label.[27]

In an ambiguous reference to the mouth cancer to which Bilbo had succumbed, the *Chicago Defender* triumphantly headlined "Bilbo 'The Man' Dies; Mouth Proves Fatal." "The Man's death leaves Rep. John Rankin, his counterpart in the House of Representatives as the undisputed champion race baiter in Congress," the weekly concluded.[28]

In 1947 the American Heritage Foundation proposed that a train would travel through the United States as a traveling exhibition of the history of freedom in America. Endorsed by President Truman and Attorney General Tom Clark, "The Freedom Train" started its journey across the United States on 17 September 1947. The streamlined train was to travel through all 48 states until the January 1949 inauguration month. The 3 July 1948 issue of the *Chicago Defender* presented a drawing of the Freedom Train on its front page. The report reads: "Rededication, the period in which all Chicago is rededicating itself to the ideals that have built America, will reach its climax with a downtown parade of more than 10,000 veterans of all wars Sunday. The following day, July 5, the red, white and blue train containing 127 historic documents including the Constitution, Emancipation Proclamation, Bill of Rights and 14th Amendment, will arrive."[29] However, there were controversies in the South over whether blacks and whites could view it together.[30] The train was scheduled to arrive in Birmingham, AL on 29 December 1947. Whites and blacks were to line up separately. As John White explains: "Although whites and blacks would be on the train at the same time, they would never actually mix because a black group would not be admitted to the exhibit until the preceding white group had exited the first car and entered the second. This was the subtle twist and distorted ingenuity of the Birmingham plan."[31] As a result the American Heritage Foundation canceled the Birmingham visit. Poet Langston Hughes wrote a protest poem against a segregated freedom train and Paul Robeson recited it at his concerts.[32]

A remarkable protest song from 1948 was entitled "Freedom Choo Choo Blues." It was recorded by Tommie Jenkins with Naomi Mack at the piano for the tiny Olliet label. The record was advertised as a "True Race Recording."

The composer credits are claimed by black label owner Ollie Hunt. Naturally, being condemned to watch this celebration of American freedom and democracy in a segregated setting deeply offended African Americans, and "Freedom Choo Choo Blues" bristled with gathering impatience and militancy.

Jenkins' song derived additional resonance from the special place which images of travel, in particular by train, occupied in both the blues and gospel lyrical traditions. For a people lacking true freedom, images of mobility were traditionally very important. The blues and gospel were full of visions of escape, whether to the promised land of northern cities or to the afterlife. It was true that trains sometimes took loved ones away, but they just as often symbolized deliverance and release; in contrast, the Freedom Train brought further indignity. Jenkins emphasized that the promises of the Declaration of Independence had been a long time coming for African Americans. Only when they were needed to fight, the singer implied, were African Americans temporarily and half-heartedly included in the ranks of American democracy.

> Get up, mama, slip on your shoes,
> Daddy's gonna tell you, some real good news.

chorus:
> The freedom choo choo, it's coming 'round the bend,
> Won't you tell me, politicians, just where has it been?

> From 1776, down to this present day,[33]
> Me and my baby've been waiting for this day.

> From the cotton fields of Georgia, to the rugged coast of Maine,
> Then to sunny California, I've waited for this train.

> I've lived in a restricted district, mostly in a slum,
> Always kicked around, until my draft card has come.

> Oh, it's loaded with the Constitution, all signed up, and when
> It comes to our living, but it don't mean a thing.[34]

Had President Truman done anything to improve conditions for African-American soldiers? What was Truman's personal attitude toward black Americans? In 1911, when he was 27 years of age, Truman had written his wife:

> I think one man is just as good as another so long as he's honest and decent and not a nigger or a Chinaman. Uncle Will says that the Lord made a white man from dust[,] a nigger from mud, then He threw up what was left and it came down a China man. He does hate Chinese and Japs. So do I. It is a race prejudice I guess. But I am strongly of the opinion that negros ought to be in Africa, yellow men in Asia[,] and white men in Europe and America.[35]

Truman's grandparents had been slave owners during the Civil War and he shared the prejudice so prevalent in the state of Missouri. All his life he used derogatory terms like "coon" and "nigger."

After becoming President of the United States Truman gradually overcame some of his biases. In an emotional discussion with Walter White, executive secretary of the National Association for the Advancement of Colored People (NAACP), and other black leaders on 19 September 1946, Truman was shocked to learn about the real face of discrimination. In particular, the horrible fate of some returning war veterans stunned Truman, himself a veteran of World War I.

The story of the Monroe lynching on 25 July 1946 was one of many that White told to the President. "My God!" exclaimed Truman. "I had no idea it was as terrible as that." The details are presented by Taylor Branch: "Negro soldiers demanded that they be given at home the rights they had fought for overseas. Whites resisted these demands, especially in the South, with a ferocity that put lynchings back into the headlines. Mobs assassinated no fewer than six Negro war veterans in a single three-week period that summer. In Georgia's first multiple lynching since 1918, one of those six veterans died when a group of hooded men pulled him, his wife, and another Negro couple out of a car near Monroe, lined the four of them up in front of a ditch, and fired a barrage that left a reported 180 bullet holes in one of the four corpses. In the aftermath, state investigators in Monroe complained that 'the best [sic] people in town won't talk about this,' but they and the FBI would compile enough evidence to take before a grand jury, which, however, declined to return an indictment."[36] On 3 August photos of the battered faces of the victims were to be seen in black newspapers across the country.

Blues singer "Champion" Jack Dupree sang about the Monroe killings in his

As Talmadge's 'Fellow Countrymen' Take Over in Georgia

Termed the most cold-blooded and inhuman massacre in American history, this is how Gene Talmadge's "fellow countrymen" used their guns to maintain "white supremacy" at Monroe, Ga., last week. Two men, one of them a veteran of 5 years service in North Africa, Italy and the Pacific, and their wives, paid with their lives for failing to possess white skins. Artist Ellsworth Northern here depicts how the brutal lynching was executed. More than 60 bullets were pumped into the four bodies.

"As Talmadge's 'Fellow Countrymen' Take Over Georgia," illustration by Ellsworth Northern, *Afro-American*, 3 August 1946.

August 1946 recording "I'm Gonna Write the Governor of Georgia." Dupree had been a prisoner of war in the Pacific (probably in 1942 and 1943), as he explained to Dick Waterman: "It wasn't too bad on me because I was a cook and the Japs gave me my own room and they sent me other prisoners to do all the kitchen work. The Japs were good to the Coloreds because they wanted us to come over onto their side in the War."[37] When Dupree wrote this song he connected his own experience of discrimination to the Monroe lynchings. "Champion" Jack Dupree left the States for Europe in 1960.

> I'm gonna write the governor, tell him 'bout the Georgia state,
> Well, I'm-a tell him to do something, yes before it is too late.
>
> When I was down in the Pacific, fighting the Japanese,
> I had to go back down in Georgia, and bow down on my knees.
>
> I got people down in Georgia, that I'm afraid to see,
> Lord, I'm afraid that gang down there, Lord, they might lynch poor me.

Now, they taken out two men, and also their wives,
Well, they taken 'em out in the woods, and they taken the people's lives.

I'm gonna write the governor, tell him 'bout the Georgia state,
Well, he better do something, just before it is too late.[38]

Significantly, Jack Dupree's song remained unissued. Moses Asch, the owner of Folkways, was hardly a stranger to racial or political controversy. His influential label was home to many of the most important and outspoken releases by Woody Guthrie, Pete Seeger, and Leadbelly. Nevertheless, Asch may well have felt it unwise to issue such potentially incendiary material at this point in time. Dupree himself may also have been reluctant to see the song released, fearing personal reprisals, or a loss of bookings if theater managers considered him too controversial and likely to attract trouble from white supremacists. This was a common pattern. Artists, their managers and their labels, not to mention distributors, theater booking agencies, and radio station managers, were permanently concerned about the adverse effects which overtly political songs might have upon both their financial and physical well-being.

Ellis Arnall, the Governor referred to in Dupree's song, was a model of racial progressivism compared to the demagogic Talmadges, Gene and Herman, the spiteful race-baiters who preceded and succeeded him respectively in the Georgia statehouse. It is a moot point as to whether Dupree would have considered a letter to either of the Talmadges worth the ink, let alone a recording. Arnall, however, was one of a handful of newly elected southern progressives, who came to office with the aid of votes from returning GIs, women and those African Americans able to take advantage of the outlawing of the white primary election in 1944's *Smith vs. Allwright* decision. The moderation of men like Arnall represented some respite from the racist frenzy of the post-war years; a brief and equivocal flowering of southern racial liberalism amid the politics of racial reaction. Arnall boldly denounced the violence at Moore's Ford and dutifully ordered a full investigation.[39]

On 3 August 1946 the *New York Amsterdam News* reported that "Although President Truman was 'too busy' to see several hundred representatives of civic and federal organizations who paraded from Union Station to the gates of the White House protesting the Monroe, Ga. lynchings, Attorney General Tom Clark announced Tuesday that Mr. Truman had instructed him to investigate every angle of the case."[40]

On 28 September 1946 the same paper reported: "President Harry S. Truman told a committee of the Crusade to End Lynching that there were political matters which made it very difficult for him to issue a statement denouncing lynching when the group presented an urgent appeal to him at the White House last week to speak out against the wave of lynch terror spreading across the nation."[41]

Fears of economic or physical reprisals probably explain why Memphis Slim, Big Bill Broonzy and Sonny Boy Williamson requested that the pseudonyms "Leroy," "Natchez" and "Sib" be used to hide their identities when Alan Lomax recorded them talking candidly on racial oppression and the blues in March 1947. Significantly, these unique recordings were first issued not in the United States, but in Great Britain a decade later. A transcription was published in the USA in 1948, so at least the contents were made public, even if the recording was not issued until much later. An example of the candid way in which racial matters were discussed on this recording is the following fragment:

> Big Bill Broonzy: And I've heard them come around and say: "If you boys keep yourselves out of the grave, I'll keep you out of jail." Say: "If you kill a Nigger, I'll hire another Nigger." You know what I mean? "If you kill a mule, I'll buy another." One of those things. You ever heard that?
> Memphis Slim: That occurred to me on the levee camp, and you see, you know them fellows be so tired from carryin' logs or something like that, you know, clearin' new ground. He'd say: "Burn out, burn up. Fall out, fall dead." We had a few Negroes down there that wasn't afraid of white peoples and talked back to them. They call those peoples "crazy people."
> Big Bill Broonzy: I wonder why did they call 'em "crazy," because they speak up for their rights?
> Memphis Slim: Yeah, they call 'em "crazy."[42]

Truman's response to the racial dilemma threatening to engulf the US and tarnish its reputation abroad was to appoint a Committee on Civil Rights. While the committee was at work, Truman delivered a speech at the Lincoln Memorial on 29 June 1947. It was the first time an American President had addressed an NAACP rally. He declared to an audience of 10,000 African Americans and millions more on radio that all Americans had the right to a decent home, an education, adequate medical care, a worthwhile job, the ballot and a fair trial in court:

When I say all Americans, I mean all Americans.

Many of our people still suffer the indignity of insult, the narrowing fear of intimidation, and, I regret to say, the threat of physical and mob violence. Prejudice and intolerance in which these evils are rooted still exist. The conscience of our nation, and the legal machinery which enforces it, have not yet secured to each citizen full freedom of fear.

We cannot wait another decade or another generation to remedy these evils. We must work, as never before, to cure them now.[43]

Afterwards the *Afro-American*, perhaps with a certain amount of irony, called this speech "the strongest address on civil rights ever made by any President on a world-wide hook-up."[44]

In October 1947 the Committee published its report, *To Secure These Rights*. The document, which covered lynching, interstate transportation, voting rights and fair employment practices, was sent to Congress on 2 February 1948. Congress was hostile to the report's recommendations. Truman responded by issuing Executive Order No. 8981 on 26 July 1948, which called for full desegregation of the armed forces. Congress had no power to halt this measure.[45] Two years later the need for manpower in the Korean conflict led to less public opposition to the measure than might have been expected and the integration of the United States army proceeded without further interruption.

In the presidential election of 1948 Truman was the Democratic candidate. However, his civil rights policies had aroused such resentment among southern conservatives that a "Dixiecrat" party was formed. "The lynch-belt south is threatening a new secession," the *Chicago Defender* reported on 7 February.[46] For President the southerners nominated Strom Thurmond, the Governor of South Carolina. In June 1948 Huddie Ledbetter recorded "Equality for Negroes,"[47] a version of "God Made Us All"[48] by the Trinidad calypsonian Lord Invader. Leadbelly's biographers, who were not aware of the origins of the composition, wrote that "there are internal references in the song to suggest that he worked it up after listening to the 1948 Democratic convention."[49] Although this is not the case, events may have prompted him to select this song for performance.

> *Now, listen what I'm outlining to you,*
> *Negroes fought in World War One and Two.*
> *Some lost their lives, others lost their hands,*
> *Stood and fightin' for the United Nations.*

If the Negroes was good enough to fight,
Why can't we get some equal rights?
For God made us all, and in Him we trust,
Nobody in this world is a-better than us.

Why don't you folks realize with one another,
Like the scripture says: "Love thy neighbor."
You are Jewish or Italian,
Negroes is subjects of Great Britain.[50]

One thing, folks, you should all realize,
Six feet of dirt makes us all of one size.
For God made us all, and in Him we trust,
Nobody in this world is a-better than us.

I been hearing you speak about that old democracy,
That diplomatic and that old hypocrisy.
I think it's about time you should cut it out,
The way the Negroes is treated down South.

Awful pain, it's a rotten shame,
Like they wanna bring back slavery again.
For God made us all, and in Him we trust,
Nobody in this world is a-better than us,
Nobody in this world is a-better than us,
Nobody in this world is a-better than us.[51]

Meanwhile Henry Wallace, who had been Vice President during Roosevelt's third term and Secretary of Commerce for the first two years of Truman's first term, had become the presidential candidate of his own, newly formed, Progressive Party. Since his New Deal days Wallace had become increasingly left-wing. He urged close cooperation with the Soviet Union, wanted to turn over America's nuclear weapons to the United Nations, and sought to nationalize coalmines and railroads.[52] Nearly a third of the "Progressive Citizens of America" were women and the majority of their members were young. Many Americans viewed the new party with fear because of its Communist sympathies.[53] Since Wallace openly denounced segregation, refusing to address segregated audiences or to sleep in segregated hotels, some African Americans were attracted to the Progressive Party. These included blues and gospel singer Richard Huey, who recorded "Wallace Fit the Battle of America," released by the Progressive Party on its own label in 1948. To the tune of the well-known spiritual "Joshua Fit the Battle of Jericho," the song sums up what Wallace's party stood for. Most of the allusions in the song require no further explanation. However, "cannons for the people of Greece" refers to the $400 million aid package that had been sent to Greece in May 1948 under the Truman Doctrine to help the country maintain its independence. Greece was of vital strategic interest to the West and since the withdrawal of the British army of occupation it was in danger of falling prey to the Communists.[54]

chorus: *Wallace come to battle for America, America, America,*
           Wallace come to battle for America and Wall Street's tumblin' down.

           Yes, my brethren, the walls of Wall Street,
           Like the walls of Jericho, there they stand high and mighty.

           Around the city of the golden calf, wherein dwelleth the money changers,
           Dwelleth the gamblers,
           Who twirleth the roulette wheels of history,
           Who stacketh the cards against the wheat and the grain,
           Who loadeth the dice against those who toil and those who sweat,
           Who reapeth the harvest they soweth not,
           Who puts the steel and the oil above the flesh and the blood,
           Who paradeth the Bible and waveth the flag,
           Who drowneth the issue in brass bands and in brass hats and with brass hearts,
           Who abandon the golden rule for the rule of gold.
           There they stand, these mighty walls.
           And around them twineth the root of all evil,
           From which blooms the blossom of all sin,
           I'm talking about the sin of 1948,
           I'm talking about the sin of slums,
           The sin of Jim Crow,
           The sin of the college quota,
           The sin of restrictive covenants,[55]
           The sin of poll tax,
           The sin of want amidst plenty,
           The sin of cannons for the people of Greece,
           The sin of clubs for the pickets of America,
           The sin of no homes for the homeless,

The sin of billions for bombs and pennies for books,

The sin of a dollar a pound for butter,

The sin of thirty cents a day for sharecroppers,

The sin of profits for GE and debts for GIs,[56]

Yes, my Lord, and as old Joshua stood before the walls of Jericho,

So stands Wallace before the walls of Wall Street,

And though he has not the trump of the press,

And though he has not the trump of radio,

He has the strength of truth,

And the truth is seven times louder than thunder,

And that thunder's rolling, rolling over the land,

It's that same thunder that's thundering over the world,

Yes, my Lord, it's that one world thunder,

And the people are hearing, people are thinking,

People are gathering, gathering for the battle of America,

America, America, America![57]

The reverse side of the Progressive Party record is sung by the Royal Harmonaires (who were actually the Dixieaires group recording extra-contractually) and is entitled "Henry Wallace Is the Man." This song emphasizes Wallace's denunciation of segregation and recalls that the candidate had been a highly successful agricultural expert. "Some threw garbage" refers to an August 1948 visit to North Carolina where angry crowds pelted the Progressive candidate with eggs and rotten tomatoes.[58]

chorus: *Now, let us talk about him, sing about him and preach it:*
        Henry Wallace is the man!

        Well, in the good Book, so I was told,
        The prophet spoke out very bold;
        Now we have a man, his precious goal,

Gonna bring peace and happiness to our soul.
Wallace is the man for you and me,
He came to set this country free.
He traveled east, traveled west,
Worked with Roosevelt, stood the test.
He went way down in the Southern land,
Spoken the truth unto every man.

Well, he wouldn't stand for segregation,
He said: "I'm preachin' to all the nation."
Freedom to every man,
Some threw garbage from the garbage can.
They tried to scare him, his clothes were ruined,
But Wallace kept talkin' till he finished his point.
Then he shook his head and mopped his face,
Cryin': "Lord, have mercy on this wicked race!"

Now, Wallace is a farmer, he plants his seed:
His honest words and Christian deeds.
No more Depression, no more wars,
That's not what the people is sufferin' for.
Jim Crow in the land is got to stop,
Gonna bring that bottom rail up to the top.
And when he do, you can plainly say:
"There's heaven on the earth today."[59]

Although Truman was duly elected, Henry Wallace received almost 1.1 million votes, half of which came from New York state. Wallace's intervention had prevented Truman from carrying New York state. A frustrated President would later characterize Wallace as "a muddled, totally irrational man, almost incapable of uttering a coherent sentence. He was also the bitterest man I have ever encountered."[60] The Progressive Party was never influential again and Henry Wallace returned to private life, but he made an impact on the emerging southern civil rights movement, galvanizing the forces of black and white opposition to segregation.

Increasingly the President began to be seen as a politician doing his best and not as a statesman making a lasting impression. The harder Truman tried to demonstrate that he had the common touch, the less worthy a candidate for presidential office he seemed. The aristocratic Roosevelt had been a charismatic leader; Truman looked like America's shopkeeper. The Truman speeches were all too often forgettable, and among commentators there was much speculation as to whether he really was in touch at all.[61]

Truman's Republican adversary was Thomas E. Dewey, the Governor of New York state, who had been defeated by Roosevelt in 1944. Dewey was considered too artificial, and he was portrayed by some of his opponents as "the little man on the wedding cake."[62]

"Vote Democratic," the Party advertised in the Chicago Defender, "Hold the Roosevelt Line Against Reaction!" In a comparison between "The New Deal" and "The Raw Deal" the voters were reminded of the FEPC, the first federal indictment in a lynching case, the reception of Negroes in the White House, the appointments of Negroes to high Federal posts, the Negro vote in the south and employment in the Federal service.[63]

However, Truman had apparently gone into free fall in the opinion polls. On the day before the elections of 2 November 1948, Dewey led by 49.5 per cent in the final Gallup Poll as against 44.5 per cent for Truman. That night Truman drank his usual bourbon and was soon sound asleep. When he woke, Dewey had been beaten again and the percentages of the Gallup Poll had been reversed.

The Chicago Defender commented: "The Negro vote, holding the balance of power, has returned President Harry S. Truman to the White House. Ignored by all of the nation-wide polls as an 'insignificant minority' whose opinion needed no consideration, this minority has again demonstrated that 15 million Negroes can swing any national election."[64]

The seating arrangements at the Mayflower Hotel were integrated for the inaugural banquet. In his inaugural speech he re-affirmed that "all men are equal because they are created in the image of God." There were a hundred black guests at the inaugural ball, and at the inaugural gala popular black artists Lena Horne and Lionel Hampton were among the performers.[65]

Now that Truman had been elected it was time to resume his domestic reform program. In the immediate post-war years reconversion and inflation had taken priority over most social legislation, but on 20 January 1949 the revised "Fair Deal" program was presented to Congress. On 20 May 1949 blues singer Harmon Ray, who had recorded as "Peetie Wheatstraw's Buddy," sang a remarkable tribute to Truman in a song called "President's Blues."

Everybody's crying: "Truman, ooh, ooh, well, well, please let that good man be,
He's gonna do more for us than Lincoln, ooh ooh, well well, and Lincoln set us free."

Now, Mr. Roosevelt, was the other poor man's friend,
But Mr. Truman is going to outdo him, ooh ooh, well well, right on to the end.

He's gonna give us some brand new projects, like the good old WPA,
He's settlin' our bets for sure, 'cause the Lord will make a way,
He's gonna feed us when we're hungry, get a doctor when we're sick,
Now, he ain't no magician, ooh ooh, well well, but he's gonna turn a trick.

He's gonna give us spendin' money, somewhere up in the millions,
Come to think about it, it's way up in the billions,
He's gonna change my way of living, ooh ooh, well well, by changing all the laws,
He's gonna do more for his people, ooh ooh, well well, than even old Santa Claus.

Now, I'm so tired and hungry, ooh ooh, well well, I don't know where I'm going
to sleep tonight,
Lord, it may be in the White House, ooh ooh, well well, but way out of sight.

Now, that's what I like about Mr. Truman, gonna like him to the end,
If he runs in the next election, ooh ooh, well well, I'm gonna vote for him again.[66]

In a 1973 interview with Tony Russell, Harmon Ray plausibly claimed "President's Blues" as his own composition, even though the composer credit is to label operator Mayo Williams. In this song the singer compares Truman to Roosevelt, and expects him to surpass his predecessor. Truman may be a magician, but there are limits to his powers. In the fifth verse Ray may be saying that if the President lets him stay in the White House, he may have to be smuggled in through the back door. Russell concluded that the enthusiasm of Ray's mentor Peetie Wheatstraw for Roosevelt was more securely founded than Ray's admiration for Truman: "The Dixiecrat vote in Congress blocked most of Truman's plans, and the 'brand new projects' that Ray heralded in

'President's Blues' proved chimerical."[67] By the end of 1949 Congress had indeed accepted only a few of Truman's plans: minimum wage was raised, old-age benefits were extended and slum clearance was to be promoted.

The roles of the NAACP (The National Association for the Advancement of Colored People) and the labor unions became more and more important in the Truman era. Military desegregation had come about after strong pressure from black labor leader A. Philip Randolph (who had enjoyed the same kind of success in prompting Roosevelt to desegregate the war industries in 1941).[68] The NAACP had become so important that Truman had been forced to deliver his 29 June 1947 speech, although he had written a letter to his sister saying: "I wish I didn't have to make it."[69]

In addition to its legal challenges to the operation of the Jim Crow system, encouragement of black voting, and investigation of lynchings, the NAACP also sought to protect African Americans from the abuses of southern courts and jails. This role was highlighted in a celebratory December 1950 recording by the Gospel Pilgrims with lead singer Otis Jackson,[70] called "I'm So Grateful to the N.A.A.C.P."

> Well, I'm grateful to the N double-A CP,
> Well, I'm grateful to the N double-A CP,
> Oh well, they helped my mother, father, sister, brother and me,
> I'm grateful to the N double-A CP.
>
> Well, in the year of nineteen and forty-three,
> The campaign manager had a talk with me,
> These five letters, let me tell you what they mean,
> They have helped more people than you ever seen.
>
> We've been down in Georgia, Mississippi too,
> Well, we fought for human right(s) as other races would do,
> Come on and join, you don't have to fear,
> We have gone to the aid of thousands of people every year.
>
> Well, in the year of nineteen and forty-nine,
> You can remember the Florida crime,
> I'm talking 'bout Shepherd, Irvin and Greenlee,
> They were saved from the chair by the ACP.

Attorney Akerman along with the ACP,
Appealed to the court for the innocent three,
That they might live, sure as you're born,
Because reporter Ted Poston made it known,
That they are some poor mother's child,
Great God Almighty, they got another trial.

Well, now this one thing you can bear in mind,
You can depend on them any old time,
Wake them in the morning, wake them late at night,
And they will get right up to fight for human rights,
Because God on His throne's smiling down from above,
On the N double-A CP fighting for brotherly love.[71]

The National Association for the Advancement of Colored People's principal objective is to ensure the political, educational, social and economic equality of minority-group citizens of the United States and to eliminate race prejudice. The NAACP, which was founded in 1909, seeks to remove all barriers of racial discrimination through democratic processes. This mission is accomplished by seeking the enactment and enforcement of federal, state and local laws securing civil rights, and by informing the public of the adverse effects of racial discrimination. Otis Jackson sings that he was asked to support the association (as a volunteer) in 1943. As an example of its deeds Jackson refers to the case of Shepherd, Irvin and Greenlee who were "saved from the electric chair" in 1949.

Four young blacks, Walter Irvin, Samuel Shepherd, Charles Greenlee and Ernest Thomas, had been accused of raping a white girl in Groveland, Florida, on 16 July 1949. Ernest Thomas, who had escaped, was killed by sheriffs. Of the three remaining accused, Irvin and Shepherd were sentenced to the electric chair. Charles Greenlee, a boy of sixteen who did not even know the others until he met them in jail, and who had an excellent alibi, was sentenced to life imprisonment. Alex Akerman, Jr. was the attorney from Orlando who defended the "Groveland Boys." Ted Poston, a black reporter covering the trial for the *New York Post*, had influenced public opinion in favor of the accused.

The Gospel Pilgrims record was issued on Atlantic and, once more, the enlightened views of the label owners were significant in providing the environment within which such a song could be recorded and released. Brothers Ahmet and Nesuhi Ertegun, jazz- and blues-loving sons of a Turkish diplomat, were among the few owners of a commercial record label to take a stand on racial issues at that time. The Erteguns' parties at the Turkish Embassy were among the first integrated social events in Washington, DC.[72] In his autobiography Ahmet Ertegun reminisced: "I remember that my father would occasionally receive letters from outraged Southern senators saying something to the effect of: 'It has been brought to my attention, Sir, that a person of color was seen entering your house by the front door. I have to inform you that, in our country, this is not a practice to be encouraged.' My father would respond with a terse one-sentence reply such as: 'In my home, friends enter by the front door – however, we can arrange for you to enter from the back.'"[73]

In April 1951 the Supreme Court ordered a new trial, but when Shepherd and Irvin were being taken to another jail in November, Sheriff Willis McCall, who was guarding them, shot both handcuffed prisoners. Shepherd was killed, and Irvin severely wounded. The sheriff was later ruled to have acted in self-defense. At a second trial Irvin was again sentenced to death, which was commuted to life imprisonment by the new Governor, Leroy Collins. Greenlee was paroled in 1962 and Irvin only became a free man as late as 1968. Sheriff McCall had to resign in 1973 after allegedly kicking a black prisoner to death.[74]

The Groveland case was referred to as "Florida's Little Scottsboro."[75] Just as Roosevelt had been powerless in the Alabama case, Truman was unable to intervene successfully in Florida. In spite of *To Secure These Rights*, lawyers were still confronted with parochial white juries. The NAACP complained that the FBI could catch "the cleverest criminals in history," but was "unable to cope with violent criminal action by bigoted, prejudiced Americans against Negro Americans."[76]

In 1952 Atlanta gospel group the Echoes of Zion recorded a song called "Keep Still 'God Will Fight Your Battles'" which outlined the African-American presence in American military history from the Boston Massacre to the Korean War. With its stoical quietism and calls for faith in eventual divine deliverance, the song's message contrasted with the later militancy and activist appeals of some, if by no means all, African-American preachers. Nevertheless, "Keep Still" pulled no punches in condemning America's failure to live up to the preamble to the Declaration of Independence, with its bold affirmation that all men are created equal. As in Tommie Jenkins' "Freedom Choo Choo Blues," indeed as in the freedom struggle more generally, such references to America's much-vaunted but unfulfilled democratic ideals, to the rhetorical and symbolic touchstones of American civic religion, were a crucial element in the quest for support for African-American rights.[77]

chorus: *Keep still, keep still, God will fight your battles,*
        Keep still, God will fight your battle if you just keep still.

        We were with you, America, right from the start,
        We loved and served you from the depths of our heart,
        We were there in seventeen seventy-six,[78]
        In the streets of Boston our blood did mix.

        In the year of eighteen sixty-five,
        We fought to keep America alive,
        We died for the blue, we died for the grey,
        Was trustin' in God for a better day.

        In the First World War we denied you not,
        We did not run when the battle got hot,
        We died for England, Belgium and France,
        We died that democracy might have a chance.

        Dorie Miller[79] lies sleeping at the bottom of the sea,
        Down in Georgia was a great massacre,[80]
        Our boys were fighting to keep the Reds on the run,
        Down in Florida our homes being bombed.[81]

Our boys were fighting in far off Korea,
For America and the ones they loved so dear,
Their blood has flowed in foreign lands,
They're coming home to take a stand.

Cruel men may say or do what they may,
But the righteous will see a better day,
Before God's Kingdom will crumble and decay,
Heavens and earth will pass away.[82]

In 1940 labor leader Philip Murray had succeeded John L. Lewis as president of the Congress of Industrial Organizations (CIO). The CIO had seven million members and Murray was a very powerful man, but Truman resented the fact that Murray had supported Henry Wallace in the 1944 campaign. Moreover, the unions had organized strikes in 1946 that had caused Truman a great deal of irritation. In 1948 the two men finally concluded a truce, and when Murray phoned Truman to congratulate him on his election victory both men were in tears.[83] Four years later, on 9 November 1952, Philip Murray died and the C.I.O. Singers (later known as the Sterling Jubilees of Bessemer), a group of steel laborers from Birmingham, Alabama, recorded a tribute disc comprising "The Spirit of Phil Murray" and "Satisfied." The record was sold at a CIO convention in Montgomery, Alabama.[84]

☆   ☆

Tiger Records

BIRMINGHAM ALABAMA

"THE SPIRIT OF PHIL MURRAY"

"C. I. O. SINGERS"

100

The Spirit of Phil Murray

chorus: *Let the spirit of Phil Murray live (on and on),*
         Lord, let his spirit (live right on).
         Let the spirit of Phil Murray live (live on and on),
         God has called Mr. Murray home.

         Well, in nineteen hundred and forty-two,
         Labor leaders didn't know exactly what to do.

Mr. Murray smiled, said: "I'll be your friend,
I'll fight for the rights of the working men.

Well, when I die I want to be straight,
Where I can enter my God's Pearly Gates."
Now, every working man in this land,
Now, don't forget the deeds of this wonderful man.

Well, in nineteen hundred and fifty-two,
God called Mr. Murray, say: "Your work is through.
Your labor on earth have been so hard,
Come up high and get your reward.

You've been loved by everyone 'most,
You fought a good fight, you finished your course."
Now, the people in the land they begin to worry,
When they received a message they lost Phil Murray.

The Congress Industrial Organization assembled,
The whole world began to tremble.
Men, women and children cried,
When they heard the sad news Mr. Murray had died.

He was the CIO's loss, but he's Heaven's gain,
In the day of resurrection we'll see him again.
Now, good God almighty, our best friend is gone,
I, I want you boys to help me just to sing this song.[85]

Satisfied

chorus: Oh, satisfied, satisfied with Jesus, satisfied, my soul's been satisfied,
God said he would be my compass, God said he would be my guide.
Oh, I looked at my hands, my hands looked new,
I looked at my feet, and they did too,
Ever since that wonderful day my soul's been satisfied.

Well, you read in the Bible, you read it well,
Listen to the story, that I'm 'bout to tell.
Christ's last Passover, he had his communion,
He told his disciples: "Stay in union.
Together you stand, divided you fall,

Stay in union, I'll save you all."
Ever since that wonderful day my soul's been satisfied.

Well, you read in the Bible to understand,
God must have been in this mighty plan.
Men working hard day by day,
Working overtime, getting little pay.
Now, the people in the land they began to worry,
But God sent a man called Phil Murray.
He called him loud, He called him low,
Said: "I want you to take care of the CIO."
But one Sunday morning about one-thirty,
Had a cerebral hemorrhage, the world was worried.
Well, He called him loud, He called him low,
Said: "With me, disciple, you must go,
To Canaan land where you'll be safe,
I prepared a man, now, to take your place.
Now, tell the working mens they need not fear,
Walter Reuther gonna be their engineer."[86]

By their derivation (several lines were borrowed) these songs again show how influential Otis Jackson's "Tell Me Why You Like Roosevelt" was (cf. *Roosevelt's Blues*). Walter Reuther (1907–1970), who was already president of the United Automobile Workers of America (UAW), succeeded Murray in November 1952.

During the Truman administration only eleven blues and gospel recordings that deal with civil rights are known to have been recorded. Josh White denounced discrimination in daring fashion, Brownie McGhee and Leadbelly sang about the reality of Jim Crow, the Golden Gate Quartet and Leadbelly attacked discrimination on the basis of skin color, Andrew Tibbs sang about the death of Theodore Bilbo, Tommie Jenkins announced the arrival of the Freedom Train, "Champion" Jack Dupree and the Echoes of Zion commented on the Monroe killings, and the Gospel Pilgrims and the Echoes of Zion referred to the case of Shepherd, Irvin and Greenlee. The corpus is small, but at least one song was devoted to most of the major landmarks in the civil rights struggle. As such they present a quantitatively modest, but qualitatively impressive musical response to the struggle for African-American freedom, and one which is probably the visible and audible sign of a larger body of unrecorded protest songs. Evidently the reasons for the scarcity of the topic were repression and fear of reprisals on the part of both the singers and the record companies. Initially black protest songs were perceived as having no commercial appeal and fear of offending radio advertisers and sponsors prevented them from being broadcast.

In the field of civil rights Truman certainly promised more than he achieved. A Truman aide later explained that the strategy was "to start with a bold measure and then temporize to pick up the right-wing forces. Simply stated, backtrack after the bang."[87] Nevertheless, Truman was the first American President to endorse a civil rights program. After he ordered the desegregation of the armed forces, his 1948 re-election was in serious jeopardy because of his stand on civil rights. Truman had learned to conquer his own bias, but there was too little concrete progress in civil rights under his presidency.

4 SAY A PRAYER FOR THE BOYS IN KOREA

During World War II, the Japanese had occupied the Korean peninsula, much to the resentment of the indigenous population, who fought a spirited guerrilla campaign against their oppressors. After the war, the US supported the creation of two separate Korean states to prevent the Communist leader Kim II Sung controlling the entire peninsula. Kim, however, never relinquished his dream of reuniting his homeland. Recent research has shown that Kim II Sung sent 49 telegrams to Moscow, begging Stalin for permission to invade the South. Total victory was within easy reach, Kim II Sung argued.

Upon Japan's surrender, civil war had raged in China from 1946 to 1949. On 1 October 1949 Mao Zedong's Communists had established the People's Republic of China; partly because Stalin wanted to reassert his and Russia's leadership of the Communist world, he finally consented to the Chinese invasion of South Korea.[1] If he had known that the United States would counter-attack in response, Stalin would presumably not have given permission. On 25 June 1950 the North Korean army crossed the 38th parallel that had divided the country since 1948.

President Truman was afraid that this might constitute "the opening round in World War III."[2] The South Koreans appeared unable to stop the advancing troops from the North, and the President sent American soldiers overseas again,

Men of the 24th Infantry move up to the firing line in Korea, 18 July 1950. US National Archives 1385.

a decision which he considered the most difficult of his presidency. The Russians had been boycotting the UN Security Council since January because the UN had failed to replace the Nationalist Chinese representative on the Security Council with a Communist one.[3] As a result Truman succeeded in acquiring United Nations support for international intervention (Truman preferred the term "police action") under American leadership.

General Douglas MacArthur, the Allied commander of the Japanese occupation in 1945–1951, flew to Korea and asked for two divisions of ground troops. Just as in several blues and gospel lyrics from World War II, MacArthur appears as the war hero *par excellence* in songs about the Korean War.[4] In December 1950, the Otis Jackson Quartet (as the Gospel Pilgrims) recorded "Korea – Fightin' in the Foreign Land," in which MacArthur's role is consistent with the legendary status he had acquired after his exploits in World War II. In reality the General was called in by the President only after Congress had already decided to support the "police action."

chorus: Oh, well, now, the battle in the foreign land, done got started again, (3×)
               Children, you better run to God, you'd better pray.

               Well, way over 'round the Pacific Ocean, in a place we call Korea,
               There's a big crowd of people has gotten together, tryin' to overthrow the US plans.

               It was May, June or July, when this awful thing began,
               They started shootin' and killin' the women and men,
               It's a scandal and a shame!

               Then MacArthur contacted Truman, then Truman got troubled in mind,
               Then he called to Congress, and Congress assembled, said: "We gotta make up our mind."

               Then Congress told MacArthur: "Use every available man,
               Because through God's will and His mighty hands, we'll save the US band."[5]

Oblique use of African-American admiration for MacArthur is also made in the November 1950 recording "Who Will Your Captain Be" by the Selah Jubilee Singers, as they remind their listeners who the real captain is in the Christian worldview:

chorus: Oh, tell me who, who will your captain be, while fighting the enemy?
               Well, you're going to need a man of war to bring you victory.
               Oh, tell me who, who will your captain be, while over the deep blue sea?
               Well, you're gonna need King Jesus all the way.

               We have faith in General MacArthur, Mr. Winston Churchill too,[6]
               All of the military leaders, for they know just what to do.
               But there is one great leader, who is far beyond compare,
               He will cheer you, keep you, keep you in his care.

               Now, let us choose a captain, who's far beyond atomic power,
               His strong-armed protection, will cheer you every hour.
               Your battle He will fight, and will bring you to the light,
               He will hold you in the hollow of His hand.[7]

The Cold War was heating up once again, and in his 1951 "War News Blues" Texas blues guitarist Sam "Lightnin'" Hopkins (1912–1982) described the fear of World War III.

You may turn your radio on soon in the mornin': sad news every day,
Yes, you know I got a warning: trouble is on its way.

Poor children runnin' and cryin': "Oh, mama, mama, now what shall we do?"
Yes, she said: "You'd better pray, childrens, same thing is happenin' to mama too."

I'm gonna dig me a hole this mornin', dig it deep down in the ground,
So if they should happen to drop a bomb around somewhere, I can
hear the echo when it sound.[8]

One of the first blues artists to sing about the Korean War was Antoine "Fats" Domino (b. New Orleans, 1928), who was by then on his way to world fame as a popular rhythm and blues artist. In his September 1950 "Korea Blues" Fats revives an old tune to express dislike of the draft, but expresses confidence in the fighting spirit of the soldiers and entrusts the outcome to God. The song is full of bugle blasts by its composer, trumpet player Dave Bartholomew.

Uncle Sam ain't no woman, but he sure can take your man,
He's takin' 'em day and night, to go to Korea and fight.

Fats Domino, North Sea Jazz Festival, The Hague, 14 July 1985. Photo by René van Rijn.

> The people over there have messed up, they have made it very rough,
> We'll have to go there and show 'em, what it means to be real tough.
>
> So pray for me, baby, I'll be thinkin' of you day and night,
> And with the help of the maker, everything will be all right.[9]

Although, as we have seen, re-enlistment had meant an escape from poverty for some veterans in the latter half of the 1940s, service in Korea was hardly an enticing option. In his October 1950 recording of "Back to Korea Blues" Chicago blues pianist Sunnyland Slim (1907–1995) voiced the stoicism of the World War II veterans who had to "go back to that army."

> I was layin' in my bed, turned on my radio,
> All I could hear, was the news about the war.
>
> Way up in the sky, airplanes flyin' just like birds,
> Well, I got my questionnaire this morning, and, you know, I sure got to go.
>
> Fightin' over in Korea, and you know that ain't no fun,
> Every minute in the day, I can't hear nothin' but noisy guns.

spoken: Talk to me, Snooky! Play it, Leroy![10]

> I got to go back to that army, but I hate to leave my baby behind,
> 'Cause duty has called me, you know I've got to go.[11]

In his July 1950 "Classification Blues" Andrew "Smokey" Hogg has not received his 1-A card (indicating that he is physically fit for military service), but he is highly motivated to "stop them Communists." "Smokey" Hogg was a veteran of World War II and as such his expectations were not illusory, but the pattern of his recording career indicates that he did not make it to Korea.

> I don't have a 1-A card, but I'm looking for my classification every day,
> We got to stop them Communists, oh man, from comin' this way.
>
> We didn't start no trouble, but look like we done got to end,
> Good old USA say: "Never mind going, if they take women and men."
>
> The sea don't get too wide, the air don't get too high,
> We will look to God to our trouble, he gonna save our children's lives.
>
> I knew this war was coming, I could feel it eight or nine months ago,
> But when this trouble is over, we won't be bothered no more.[12]

In a brilliant tactical pincer movement MacArthur ordered an amphibious landing at Inchon, on the northwest coast of South Korea, on 15 September 1950. As a result of the Inchon invasion, Seoul was retaken on 26 September and on 1 October the North was forced back above the 38th parallel. Many argue that the "police action" should have been terminated here. However, MacArthur had convinced Truman that the Chinese would not interfere if UN troops continued to advance northwards, and received the President's permission to cross the 38th parallel in order to unify the Korean peninsula. Just like Roosevelt, Truman had deferred to the advice of the Joint Chiefs, and supported their conclusions when he felt sufficiently informed.

UN troops invaded the North on 7 October and occupied the capital Pyongyang on 20 October. Just as Stalin had been mistaken about the American reaction, Truman had miscalculated Chinese opposition. On 6 November China entered the war, and with massive Chinese help the North managed to recapture Pyongyang on 5 December 1950. From 1950 onwards, the enemy in blues and gospel lyrics was referred to as "the Communists" or "the Reds." The absence of such a designation before the Chinese intervention may be evidence of a feeling that the drive for Korean unification was a purely indigenous nationalist movement. In the 1951 song "Go and Tell the Reds We're Gonna Win" by the Memphis-based Sons of Jehovah, patriotism reigned supreme and recalled similar songs in World War II.

chorus: *Won't you go, and tell the Reds, we're gonna win, we're gonna win?*
         Won't you tell them just like we told the rest that we won't never be in debt.

      If we would all get together all over the land,
   We could lick the Reds like we did Japan.
      We got strong armies and airplanes too,
   Show the other nations what we can do.
      Listen everybody in the USA:
   Buy a great big bond every payday.

   Let's keep our defense, big and strong,
   So all our boys can soon come home.
   We got a lots of scrap iron, metal, copper and tin,
   Stronger than we were when we took Berlin.
   We've got a strong defense along the line,
   That's the reason we're skimping stuff of mine.
   We hate war, we hate jealousy,

But it seems we gotta fight to maintain peace.
The people are united nearly everywhere,
To get down on their knees in prayer.
When your burden gets heavy upon your back,
Call on God he'll be your battle-axe.
Listen everybody, both young and old,
We're gonna keep on fighting to save your soul.
We're gonna keep on fighting night and day,
And keep America the home of the brave.
We're gonna keep on fighting day and night,
Till my God make everything all right.[13]

Back home, the "Jody" theme was revived now that another war was raging. In "No Jody for Me" from 1951, blues singer "Big Mama" Thornton (1926–1984) has learned her lesson and vows that the "Jody Man," the proverbial stand-in lover of the women back home, will not fool her this time:

Well, if my man goes to war again, I am going to use my head this time,
'Cause when he came home before, I didn't have a measly dime.

I met a no good Jody fooled me, well, and spended up all my dough,
Then when the war was over, baby, Lord, he didn't show up no more.

Well, when my man came back home again, he really took me by surprise,
He gave me a good beating, and blacked both of my eyes.

I hear what Jody say, he loves me, well, I know it's just a lie,
'Cause if Uncle Sam can't use him, why, oh why should I try?[14]

During January 1951 the Korean War reached a critical point. On the 4th the North had again invaded the South and recaptured Seoul. Eleven days later the Communists were stopped, and on the 20th the United Nations branded China the aggressor. Thousands of American soldiers were dying on the battlefields and Mississippi-born guitarist J. B. Lenoir (1929–1967) recorded a fatalistic "Korea Blues" in which fear of death in action is combined with the specter of the Jody back home. This recording from late 1950 is the first song in which the Chinese are mentioned.

Advertisement for Jimmy Rogers, "The World Is in a Tangle,"Chess 1453, and J. B. Lenoir, "Korea Blues," Chess 1449. *First Pressings*, March 1951.

Lord, I got my questionnaire, Uncle Sam's gonna send me on away from here,
He said: "J.B., you know that I need you, Lord, I need you in South Korea."

Sweetheart, please don't you worry, I just began to fly in the air,
Now if the Chinese shoot me down, Lord, I'll be in Korea somewhere.

I just sit in here wonderin', who you gonna let lay down in my bed,
Wouldn't hurt me so bad, think about some man a-snorin' in your face.[15]

Three years later, in October 1954, Lenoir recorded "I'm in Korea." Despite the topographical details, Lenoir never actually fought in Korea. Again fear of death is mingled with the fear of losing the woman left behind.

Yes, I am in Korea, northeast side of Kamp'o,[16]
Lord, I don't have no idea, I never will see you no more.

I'm on a hill called 10-62, machine guns firing all over my head,
Darling, I was thinking about my kids and you, if I die what you gonna do?

I begin to wonder, have you forgot just what I said?
Don't let nobody, lay their head down in my bed.[17]

On 14 March 1951 a Gallup Poll indicated that only 26 per cent of the American people still supported President Truman. By the end of that month 57,120 American soldiers had already died in Korea, although the number of South Korean dead was three times higher.[18] Contemporary blues lyrics were showing increasing disillusionment and despair, as demonstrated in two record-ings, "Missing in Action" and "Got My Call Card," made for the Memphis-based Sun label by blues artist L. B. Lawson (b. 1929) in January 1952. By the end of the war 4821 American soldiers (14 per cent of the total number of US casualties) were "missing in action," and declared dead.[19]

Missing In Action

Well, they said I was missing in action, they thought that I was dead,
But the good Lord then He come to me, said: "Son, don't worry your head."
Oh, yeah, I know the Lord was on my side,
Yes, my mother she's back on earth, says she's worried about her child.

Now, she said: "Son, don't you worry about the night being long,
I know you're way over here in Korea, you know you're a long old way from home."
They say I was missing in action, by the help of the Lord, they got that wrong,
Yes, I know mother's gonna jump and shout, Lord, just when I get back home.

Yes, now you know the day they captured me, and I fell down on my knees,
I said: "I want everybody just to hear me, Lord, I wanna pray one time, if you please."
I said: "Lord, have mercy, will you please make a way?"
Yes, you know I was missing in action, Lord, I was helping the ROK.[20]

Got My Call Card

Well, I got my questionnaire, yes, I got my call card too,
Ooh, oh, oh! Lord, just what I'm gonna do?
Yes, my brother's gone to the army, Lord, and they tryin' to get me too.

You know I had a friend once, across the water, he was so dear to me,
You know that atom bomb done exploded, you know he done disappeared, don't you see?

Oh, yeah, they tell me, that we'll never meet again,
Yes, they tell me over in Korea, said they done lost a many men.

Yes, they say he was missing in action, but I don't believe that's so,
They done dropped a bomb, I know they didn't have to just let him go.

Ooh, oh, oh! Lord, now what I'm gonna do?
Yes, I swear he's missing in action, Lord, and they're coming after you.[21]

The singer here does not believe that his friend is "missing in action," but thinks that an atomic explosion annihilated him. Lawson may be looking back to World War II, when Allied prisoners were indeed among those killed by the atomic bombs. If so, he is worrying that Korea might see a further use of atomic weaponry.

He had good reason, for on 30 November 1950 Truman had even allowed himself to say to journalists that use of the atomic bomb was under "active consideration."[22] The resulting panic led to a crisis in leadership and the President's "mental competence and emotional stability" were questioned.[23] During the Chinese onslaught of late 1950 and early 1951, many Americans lost faith in their President's ability to handle the escalating crisis.

Truman had always detested General MacArthur, who, unlike the President, would have liked to move quickly from consideration to deployment of nuclear weapons to end the Korean War. Truman considered MacArthur conceited and over-ambitious, calling him: "Mr. Prima Donna, Brass Hat, Five Star MacArthur."[24] Tensions between them grew to such an extent that on 10 April 1951 Douglas MacArthur was relieved of his command for "rank insubordination" and unwillingness to conduct a limited war. A contemporary cartoon said it all, when it showed a senator saying: "Who does Truman think he is? President of the United States?"[25]

"Old soldiers never die, they just fade away." On 19 April a record 30 million radio listeners heard the General quote the sentimental Frank Westphal song

Army General Douglas MacArthur inspecting troops of the 24th Infantry. US National Archives 1375.

"Old Soldiers Never Die (They Just Fade Away)" in his historic farewell speech before the House of Representatives. The next day seven and a half million people gave him the greatest ticker-tape parade in history. A few days later, on 26 April 1951, blues guitarist René Hall (1912–1988) opportunistically recorded the song with vocalist Courtland Carter.[26] It was virtually MacArthur's last hurrah. Popular support for MacArthur waned after the Senate's investigation of his dismissal. After years of seclusion in New York City, the Lion of Luzon died in 1964 at the age of 84.

Judging from all the blues and gospel songs recorded in praise of the General, few African Americans seem to have been concerned about Thurgood Marshall's view of MacArthur as a racist. Marshall visited Korea at Truman's request to review the treatment of black soldiers.[27] However, after MacArthur's dismissal, war correspondent James L. Hicks of the *Afro-American* wrote a front-page article subtitled "Tan Yanks won't shed any tears over his removal," in which he called the general a "backer of Jim Crow," and claimed that segregation was allowed under his command. Hicks found that most colored service personnel in the Far East considered MacArthur to be a great military strategist, but that, in spite of the President's directives on segregation, the general always permitted racial discrimination to exist in his command. Several harrowing examples were given to support these opinions. The paper concluded with an editorial entitled "We Shed No Tears" in which it stated that the "arrogant militarist" was "one of the few remaining disciples of the white imperialistic domination school glorified by Rudyard Kipling."[28]

In July 1951 peace negotiations began at Kaesong, but a rapid conclusion to the war was not forthcoming. Blues singer Willie Brown drove the message home in a "Korea Blues" recorded in Atlanta on 30 August 1951.

> Well, the war in Korea is never over, Uncle Sam's calling boys every day and night,
> And with all the screamin', clawin' and bloodshed, you have never seen the sight.
>
> But, mother, don't you worry, your boy will be home again some day,
> But all we can do now, is fall on our knees and pray.[29]

Sherman "Blues" Johnson compared the Korean War unfavorably with World War II when he sang "Lost in Korea" in September 1952. Memphis studio operator Sam Phillips, who had previously recorded Johnson for Lillian McMurry's Trumpet label, "later spent hours laboriously dubbing over bomb effects, again and again, until he had approximated the whistlings, shudderings, and far-off rumblings that he heard in his imagination."[30]

> Baby, please, write me a letter, because I'm lost and all alone,
> Well, I have no one to love me and I'm a million miles away from home.
>
> Well, my days are miserable, baby, and my nights are lonesome and cold,
> When this war in Korea is over, I'll be as happy as a two-year-old.
>
> World War Two was bad, but this is the worst I've ever seen,
> Every time I think it's over, I wake up and find it's just a dream.[31]

During 1952, a year of complicated negotiations, several prayers for peace were recorded. One of these was "Say a Prayer for the Boys in Korea" by the Evening Star Quartet, a song composed by their first tenor, Joseph Cook.

> Oh, why don't you say a prayer for our boys in Korea,
> That are fighting and dying over there?
> Lord! 'Struction on every hand,
> There is blood running in the sand.

chorus: Won't you say a prayer for our boys in Korea?

> In the year nineteen hundred, you know of fifty-one,
> When another war, child, had to be born.
> You know the Communists stuck out their paw,
> And they brought our country into war.

> I said, Mother, I hear you pray, I know what you're praying for,
> You're praying to God our father, for Him to stop the war.
> If everyone would kneel and pray,
> The war would end one day.

> "Mother, you keep on praying," I said: "Father, you pray too,
> To our Heavenly Father, carry our soldiers safely through.
> You know they're fighting over there,
> And God knows, they need your prayer."

> I said: "Lord, bless my mother, Lord, bless my father,
> Dear Lord, bless our soldiers over there."
> Yes! Every night and day,
> You will always hear me say:

> Said: "Our Father, who art in heaven,
> Please protect our soldiers in Korea.
> Lord, hold 'em in your mighty hand,
> Bring peace to this land."

> I said: "This is our prayer for our boys in Korea." Amen![32]

With the Korean situation still unresolved and public support declining still further, on 29 March 1952 Harry Truman unexpectedly concluded a speech in Washington by saying: "I shall not be a candidate for reelection. I have served my country long, and I think efficiently and honestly. I shall not accept a renomination. I do not feel that it is my duty to spend another four years in the White House."[33]

As campaigning got under way, Louis Jordan introduced the various candidates

Sergeant First Class Major Cleveland fighting with the 2nd Infantry Division. US National Archives 1426.

for the Presidency and gave some light-hearted advice on how to vote in his 8 May 1952 "Jordan for President."

spoken: *All right, folks of this strivin' community:*
          If I'm elected your President,
          Every Sunday evening at two-thirty,
          I'll entertain all your kiddies on the White House lawn.

spoken: *All right, folks: if you send me to Washington as your leader,*
          I'll personally see to it that every living American gets his portion, (after I get mine.)

spoken: *All right, folks: we all are worrying about the coming election,*
          But you know, folks, we gotta make the proper selection.
          And I wanna get all you people straight about all the candidates:

          Now, if you want a man with a good offer,
          Then cast your ballot for Kefauver.[34]
          And you can rest and be assured,
          You'll get no graft from Taft.[35]

But if you want administration that will groove you,
That will move you, and keep you sent:
Vote for Jordan for President!
That's me, folks, on the swing ticket.

Now, if you want to get the military bit straight,
We all know that MacArthur would be great.[36]
And if you want a hipster, that'll take no sassin',
Then vote for Stassen.[37]
But if you want to walk on the sunny side of the street,
With a candidate with a beat,
Vote for Jordan for President!
That's right folks!

You know, folks, I ain't runnin' no chicken in the pot campaign:
Everybody's gonna drink champagne!
And in every city I'm gonna install a rhythm committee.
(Pass out them cigars there, boy!)
And on my birthday everybody in the USA is gonna get new shoes,
We're goin' dancin', nobody will get the blues.
No longer will I be on a phonograph record:
I'm gonna be on Congressional Record!

If you want the man of the hour,
Then vote for Eisenhower.[38]
And, ladies and gentlemen:
Don't sit there and sob,
'Cause Truman don't want the job.
But if you want a candidate that's real cool,
Don't vote for the elephant or the mule:[39] *Vote for me!*
Vote for Jordan for President!

Folks, if you send me to the White House, we all will serve – time!
Vote for Jordan for President!

I'll put everybody on Relief!
Vote for Jordan for President!

If you wanna hustle with Russell, go ahead![40]
Vote for Jordan for President!

Folks, if you stick with me, I'll put everybody in the race!

Vote for Jordan for President!

Write in for me, folks![41]

"Jordan for President," Louis Jordan at the Strand Theater, c. April 1952. Author's collection.

DECCA

SAMPLE COPY; NOT FOR SALE

Fox Trot
Vocal Chorus By
Louis Jordan
And Ensemble

JORDAN FOR PRESIDENT
(Louis Jordan)

LOUIS JORDAN
And His Tympany Five

28225
(82834)

It is easy to see why Louis Jordan was such a popular artist. The infectious rhythms and melodies of his songs were combined with sharp-witted lyrics. This monologue, a composition by the artist himself, is full of puns: "swing ticket" on musical and political swing, "I'll put everybody in the race" on the electoral and the black race. In the final line Jordan urges a "write-in" vote on the ballot, but obviously no African-American candidate was going to be listed. It would of course have been unthinkable for a black man to become a candidate for the Presidency in 1952. Jordan was a marvelous entertainer who did not present a serious alternative manifesto and who consequently was not perceived as a threat by the white establishment.

The Republican candidate, General Eisenhower, foresaw that a promise of peace in Korea could lead to a Republican victory. On 24 October Eisenhower appeared on television and announced that he would go to Korea to end the war.[42]

President Truman was ignored in the Korean blues and gospel lyrics. He is certainly not hailed as the ideal wartime leader, as had been the case with FDR.

In contrast, there is sadness and frustration about the many victims of war and the absence of a peace settlement. Whereas Roosevelt and MacArthur were adept in the field of public relations, Truman had great difficulty in maintaining a positive image.

An amusing sketch entitled "Male Call" about the ongoing war in Korea was recorded on 30 May 1953 by guitarist Emmitt Slay and pianist Bob White. Bob White, who may be responsible for both voices, composed the song; the title is presumably a pun on "Mail Call," the moment when mail is distributed to soldiers.[43]

> Hey, man. Here's a letter that you missed at mail call this morning, and I picked it up for you.
>
> Thanks, my man. (sound of letter being torn open) It must be from my boy telling me about my wife. I told him to look out for her. She's a good girl. Would you read this for me? I can't read, you know.
>
> Sure. "Dear Buddy, how are things over there in Korea? I sure envy you over there in the thick of things. I was over to see your wife last night, and while I was there, your brother-in-law, Smelly, dropped in. He was wearing a pretty brown suit, the one that you bought just before you left. Your wife gave it to him because she said, most likely it would be out of style by the time you got back. Three or four other couples dropped in, and I guess we killed about four or five cases of beer. We offered to chip in to pay for it, but your wife wouldn't let us, because she said that you send her twenty-five and thirty extra dollars to do with as she wishes. We thought your wife would be a little shaken up after the accident she'd had last week with your brand new Cadillac, but you'd never know she'd had a head-on collision and it smashed your car to bits. The other driver, he's still in the hospital, and he's threatenin' to sue. But we all admire your wife's courage by her willingness to mortgage the home to pay the bill. But to get back to the party – you should have seen your wife doing her interpretation of Rose Hathaway.[44] She was still going on strong when we said good night to her – and Claude. Oh, I guess you know Claude. Claude's rooming at your house. He says that your wife can cook bacon and eggs better than anybody else in the world. Well, buddy, I guess I might as well bid you good night now. I can see across the street from my window into yours, and your wife and Claude are having a nightcap. He's got on a pretty smoking jacket, the one that you used to love to wear so often. Well, buddy, good night. But do me one big favor. Give all of those Communists heck, huh?"
>
> Hey man, what you doing with that gun? Put that gun down! (pop) Hot dog! I gave him the wrong letter.[45]

The soldiers were eager to return home, but would the new President do what he had promised? Dwight David Eisenhower (1890–1969), who had been raised on a farm in Abilene, Kansas, went to West Point military academy in 1910. With his keen interest in sports and history this seemed a logical choice for an athletic, good-looking young man. His biographer reports that he did not suffer under the harsh regime, but instead delighted in finding ways to escape the strict rules of military training.

In World War I Eisenhower distinguished himself so much by his administrative skills that he became an aide to General Douglas MacArthur.

By the time of World War II General Eisenhower had risen in rank to become commander of the Third Army in 1941, and Supreme Commander of the Allied Forces in Europe in 1944. His strategic vision made him an ideal leader. As he himself once pointed out, "the art of leadership is making the right decisions, then getting men to *want* to carry them out."[46] After the defeat of the Nazis Eisenhower was arguably, as his biographer Stephen Ambrose concludes, "the most successful general of the greatest war ever fought."[47]

In 1948 the popular war hero felt he was not ready for political office, accepting instead the post of president of Columbia University. However, when Truman asked him to become NATO commander in 1950, he readily accepted.

In February 1952 Eisenhower finally decided to run as the Republican candidate for the presidency, with Richard Nixon as his running mate for the vice presidency. As his opponent, the Democrats eventually nominated the Governor of Illinois, Adlai Stevenson.

Meanwhile the Korean War continued. As had been the case with the Japanese after Pearl Harbor,[48] the Chinese foe quickly became the subject of great racist abuse. Although African-Americans were on the receiving end of discrimination at home, many quickly fell into the habit of inflicting it on other ethnic groups, whether in an effort to show their patriotism or to elevate themselves in America's racial pecking order. Blues guitarist "Homesick" James (b. Tennessee, 1914) stereotypes the Chinese as ruthless rice-eating killers in his January 1953 recording "Wartime." There is no need for American soldiers "to weep and moan," James argues with tongue in cheek, for while they are fighting the Chinese, he will look after their wives.

Homesick James, NBBO Blues Festival, Amstelveen, The Netherlands, 27 October 1973. Photo by Hans ten Have.

Every time I pick up a newspaper, I can read something about the war,
Well, now, you know, all these Chinamens do is eat rice,
  and they still out to take some good man's life.

Uncle Sam is fixing up your questionnaire, boys, Lord, your examination, Lord,
                                and your class card too,
Yes, you know I ain't got no right to worry, always got a smile, man, on my face.

Well, some of you gone to the army, boys, ain't no need you to weep and moan,
Well, she always got a smile on my face, well, I'll be laying 'round your house a-tryin'.[49]

In the 1960s the New York-based Spivey label issued a Chicago Blues album, which contained a "Korea Blues," thought to have been recorded some time previously. Although the artist was given by Spivey as J. B. Lenoir, this has long been disputed.[50] It has been suggested that the singer was actually Chicago guitarist

Eddie "King" Milton, who had recorded the same song as "Love You Baby" for J.O.B. Records in 1960. Whoever the artist was, like so many wartime blues the track vividly describes the estrangement between lovers brought about by the forced separation. Milton's wife had shown rather more independence than the singer had bargained for. He refers to his unexpected return home on Independence Day, normally a day of celebration, and implies that he found her with another man. With regard both to its melody and to some of the lyrics, this song was based on a prison work song. Considering the recording date, it might deal with the American Armistice enforcement.

> Love you, baby, yes, I always will,
> Love you, baby, yes, I always will.
> Took you down town, baby, bought you some shoes,
> Took you down town, bought you everything.
> Went to the army, I stayed two long years,
> Fought twelve months in the heart of Korea.
> Sent my money to my wife and child,
> She (didn't) even write me a single line.
> Got back home on the Fourth of July,
> Knocked on her door, and she made me cry.
>
> Don't nothing matter but being back home,
> Being back home with my wife and child.
>
> Hey, hey, hey. Hey, hey, hey.
> Oh yeah. Oh yeah. Oh yeah.
> Did me wrong.
> Hey, hey, hey. Hey, hey, hey. Hey, hey, hey. Hey, hey, hey. Hey, hey, hey.[51]

An earlier song about the wartime separation of lovers is "Soldiers' Blues" from 1953 by George "Red" Callender (1916–1992) and His Sextet. Vocalist Duke Upshaw is roaming the bloody hills of Korea with his woman on his mind:

> Wonder, pretty baby, baby, do you ever think of me?
> Lot of reason to worry, baby, is because I'm across the deep blue sea.
>
> When I think about you, baby, mmm, the chills run up and down my spine,
> Yes, I wanna see you, baby, mmm, I almost just lose my mind.

As I roam these bloody hills, body cold and full of chills,
I wanna see you, baby, sometimes I think I never will.

Blues in Korea, broken as a man can be,
Won't you write a letter, baby? "Daddy, please hurry home to me!"

I've got rocks for my pillow, the cold ground is my bed,
Wanna see you, baby, yes, I almost lose my head.

Got the blues, got the blues, won't you write me, pretty baby?
"Daddy, please, hurry home to me."[52]

On 24 October 1952, during a campaign meeting in Detroit, Eisenhower had announced that he would end the Korean War immediately after his election: "That job requires a personal trip to Korea. I shall make that trip. Only in that way could I learn how best to serve the American people in the cause of peace. I shall go to Korea."[53] A fortnight later Eisenhower won the presidential elections by a 55 per cent majority, as against 44 per cent for Stevenson. It was the first Republican victory since 1928, and it was a personal triumph for Eisenhower.

Blues shouter Max "Scatman" Bailey, recording as "Little Maxie" Bailey, shows how high the expectations of the new President were in his 1953 "Drive Soldiers Drive."

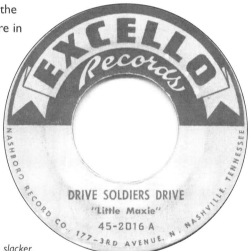

> *President Ike is a mighty man,*
> *He called for the whites and the*
> *brown and tan:*
> *"Come on boys and follow me,*
> *We gonna end this war in old*
> *Korea."*

chorus: *Drive, soldiers, drive, (drive on) (3×),*
Drive on, drive on, drive on!

Don't worry 'bout your wife and be no slacker,
Uncle Sam is your financial backer.
All you got to do is follow through,
We'll take care of you and your families too.

spoken: *Hut, hut, hut, ho! (6×)*

   Hup, two, three, four! (5×), Hup!

   Well, everybody knows that Ike's the one,
   He knows and I know there's work to be done.
   We can win this war, but make it fast,
   And Uncle Sam won't have to ration that gas.[54]

spoken: *Drive on!*

   Well, I know you boys has got a lot of ambition,
   You can tear up things with that new ammunition.
   We're in this war, but we're not alone,
   Let's finish this war, then we'll all go home.

spoken: *Hut, hut, hut, ho! (3×)*

   Look out soldiers!

   Hut, hut, hut, hut![55]

On 29 November 1952 the President-elect flew to Korea to view the situation at first hand. He concluded that a stalemate had been reached. Total victory could not be reached at a cost America was willing to bear. Eisenhower resolved that no more American lives should be sacrificed.

Negotiations for a truce contin-ued, and eventually an armistice was concluded on 27 July 1953. That very day gospel guitarist Sister Rosetta Tharpe (1915–1973) recorded a jubilant "There's Peace in Korea."

chorus: *I'm so glad, at last, there's peace in Korea, (3×)*
   Because President Eisenhower, has done just what he said.

   We're hoping there will be no more misery and no more sadness,
   No, no, no, no, no more dying, there'll be in the land.
   Hope we'll have happiness and joy and peace of mind,
   Because we know God has made this world, and made it for the good and kind.

I'm saying to all you mothers: "Now don't you weep and moan,
I know that you are glad, because your sons are coming home.
Now, you wives, sisters and brothers, you can wipe your teary eyes,
Because, sure as I'm singing, the sun has begun to shine."[56]

Texas blues guitarist Sam "Lightnin'" Hopkins recorded several songs about the way in which war influenced daily life in the United States. Two days after the Sister Rosetta Tharpe recording Hopkins waxed "The War Is Over," casting himself in the role of a returning soldier who could return to his mother and his "used to be."

Yeah, you know the war is over, now I've got a chance to go back home,
Yes, you know, if that woman done spent all my money, I'm gonna whup
her for doing me wrong.

Yeah, you know, that's what mother been praying, for 'em to send her poor child back home,
Yes, but you know, it's a sin and a shame for him to come back, find every dime he made is
gone.

Now, the war is over, baby, now, ain't you glad?
You know, you can get back, and that old used to be, have the same good times you used to
have.[57]

John Lee Hooker in "Build Myself a Cave,"[58] Lightnin' Hopkins in "War News Blues,"[59] Honeyboy Edwards in "Build a Cave,"[60] Jimmy Rogers in "The World's in a Tangle,"[61] Arthur "Big Boy" Crudup in "I'm Gonna Dig Myself a Hole"[62] and Robert Lockwood & Sunnyland Slim in "I'm Gonna Dig Myself a Hole"[63] had all sung about burrowing underground either to escape (nuclear) bomb attacks, or to escape the draft. Now it was time to "move right out the ground" and to return home, as Arthur "Big Boy" Crudup (1905–1974) sang in "The War Is Over," a November 1953 sequel song.

Yes, the war is over, I'm gonna move right out the ground,
Darling, I wanna find you, baby, when your man not hanging around.

I want you, baby, you know I want you for my own,
I want you now, darling, each night now in my arms.

spoken: *Oh, Lord, play it for me, man, play it for me!*[64]

Black soldier returns, 1953. US National Archives 1520.

Yes, I'm coming home, darling, I want you by yourself,
You know the war is over, baby, I don't want nobody else.

I'm diggin' away, I'm gonna move right out the ground,
You know the war is over, baby, no man now hangin' around.[65]

As the soldiers were coming home from Korea, female vocalist Dell St. John recorded "Welcome Home Baby" with alto saxophonist King Perry & His Orchestra in October 1953.

I feel so glad, my baby's coming home,
I've been so sad, I've been so all alone.

He's been gone since April fifty-two,
I've been so lonesome, I didn't know what to do.

Welcome home, my love, (4×)
I'm glad you're back and I thank the Lord above.

When he gets home, we're gone have a ball,
We're gonna get real high and that ain't all,

Been waitin' to hear from Panmunjong,
Korea's through fightin' and baby's coming home.

Feel so gay, my baby's coming home today,
Gonna thank the Lord and get right down and pray.

Welcome home, my love, (4×)
I'm glad you're back and I thank the Lord above.[66]

President "Ike" had kept his word and he was as popular as ever. A few days after the signing of the peace treaty, the Keys of Heaven, an obscure male gospel group, sang his praises in their August 1953 "Let Your Light Shine on Ike."

chorus: *Oh Lord, let your light, let it shine on Ike,*
That he might lead us, lead us safe day and night.

When Ike was striving to win the vote,
Mothers prayed: "God, give him hope."
He's our leader, of today,
God, guide him, on the way.

War is over, in Korea,
Battle is ended over there.
Every mother's son did no wrong,
Now it's ended, return home.

Oh Lord, oh Lord, oh Lord, oh Lord,
I know you heard, I know you heard, I know you heard,
Some mother, somebody's mother, somebody, somebody's mother,
On her knees, cryin': "Lord, oh Lord, please Lord, oh Lord, oh Lord."[67]

At least ten blues singers served in Korea. Nat Foster (no dates) was a maintenance clerk with the 540th Transport group in Chanchon, from where he sent lyrics, credited to N. A. Foster, Jr., Army Pfc. F-6456, to New York music publisher Joe Davis.[68] William "Soldier Boy" Houston (no dates) sang that he had been in the army since 1941, and that he was sent to the Philippines in 1943, coming home in 1945. In an unissued 1953/54 song he sang about leaving Korea, although there is no conclusive evidence that he served there.[69] Johnny "Big Moose" Walker (1927–1999) played piano in the Seoul Officers' Mess.[70] Alford "Chicago Pete" Harrell (1931–2001) served in Korea in the early 1950s.[71] Sammy

Lawhorn (1935–1990) spent most of 1953 through 1958 in military service. This included a stint in Korea, where he was aerial photographer for the Navy and got wounded in action.[72] Little Joe Blue (1934–1990) signed up with the US army in 1953 and went off to Korea for three years "to give it a try."[73] J. B. Hutto (1929–1983) served as a draftee in the Korean War in the early 1950s, driving trucks in combat zones.[74] J. D. Nicholson (1917–1991) served in Korea in the early 1950s.[75] Rudy Ray Moore (who does not want to reveal his date of birth) served in Korea, where he put on comedy shows in which he sang, danced, emceed and told jokes. He was discharged in 1953.[76] Memphis blues singer Velba Lee "Little" Applewhite (b. 1933) also served in Korea. He fought at the Russian border and was in the long march back. He got frostbite, said the shells were falling like rain and he thought he would never get out alive.[77]

Iverson "Louisiana Red" Minter (b. 1936) lied about his age to join up, served in US Army Air Force in Korea in a labor battalion, and sang the blues at service clubs from 1951 to 1953.[78] In 1994 he recorded a "Korea Blues" in Greece. Yet again this song brings out the estrangement between two lovers caused by the outbreak of war. Red is so desperate that he is ready to enlist again. In real life he did just that and is both a Korea and a Vietnam veteran.

> In this cold war in Korea, wonder what you're doing in the USA?
> Well, you sent me your picture and you tored my life up today.
>
> Said: "Red, I don't love you, got a brand new man,"
> Ain't that something to tell a soldier, when he's fighting in another land?
>
> I got the first letter, you sent to me,
> It was you and your wedding and my best friend, George, you see?
>
> Ain't that a something to send a soldier that's fighting in another land?
> Well, that's alright, baby, one day you're gon' overturn your hand.

spoken: Well, alright, man! Mm!

> When I get out of this army, I might re-enlist,
> 'Cause what I got in this letter, I just can't stand no more of this.
>
> Hey, hey, baby, why you do a soldier fightin' in another land?
> Well, I tell you this letter, Lord, done sho 'nuff changed this man.[79]

Louisiana Red, The Netherlands, mid-1970s. Photo by Diny van Rijn.

On Armistice Day (27 July 1953) army strength was at its peak. On that day there were 302,483 American soldiers in Korea. The National Archives and Records Administration states that 33,642 American soldiers died in the Korean conflict, 29,014 (= 86 per cent) of whom are listed as "Caucasian" and 3123 (9.3 per cent) as "Negro."[80] It is estimated that 8 per cent of the American soldiers in Korea were black.[81] These percentages do not differ very much from general population statistics, so that we can conclude that the number of black soldiers who died in Korea as a result of hostile action or who are determined to have died while missing or captured is proportionate.

When the war started there were about 40 million people living in North and South Korea. One of the more generally accepted estimates states that there were about four million casualties among those 40 million people, three million in North Korea and one million in South Korea. Three and a half million of them were civilians.[82]

After President Truman's decision to desegregate the American forces, most of the military had been integrated by the outbreak of war in 1950. Only the 24th Infantry regiment remained an identifiably African-American unit. Because of the poor quality of its (white) officers, the long history of segregation, and the second-class treatment of black soldiers, the combat record of the 24th was poor. It was disbanded on 22 September 1951. A group of social scientists studying the results of integration concluded that black soldiers performed better when not restricted to segregated units, and that the effectiveness of the army was considerably enhanced by integration.[83]

Today the Korean conflict stands as another milestone in the integration of the United States army. Looking back on the war on 30 July 1953, the *Chicago Defender* concluded: "The Jim Crow barriers began to crumble under General

Private First Class Edward Wilson of 24th Infantry with leg wound.
US National Archives 1394.

Douglas MacArthur as Far East commander. But it was General Matthew Ridgeway who in a forthright manner ordered an end to Army segregation in the Far East."[84]

Black Korean veterans returning to the South still found Jim Crow at home. A November 1952 report in the *Afro-American* stated that: "Trainees as well as overseas veterans are shocked at conditions at the Ft. Sill (Oklahoma) Artillery School. Clubs and houses are for whites only. Even children are barred from public schools on the army post. Yet a 'policy of opportunity' is supposed to exist in the Armed Forces."[85]

In the many blues and gospel lyrics the Korean War is chiefly noted for its destruction and bloodshed. The many casualties and the high proportion of soldiers missing in action were deplored. Xenophobic feelings, which were so prominent in the fights against the Nazis and the Japanese, though not entirely absent, were somewhat less virulent, and mingled with anti-Communism, a sentiment every patriotic American was supposed to endorse. The other United Nations countries that took part in the police action (United Kingdom, Canada, Turkey, etc.) are rarely mentioned, which is in contrast to the situation in World War II, when there was a greater awareness of the actual contribution. The fear of a third World War is evident. In spite of his misplaced confidence that the Chinese would not enter the war, and the subsequent Chinese victories, the singers still hailed General MacArthur as the great hero of war. Predictably, gospel singers put their trust in Jesus.

The Korean War had helped to define Communism as the greatest threat to world peace and the United States as leader of the fight for freedom and democracy abroad. African Americans were generally patriotic during the war, but they seemed anxious for the war to be over and done quickly. They were more resigned to doing what needed to be done, and generally did not expect the war to generate changes in their situation at home, as they had in World War II.[86]

5 THINGS ARE SO SLOW

Now, I'm livin' in the White House, just tryin' to help old Ike along,
And tryin' to make an amendment, for things Harry left undone.

I don't need no pilot, to chauffeur me in no jet,
Because I'm kind of in a hurry, I'll have to ride Space Cadet.[1]

I want to live in paradise, make servants out of kings and queens,
Now, don't shake me, please, darling, this is one time I wanna finish my dream.[2]

Dwight D. Eisenhower was inaugurated as President of the United States on
20 January 1953. Eight days earlier blues guitarist Johnny Shines (1915–1992) had
recorded "Livin' in the White House," a song that was to remain unissued until
the 1960s. Shines sang that Ike had "to make an amendment for things Harry left
undone." Among these "things" the war in Korea was one of the most important. Under Truman some advance had been made in the field of equal rights,
notably the desegregation of the armed forces, but the point of the song is in the
last line, where it is made clear that Shines – and by extension black Americans –
can only dream of political and economic power.

To blues singers the White House was a remote and far-off place, the stuff of
fantasies. "Livin' in the White House" belongs to a sub-genre of blues songs from

Johnny Shines and Robert Lockwood, Vera, Groningen, The Netherlands, 14 October 1979.
Photo by René van Rijn.

the late 1930s onwards, in which the singer is asked to come to the White
House to help the President out or to become President himself. Examples are:
Big Bill Broonzy, "Just a Dream (on My Mind)" from 1939, Eddie Vinson, "Just a
Dream" from 1945, Gene Phillips, "Just a Dream (It Was a Dream)" from 1947,
Louis Jordan, "Jordan for President" from 1952, and Louisiana Red, "Red's
Dream" from 1962. Of course, at the end of such songs this turns out to be
either a dream or decidedly wishful thinking.[3]

Dwight David Eisenhower was the last President born in the nineteenth
century and the first Republican in the White House since 1933. When he took
office he had little support among African Americans. Indeed, in 1952 Adlai
Stevenson, the Democratic candidate, received 73 per cent of black votes, a
4 per cent improvement over Truman in 1948.[4] In the 1954 recording
"Democrat Blues" by Detroit guitarist John "Bobo" Jenkins (1916–1984) we are
reminded that it was the Democrats who had put the people "on their feet"
after the Depression, while the Republicans are characterized as the party of
recession, unemployment and hunger. A high percentage of women had voted for
Eisenhower, and Jenkins upbraids his girlfriend for joining them, while remaining
confident of a Democratic victory in 1956.

Well, do you remember, baby, nineteen and thirty-one?
That's when the Depression, baby, just begun.

chorus: *Yes, darling, if you know what I'm talking 'bout,*
Well, the Democrats put you on your feet, baby, you had the nerve to vote 'em out.

You didn't have to plant no more cotton, baby, you didn't have to plough no more corn,
If a mule was running away with the world, baby, you'd tell him to go ahead on.

Well, do you remember, baby, when the steel mill shut down?
You had to go to the country, 'cause you couldn't live in town.

spoken: *Yeah, man, play it a long time! Nineteen fifty-six! Beat 'em, beat 'em!*

Well, do you remember, baby, when your stomach was all full of slack?
Somebody help me, get them Democrats back.[5]

Jenkins had written his "Democrat Blues" on Election Day, 1952. It is a good illustration of the exploitation by record companies of black talent at the time, for Jenkins was paid $25 for the recording by the Chess Record Company and claims he never received any royalties. When interviewed in 1970 Jenkins remembered the circumstances: "Then I wrote a record they call the 'Democrat Blues' and I really didn't have no idea of going out in the music world with it, but when they elected Eisenhower as president, I says: 'I'm gonna start doing something, because these factories gonna shut down.'"[6] In a later interview he explained that the song was really about the Great Depression, and the especially hard economic times that plague the poor during Republican administrations.[7]

"Democrat Blues" sees exercise of the franchise as a chance to put things right. The song is very engaged with politics and as such it presents a new point of view among blues singers. In Jenkins' Detroit home, or in most northern industrial cities, the black vote was far more influential than in the South, where

"It's Still Waiting There, Ike," cartoon, artist unidentified, *Afro-American*, 22 November 1952.

most blacks were still disenfranchised. The estimated percentage of blacks registered to vote in the eleven southern states rose from 3.0 in 1940, to 12.0 in 1947, 20.0 in 1952 and 29.1 in 1960. These regional statistics concealed even lower figures in some states. In 1952, for example, Alabama and Mississippi lagged behind the southern average with only 5.0 and 4.0 per cent of black voters respectively.[8]

Another blues singer who invested his hopes in the election year of 1956 was blues pianist Memphis Slim (1915–1988), whose March 1954 song title, "Four Years of Torment," leaves no room for misunderstanding about his opinion of Eisenhower's first presidency. The Republicans have taken his money, so he cannot afford to pay the phone bill, his wife has left him and he has had to mortgage his house to raise money. He blames "the youngsters and their mothers" for the Republican victory of November 1952.

Started back in November, in nineteen and fifty-two,
When the youngsters and their mothers, brought in another crew.

chorus: *Four years of torment, what are we going to do?*
Next time we'll know better, if we can just see it through.

Can't call for no help, they've taken out my telephone,
Got no money, lost my wife, even mortgaged my happy home.

Asked my friend for some money, but this is really sad,
His story was so touching, he got the last dime I had.

In nineteen and fifty-six, we will start all over again,
You can bet your bottom dollar, that crew will never get back in.[9]

Slim's analysis was not inaccurate: Eisenhower had to a large extent been elected by "youngsters and their mothers." According to Arthur Schlesinger Jr., "Almost thirteen million 'new' voters – one third were too young in 1948 and the rest had not voted then – provided significant support for the General. The young supported him 57–43 per cent."[10] "Gallup and Harris both estimated that about 17.6 million women voted for Eisenhower and about 12.7 million for Stevenson."[11]

In the spring of 1954, during the aftermath of the Korean War, the United States suffered a modest recession. Because Dwight Eisenhower was the first Republican President since Herbert Hoover, who had become synonymous with the Wall Street Crash of 1929 and the ensuing Depression, fears of another Republican recession were very high.[12] Eisenhower himself called it "the skeleton in the Republican closet, locked in by demogogues [sic]."[13]

The most bitter and personal attack by a blues singer on the President was "Eisenhower Blues" from October 1954, recorded by blues guitarist J. B. Lenoir.

Hey, everybody, I'm just talking to you,
I ain't telling you jive, but this is the natural truth.

chorus: *Mm, mm, mm, I got them Eisenhower blues,*
Thinking about me and you, what on earth are we gonna do?

My money's gone, my fun is gone,
Way things look, how can I be here long?

Taken all my money, to pay the tax,
I'm only giving you peoples, the natural facts,
I'm only telling you people, my belief,
Because I am headed straight for relief.

Ain't got a dime, ain't even got a cent,
I don't even have no money, to pay my rent,
My baby needs some clothes, she needs some shoes,
Peoples, I don't know, what is I'm gon' do?[14]

In a 28 October 1963 letter to British blues writer John Broven, J. B. Lenoir claimed that "Eisenhower Blues" was banned by the government: "I create music in my sleep sometime Oh its a long story of things I see in my sleep you ask me about Eisenhower Blues, well let me tell you something about the record, after the record had been released they heard it and sent a may from Washington and stoped it because his name was in it and why I do not know. That's why it was changed to Tax Paying Blues. When I recorded that Record I saw what was going to happen 5 years ahead, now you listen to Tax Paying Blues and you will see what I am talking about" [all *sic*].[15]

In "Tax Paying Blues"[16] Lenoir simply changed the name "Eisenhower" into "Taxpaying." J.B.'s letter lends credence to the theory that the less offending alternative was recorded on the same day as "Eisenhower Blues."

In the early 1970s, this account was the subject of a debate in the American blues magazine *Living Blues* between writers Pete Welding and Mike Rowe. Finally

Living Blues phoned producer Al Benson of Parrot Records, who stated that "the U.S. government had nothing to do with the case. He says that the song's reference to Ike was deleted and the title changed to 'Tax Paying' solely to 'appease' the Republican management of a Chicago radio station. Although this could be considered 'political pressure' in a sense, surely if the government itself had intervened, it wouldn't have been only through one radio station in one city."[17] Benson's account is a persuasive one; apart from First Amendment rights, it seems quite implausible that the US administration should have heard – let alone been worried about – a record by a black musician on a small Chicago label. No doubt it made Lenoir happier to believe otherwise, and supported his image as a political gadfly.[18]

The end of the Korean War threatened to deepen the economic difficulties Ike faced. After the Panmunjom truce of 27 July 1953 most American soldiers were withdrawn from Korea and war production decreased significantly. In addition to this reduction in defense spending, the government placed restrictions on the money supply to prevent inflation. British economist Colin Clark predicted a massive depression with almost seven million people unemployed unless drastic measures were taken.[19] The economy duly went further downhill in September 1953 and there was widespread alarm in the final quarter of the year. One of the first blues singers to comment on the decline was guitarist John Brim (b. 1922) in his March 1954 song "Tough Times" that he had written together with his wife Grace (1924–1999). Brim sings that he has lost his job, has no money to buy food, and fears a repetition of the Depression of 1932. When I asked for his opinion about Truman and Eisenhower Brim replied: "I never was too political, I think the government does pretty fair."[20]

> Me and my baby was talking, and what she said is true,
> Said: "It seems like times is getting tough, like they was in thirty-two.
> You don't have no job, our bills is past due,
> So, now tell me, baby, what we gonna do?"

chorus:
> Tough times, tough times is here once more,
> Now, if you don't have no money, people, you can't live happy no more.

> I had a good job, working many long hours a week,
> They had a big lay-off, and they got poor me.
> I'm broke and disgusted, in misery,
> Can't find a part-time job, nothing in my house to eat.

spoken: *Come on, Eddie!*[21]

> *I went down to the grocery store, said, I'll get a little more food on time,*
> *The man said: "Wait a minute, see how do we stand?"*
> *Said: "I'm sorry to tell you, you too far behind."*[22]

For Johnny Fuller in his recording of "Hard Times" the 1954 recession prompted a return to the South (Fuller was born in Mississippi in 1929 and died in Oakland in 1985), where one could still "raise hogs and corn." A similar feeling had earlier been expressed by Smokey Hogg in his 1947 song "High Priced Meat," which was discussed in Chapter 1 (on Reconversion). Given the mass African-American exodus from the South to the North and West during the twentieth century, thoughts of return are quite ironic, particularly with Jim Crow still firmly in place in the South.

> *Times done got hard, well, I believe I'll go back home,*
> *Well, I'm goin' back, where I can raise hogs and corn.*
>
> *On that next train south, you can look for me home,*
> *Well, I wanna give a big celebration, well, in the place where I was born.*
>
> *Well, goodbye, goodbye, tell everybody I'm gone,*
> *Well, if times don't get better, you will find Little Johnny at home.*[23]

In January 1954 there were three million people on the dole, almost 5 per cent of the civilian labor force. The President was determined to fight the looming recession without panic, which became hard indeed when February yielded an even worse unemployment figure of 3.6 million. For blues singer Jimmy McCracklin (b. 1921), who had experienced the 1932 Depression as a child in St. Louis, "the panic was on" again in 1954.[24]

chorus: *The panic's on, wonder what are we going to do?*
>   *Lord, it reminds me of, nineteen and thirty-two.*
>
> *I used to could take fifty dollars, you know, and spend it free and wild,*
> *But now times have got so hard, been hurtin' me to spend four or five.*
>
> *I lost my job today, after all the time I had spent,*
> *And now I don't even have no food at home, do you know I owe for my rent?*

I don't want to rob and steal, you know that ain't no doubt,
I've been drawing Social Security, but, people, now it have run out.[25]

By March 3.7 million people, or 5.8 per cent, were out of work. Eisenhower had so far refused to implement a massive program of federal intervention or an increase in individual income-tax exemptions.[26] In his 1954 "Depression Blues" blues guitarist "Gatemouth" Brown (b. 1924) urged women to find themselves a "sugar daddy" to support them, for the Depression would no doubt place their husbands in the soup line.

chorus: *I'm gonna tell all you women: "You'd better find yourself a man,*
Because the depression is comin', and you'll be needin' a helpin' hand."

Now, all you ponytails, TV mamas[27] *too,*
Yes, you run around here braggin' what your old man can do,
You say he makes plenty money, and spends it all on you,
But if he keeps that up, he'll be on the soup line too,
Depression blues, oh, I hate depression blues.

My papa stole a chicken, my mama fried it hard,
The reason why she did that: he couldn't steal no lard.
Depression blues, oh, I hate depression blues,
Depression blues, oh, I hate depression blues.[28]

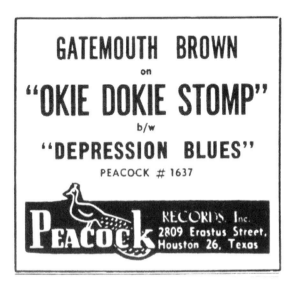

Advertisement for Gatemouth Brown, "Depression Blues," Peacock 1637. *First Pressings*, July 1954.

Gatemouth Brown, NBBO Blues Festival, Zodiac, Amstelveen, The Netherlands, 25 February 1972. Collection Guido van Rijn.

In November 1955 vocalist Dave "Dizzy" Dixon recorded a humorous sketch about the growing soup lines. Although Dixon only dreams that he is in the soup line, this return to 1932 must be a "kind of premonition." Dixon makes his political opinion clear. He thinks that the Republicans are again responsible for a depression and that the Democrats should return to save the country.

> I had a dream the other night, it's lingerin' on my mind,
> I dreamed that times was hard again and I was standin' in a long soup line.
> I don't know exactly where I was or how I got in that position,
> But it must have been a warning, some kind of a premonition.
> Now, they wouldn't give us very much soup, just hardly enough to see,
> But when I got back in line for the second time, now, this is what he said to me:

chorus: Get out of that line, man, you had one bowl, you know,
> Ain't no need of you standin' there beggin', 'cause you ain't gonna get no more.
> Should have saved your money when times was good, you was working every day,
> When you got them great big pay checks, you didn't do nothing but throw 'em away.

Now you had a little money in the bank downtown, you went and drawed that out,

Now you're beat out on the ground, just as raggedy as a can of kraut.

You wasn't drinkin' nothin' but the best of whiskey, I never did see you sober,

You should have knowed the day was comin' when all your good times would be over.

Now, you ain't had no dependents, no, no, nobody but yourself,

Now comes the time you need that money, you ain't got a penny left.

spoken: *Junior, get out the back of that line!*

What you think you are? Privileged class or something?

No, I ain't givin' up nothing, you might as well move back.

Get on back out of that line, man.

All right, I'm gonna call the police for you!

But that old man made me awful mad, standin' there gonna loud-talk me,

Me, I was wobblin' in my knee, just as hungry as I could be.

I said, now looka here, man, you done said your say, so sit back and relax,

When I made all that money with no dependents I paid it right back in tax.

And how did I know these people would make that same mistake, my friend?

Forget all about depression and let that party take over again.

Anyhow, I think it's an awful disgrace that you had the nerve,

To stand here before my very face, tellin' me what I don't deserve.

Now, I'm entitled to this old mess of soup, and I think I done got you told,

So since I'm next for serving, would you pass me another bowl?

Now, wait, as a very special favor, I'll tell you what I want you to do,

This time put in a spoon of beans and just a few crackers too.

So get out, oh, get out, 'cause you ain't gonna get no more.[29]

Pressure on the President was mounting. Had he not promised to act at the first sign of a recession?[30] Eisenhower first wanted to see if the recession would continue, but he claimed that his government was certainly ready to act if really necessary.[31] In the meantime J. B. Hutto (1926–1983) voiced the despair of the man who was laid off. His car is repossessed because he cannot keep up the loan payments on it to the finance company. Hutto looks back to 1944 when the economy was strong in his "Things Are So Slow" from October 1954:

> I went to work this morning, was all set to start,
> My boss walked up and told me: "Sorrow in my heart."
>
> "Things are so slow, don't think we need you any more,"
> He told me: "Things is so slow, don't think we need you any more."
>
> I had to tell my wife, she didn't fuss,
> Finance took the car, we had to ride the bus.
>
> "Things are so slow, don't think we can ride any more,"
> I told her: "Things is so slow, don't think we'll be riding any more."
>
> I had a dream last night, I was standing in a great long line,
> A line like they had, boys, in nineteen twenty-nine.
>
> "Things were so slow, don't think I'll make it any more,"
> I said: "Now things is so slow, don't think I'll make it any more."
>
> In nineteen forty-four, everything was going along strong,
> I say it's ten years later, boys, and everything's gone wrong.
>
> "Things are so slow, don't believe I can make it any more,"
> I said things: "Now, things is so slow, don't think I can make it any more."[32]

There had been optimism about an end to the recession during April and May and on 11 June 1954 Dr. Arthur F. Burns, the chairman of the President's Council of Economic Advisers, reported that recovery was now under way.[33] By July it became clear that the downturn had ended and that America had moved from a wartime to a peacetime economy without having encountered a major collapse. Eisenhower was proud to have accomplished the transition "from federal to private spending, from armaments to consumer goods." He felt he had established faith in the concept that economic recovery is the work of the people and that the government should merely provide the foundation. The

President's faith in the inherent strength of the economy itself had not betrayed him.[34]

Poverty was still there, of course, with African Americans disproportionately represented, and the blues singers blamed the President for high taxes. Eisenhower had refused to make cuts in income and excess profits taxes until he had a balanced budget.[35] Blues singer J. B. Lenoir held him personally responsible in his September 1955 "Everybody Wants to Know (Laid Off Blues)." It is an even more outspoken version of his 1954 "Eisenhower Blues." Blues writer Mike Rowe has called its lyrics "positively revolutionary."[36]

spoken: *Hey, Little Brother,[37] did they get you?*
                   Uh-huh!
              They got me too! And you know I'm mad!

              One thing I hate: they all got me in a hovel,
              Laid off my sister and my brother,
              Reached back and got my dad and mother.

chorus: *Uh, uh, uh, I got them laid off blues,*
              Thinking about me and you:
              What the President gonna do?

              Taken all my money, to pay them tax,
              I'm just givin' you people, the natural facts,
              Everytime I look around, it's payin' tax, tax, tax,
              You have taken all my money, and will not give me none back.

              You rich people, listen, you better listen real deep:
              If we poor peoples get so hungry, we gonna take some food to eat.[38]

One of the musically most primitive of blues artists, Sam Wilson from Detroit was called "One String Sam" because of the nature of his instrument. The "Motor City" was one of the worst hit towns during the short-lived recession. In January 1954, 107,000 workers in the area (7 per cent of the labor force) were unemployed.[39] In his "I Need a Hundred Dollars" from 1956 Wilson harks back to 1933 by employing a stanza from Walter Roland's "Red Cross Blues."[40]

You know, I talked with mother this morning, mother talked with the judge,
I couldn't help eavesdropping, you know, understood the words.

chorus: *She said: "I need a hundred dollars, you know, I . . .*
You know, I need a hundred dollars, just to go my, my baby's bond."

You know, me and my little girl got up this morning, she said she wanted a Frigidaire,[41]
Told her the icebox was leaking, baby, freeze my ice myself.

You know, I, I left her mother standing, baby, in her doorway crying,
Come begging and pleading: "Don't mistreat the little girl of mine."

spoken: *Yeah, I need that hundred dollars.*

You know, my houselady come telling 'bout, wanna talk for an hour,
Wanna go to the Red Cross, people, you know, for a sack of Red Cross flour.[42]

As we have seen, blues singers like Bobo Jenkins and Memphis Slim had high hopes for the election year of 1956. Would the Democrats return? What kind of President did the black population need? Vocal group the Treniers had the answer in "(We Want a) Rock and Roll President." Although this August 1956 song is really about selling rock and roll records, it still shows that awareness of the political process, and acceptance of it as part of life, was growing among African Americans.

We want a Rock and Roll president,
A president who rocks and rolls,
We want a man, who digs our kind of rhythm,
Republican or Democrat, we with him.

We want a Rock and Roll president,
And we Rock and Rollers can swing that vote,
We'll tell our fathers, mothers, relatives and others on their trip to the polls,
To vote for a president who rocks and rolls.

spoken: *Vote for me!*[43]

As in 1952, the Governor of Illinois, Adlai Stevenson (1900–1965), was the Democratic candidate. There was only one blues song devoted to Stevenson. West Coast piano player Clarence "Candyman" McGuirt (1925–1979) and vocalist Geneva Vallier recorded a parody of the popular song "Wake the Town and Tell the People" entitled "He's a Friend" in September 1956:

Wake the town and tell the people, sing it to the Moon above,
Wake the town and tell the people, that the nation needs Stevenson.

He's a friend of the people, let's declare a holiday,
Send out all the invitations, to the citizens of the USA.

Vote for Adlai Stevenson, he's a friend of the people,
He's for democracy in action, he's for better schools and fair wages too.

To the farmers he'll keep his promises, he's the one I am told,
He's for international trade, small businessmen and foreign aid.

Wake the town and tell the people, shout it from the highest steeple,
Ring your friends' and neighbors' doorbells, the who- who- who- whole day through.

Wake the town and tell the people, Democrats and Republicans too,
To vote for Adlai Stevenson, he, he is a friend to you![44]

Although 73 per cent of African Americans had voted for the eloquent Stevenson in 1952, this time the percentage dropped to somewhere between 60 and 65 per cent. He inspired the African-American electorate so little that black votes for war hero Eisenhower rose by 11 per cent in the largest black district in Chicago, in Harlem by 16.5 per cent and in Memphis by 25 per cent.[45] The relatively good economic times, and civil rights leader and Democratic Congressman Adam Clayton Powell's endorsement of Eisenhower, were major influencing factors also. At the time Powell was being accused of tax evasion, but when questioned about his motives for supporting the Republicans, he maintained that disappointment with the Democratic Party had been the sole reason for his switch.[46]

Eisenhower was re-elected – still heavily dependent on southern white votes. Although the *Brown* decision against segregated schooling in 1954 and 1955 had thrust race relations to the fore, the former General had generally managed to evade the topic of desegregation, while the Democrats evidently could not afford to raise the issue themselves. "At what cost to the nation's children, and especially those who were black and lived in the South, no one can say," Eisenhower's biographer Stephen Ambrose comments.[47] Eisenhower would not, however, be able to avoid the issue in his second term, when the Little Rock crisis put his handling of the desegregation issue under the media microscope.

Another crisis occurred a few days after the shameful events at Little Rock in September 1957, which are dealt with in the next chapter. Dr. Edward Teller, the father of the hydrogen bomb, called it a greater defeat for the United States than Pearl Harbor.[48]

On 4 October 1957 the Soviet Union launched the first artificial earth satellite, *Sputnik*, which circled the earth for 57 days, sending scientific data back to Earth. The Russians had won the space race and Americans, who were not accustomed to second place, blamed Eisenhower. A crisis of confidence gripped the nation. To make things worse, *Sputnik 2* was launched on 3 November. It stayed in orbit for 162 days, after which it burned up in the earth's atmosphere, killing the first cosmonaut, the dog Laika. By the end of 1957, Roosevelt Sykes recorded a topical sexual metaphor on the subject in his song "Sputnik."

> Listen, Mr. Khrushchev, I heard a lot of talk,
> Satellites and missiles and Eisenhower's fault.
> But now you better listen, to what I got to say,
> The thing I'm gonna tell you, man, it make your hair turn grey:

chorus:
> I got a satellite baby, with a red-hot style that's new,
> Yes, I got a satellite baby, that can rock me the whole night through,
> She can make more speed than Sputnik number two.

> Now, you talk about your Sputnik, and your hound dog crew,
> I got a rocket baby, faster than the Asiatic Flu.

> Yes, I got a hot rocket baby, can leave you any time,
> Yes, I got a hot rocket baby, will leave you flying blind,
> When she gets in gear, you think it's the end of time.

spoken:
> Somewhere way out in space, somewhere way out in space![49]

Once the 1954 recession was over, Eisenhower had to fight inflation. Each week the economic figures were carefully analyzed and an effort was made to reduce federal spending "to produce a surplus for partial payment on the staggering national debt," as the President himself phrased it.[50] In 1957 federal income went down again and Eisenhower experienced his second economic crisis. The Memphis-based Sons of Jehovah invoked the past strength of the dollar in their 1957 "High Cost of Living." Although the current President is not mentioned, the reference to Abraham Lincoln, the Emancipator, is pointed.

chorus: *Well, the cost of living, boys,*

      It is so high, it is so high, it is so high,

   The cost of living, boys,

      It is so high,

      It's a crying shame what a dollar will buy.

Well, way back yonder in olden days,

When Abraham Lincoln freed the slaves,

Five dollars worth of groceries was all you needed,

To last you and your wife all the week.

But now it's different, the cost has raised,

Five dollars worth will hardly, uh, last two days.

Think a little bit, you take a buffalo nickel,

You can't even buy yourself, uh, one dill pickle.

Now if you only got a dime, you may as well stay home,

You can't even buy yourself a can of corn.

You take a quarter, it's large in size,

But it's a shame to even mention what it will buy.

You take fifty cents, most of you know,

If that's all you got, you're already broke.

You take a dollar bill, it's only that in name,

The way it's shrunk it's a sin and a shame.

They'll take your dollar bill and do it like that:

Ninety-seven cents and don't forget the tax.[51]

As ever, hard times in the blues were linked to romantic disappointment. Since the recession, blues guitarist B. B. King (b. in Mississippi in 1925) has lost the opportunity to womanize. He cannot afford expensive liquor anymore, and makes a plea to the White House to help him out in his July 1958 composition "Recession Blues."

Since this recession I am losing my baby, because the times are getting so hard,

Yes, I have to stop running around, man, you know it's breaking my heart.

Yes, I can't afford no liquor, all I can buy is beer and wine,

Well, I can't get my baby what she wants, and she stays cross all the time.

spoken: *Yes, help me! Yes, all right!*

B. B. King, North Sea Jazz Festival, The Hague, The Netherlands, 18 July 1982. Photo by René van Rijn.

> *Well, please, somebody, please go up to Washington for me,*
> *Yes, think about us out here, help to get me out of this misery.*[52]

Tommy Dean's vocalist Joe Buckner intends to call the President to account in his May 1958 "Recession." In fact prices were not really that high in 1957/58. The following numbers show the consumer price index for the Eisenhower years: 1953 (0.8 per cent), 1954 (0.7), 1955 (0.4), 1956 (1.5), 1957 (3.3), 1958 (2.8), 1959 (1.5), 1960 (1.7).[53] "Congress calls this a recession, but it smells like depression to me," Joe Buckner sang. Perhaps he was exaggerating a bit, in the interest of selling his record or making political capital.

> *Hey, operator, get me the White House on the phone,*
> *Let me speak to the man in charge, see if he knows what's going on.*
> *Boy, boy, boy, things ain't like they used to be,*
> *Congress calls this a recession, but it smells like depression to me.*

Hey, Mr. landlord, tell me how much rent I owe,

When I get it, then you get it, no use knockin' on my door.

Boy, boy, boy, times are tight as they can be,

Congress calls this a recession, but it smells like depression to me.

Hey, General Motors, come get your Cadillac,

I'd bring it in myself, but I ain't got bus fare back.

Boy, boy, boy, where can all that money be?

Congress calls this a recession, but it smells like depression to me.

Hey Mr. Senator, remember nineteen and thirty-two,

If you can't think back that far, let me tell you what to do:

Bring back the WPA, the PWA and call out the triple A too,

We need AID, dear brother, AID, PDQ,[54]

Congress calls this a recession, but it smells like depression to me.[55]

The specter of the Crash and the Depression haunted many of the blues of the Eisenhower years. It is striking how many blues artists referred to the years 1929, 1931 or 1932 in contemporary blues songs: Jimmy McCracklin, John Brim, J. B. Hutto and Bobo Jenkins in 1954, Tommy Dean in 1958 and Detroit guitarist Mr. Bo (= Louis Bo Collins, 1932–1995), witnessing "Times Hard" in 1959 or 1960.

Hard times, hard times, hard times is here once more,

Well, I don't have no money, don't have no place to go.

Yes, they said things would get better, in a few months or so,

Yes, darling, I remember, that was a few years ago.

spoken: *Ah! Oh, yeah!*

Yes, things have really gotten bad, like they were in nineteen thirty-two,

Well, I don't have no job, all I do is walk around and sing the blues.

spoken: *Oh, yeah!*[56]

1957 being a recession year, the President refused to spend excessive amounts on space research. "Look, I'd like to know what's on the other side of the Moon, but I won't pay to find out this year!" the President exclaimed during a Cabinet meeting.[57] Not until 31 January 1958 would the United States launch *Explorer 1* from Cape Canaveral. Several unmanned satellites were to follow in

Mr. Bo, Blues Estafette, Utrecht, The Netherlands, 20 November 1993. Photo by René van Rijn.

the late 1950s. The Russians had their Sputniks and Lunas, the Americans their Vanguards and Explorers. The Russians were triumphant on 4 October 1959 when *Luna III* took the first photographs of the then unseen, dark side of the Moon.

Blues singer Harmonica George recorded an instrumental entitled "Sputnik Music"[58] and the gospel singers uttered warnings. "God Made the Moon to Rule the Night," Lawrence Roberts sang in June 1958. Man belongs on earth, not on the Moon:

To those who don't understand, and think they're right,
God made the Moon, as a lesser light,
He hung it high, and said: "Shine bright,"
God gave the Moon, dominion over night.

And he didn't set up (no transportation), and he didn't give (no explanation),
And sending up Explorers is all in vain,
Oh, the Bible don't speak (no population), from this here (no other nation),
God made the Moon to rule the night.

And he didn't set up (no transportation), and he didn't give (no explanation),
And sending up those Vanguards is all in vain,
Well, the Bible don't speak of (no population), from this here (no other nation),
God made the Moon to rule the night.

And if you make it to the Moon,
Tell me what you gonna look for,
Tell me what you gonna seek,
Tell me what you gonna find.

If you're looking for joy, (it's right back here),
If you're looking for love, (it's right back here),
If you're looking for peace, (it's right back here),
God made the Moon, (oh yes, to rule the night).[59]

Similar worries occupied Sister Dora Alexander's mind in March 1958. Accompanied solely by her tambourine, she warned "wicked Russia" to "Let God's Moon Alone."

Oh, Russia, let that Moon alone,
Russia, let that Moon alone,
Moon ain't worryin' you,
Oh, Russia, let that Moon alone.

God told you: "Go and till the Earth!"
God didn't tell you to till the Moon,
You better let that Moon alone.
Oh, Russia, let that Moon alone.

You can make your Sputnickels, [sic]
And your satellites;
You can't catch God's Moon,
Let God's Moon alone.

The Moon ain't worryin' you,
The Moon ain't worryin' you.

God told Man to till the Earth,
God didn't tell you to till the Moon,
You better let that Moon alone,
The Moon ain't worryin' you.

Oh, wicked Russia, get down on your knees and pray,
And let God's Moon alone;
The Moon ain't worryin' you,
The Moon ain't worryin' you.

God put the Moon up there to give you light by night,
You better let God's Moon alone;
The Moon ain't worryin' you,
Better let God's Moon alone.

The Moon ain't worryin' you.
Oh, Russia, get down on your knees and pray,
Let God's Moon alone.[60]

But the gospel singers were not the only artists who had their doubts about the explanations of man's legitimacy in outer space. Popular New Orleans singer Chris Kenner (1929–1976) raised his objections in his recording of "Rocket to the Moon" from 1960. For his inspiration Kenner not only turned to the Bible, but, exceptionally, also to a popular element from classical history.

Tryin' to build a rocket, to send to the Moon,
And if they ever do, it will be way too soon,
I've heard of the satellite, Sputnik 2,
But I never thought a rocket could reach the Moon.

chorus: *A rocket to the Moon, a rocket to the Moon,*
And if they ever do, it'll be way too soon,
They're building a rocket to send to the Moon.

Nero played the fiddle while Rome burned,
Samson was the strongest man I've learned,
Noah built an ark when the world was
doomed,
Now they're trying to build a rocket
just to reach the Moon.

Now, I'm gonna tell you, how I feel,
Somethin' like the story of, eh, Adam
and Eve,
Man done got so very wise,
That he gonna set this world on fire.

Now, if they ever make 'em that
will reach the Moon,
(Which I think is way too soon,)
I'm gonna put on my running shoes,
And I'm gonna be the first one to spread the news.[61]

Pianist Eurreal "Little Brother" Montgomery (1906–1985) recorded a "Satellite Blues" in July 1960. The song portrays Montgomery as a satellite inventor who needs an (obviously phallic) rocket to search for his lover in outer space.

Now, I have started an invention and it might sound silly to you,
Now, I'm only trying to do something that no other man could do.

I made a two-monkey carrier with a electronical engine room,
Now, I was only trying to create something to go and reach the Moon.

I made a sharp pointed object, just as sharp as anything could be,
I was only trying to create something to find the other world for me.

Because my babe has gone and left me, and she must have, have gone outer
space,
Now, you know I've searched this whole wide world over and I can't find my
baby any place.[62]

Another example of the fascination for the new space age is "Z Astronaut," a 1960 recording by blues guitarist Joe Richardson, who recorded this hilarious song as "Bob Arnold & His Little Astronaut." "Z" is a humorous exam grade way beyond F, the normal lowest mark in US schools and colleges. The moral of the song seems to be that you never know what will happen to you once you enlist in the army!

spoken: *Ten, nine, eight, seven, six, five, four, three, two, one:*

chorus: *I'm an ordinary member of the human race,*
           I don't wanna be no pioneer in outer space,
           Yet here I am, the most unwilling hero you can find,
           Who needs to be an astronaut? What am I, out of my mind?

           I was just a simple country boy who wanted to enlist,
           The draft board never told me that I'd wind up like this,
           The sergeant asked for volunteers to take a trip in June,
           How was I to know he meant a rocket to the Moon?

spoken: *I wonder if this is one of them do it yourself jobs.*

           They shipped me to a hospital and gave me lots of tests,
           The competition sure was rough, but I did my very best,
           So when it all was over, I was glad as I could be,
           I knew I had come in third behind a mouse and a chimpanzee.

spoken: *And I repeat, R-E-P-E-A-T,*

spoken: *Well, if them Russians can do it, so can I.*

           The scientists say the Moon is half a million miles away,
           I hope this doggone chicken coop don't start to go astray,
           I ain't the kind who likes to fuss, I ain't the type to squawk,
           But if this thing runs out of gas, I can't get out and walk.[63]

The Roosevelt Sykes satellite song "Sputnik" from 1957 quoted earlier is the first blues to mention Nikita Khrushchev, First Secretary of the USSR Communist Party from 1953 to 1964. In these Cold War years Khrushchev and Eisenhower personified the rivalry between their nations. Tensions escalated in the election year of 1960. In nearby Cuba Fidel Castro, who had assumed power in 1959, presented a potential threat to peace, as he became increasingly radical. On 1 May 1960 a U2 reconnaissance plane was shot down in Russian airspace. The United States claimed the plane had drifted off course, but Khrushchev was adamant (and correct) that it had been on an espionage mission. On 7 May he

Lightnin' Slim (and
the author),
De Bajes,
Amstelveen,
The Netherlands,
5 February 1972.
Photo by Jan van
Veen.

made it known that the pilot, Francis Gary Powers, and parts of the plane were
held in Moscow. A proposed summit between the two leaders was called off and
Ike became very depressed.[64]

In September 1959 blues guitarist Lightnin' Slim (Otis Hicks, 1913–1974)
updated Sonny Boy Williamson's 1944 "Check Up on My Baby"[65] by adding that
Khrushchev did not play a fair political game. In his patriotic "'GI' Slim" the artist
wants to join the army.

> Now, I want all you young chicks and grown-up hens,
> I just want to tell you, about where I've been:
> From coast to coast, to the Golden Gates of Maine,
> I've chatted with the queen, babe, I've shot dope with the king.

> I heard Hitler say to President Roosevelt:
> "We got the fastest plane in the world."
> I heard President Roosevelt say:
> "That ain't so, 'cause we got planes climb like a squirrel."

chorus: That's why I'm goin' to join the army, just like any good boy should,
             I wanted old man Hitler to know, that poor Lightnin' didn't mean him no good.

> Now, when they raised the white flag, and all of us came home,
> I thought that I would settle down, and no more would have to roam.
> Now, I understand there's more trouble with those Russians over there,
> That fellow that they call Khrushchev, don't want to do it fair.[66]

At 70 and after his first heart attack, Eisenhower was anxiously awaiting retirement. Blues singer John Lee Hooker (1917–2001) hoped the Democrats would regain control. Hooker had always been and would always remain a Democrat. Just as Memphis Slim had done in 1954, Hooker blamed the "crazy women" for putting the Republican President in the White House. In his February 1960 "Democrat Man" Hooker argues that although Eisenhower did bring American soldiers home from Korea, he has failed to give them employment on their return.

> Democrats put us on our feet, these crazy women, they voted them out,
> But I don't think they will make the same mistake, won't make the same mistake no more.

> He told them: "I'll send your sons home,"
> He did just that, they sent 'em home to stay without a job,
> I declare: They won't make that same mistake no more,
> Democrats put us on our feet, these crazy women, they voted them out.

> I ain't goin' down, I ain't goin' down, no I ain't, I ain't goin' down to the Welfare store,
> Won't be long before the Democrats be back in again.

> I know the girls, I know the girls, I know the girls,
> You girls won't make that same mistake again, no more, I know you ain't,
> The men voted them in, and the women, the women voted them out.

> I ain't got no shoes, no shoes, no shoes to go on my feet,
> But I ain't goin' to that Welfare store. You know why? You know why?
> I know I'll get shoes, I'll get clothes, when the Democrats get back in again.

John Lee Hooker, North Sea Jazz Festival, The Hague, The Netherlands, 10 July 1983. Photo by René van Rijn.

Vote them in, we voted them in, mmm,
I'm a Democrat man, I'm a Democrat man, please, please, don't be no fool no more.

Mmm, mmm, I ain't goin' down, to the Welfare store,
It won't be long. Oh yeah.
I'm a Democrat, I'm a Democrat man, and I'll be until the day I die.[67]

As ethnomusicologist David Evans has explained, Hooker is one of the few blues artists to make commercial recordings by spontaneous improvisation.[68] Such recordings are usually unrhymed and loose in structure. This kind of blues is hard to accompany and forces the listener to pay great attention. In an interview with blues writer Pete Welding, Hooker commented on this aspect of his art: "On my records, lots of times I just make up the words right on the spot, right there, like I do in clubs. 'Democrat Man' — I made that up as I went along. . . . You know, though, I'm pretty good at those things, doing things like that. I don't know how I do it, but I do."[69]

Blues songs which comment on politics in the Eisenhower years show dissatisfaction with the women and the young voters who helped to elect Ike. Fears of a return to Depression conditions of the 1930s dominate. The recessions of 1954 and 1957 seem to exacerbate these fears, while inflation, unemployment and high taxes are attacked in the songs from this period. The President is held personally responsible. The blues songs show that engagement with the political process is coming to be seen as a good thing in itself. At first, much black hope was aimed at the election year of 1956, but when the Democrats did not come back in, there was something of a disengagement from politics. After the President was re-elected, he was virtually ignored by blues and gospel singers during his second term. The responses to the space race show that the religious singers took an anti-scientific view and that the secular ones mostly tried to find humor in it.

Although Eisenhower had managed to balance the budget and to stop inflation, the economy grew a mere 2.5 per cent under his administration.[70] Stephen Ambrose, his biographer, concluded that the Eisenhower presidencies were the time of "the great postponement." This not only held true of the desegregation of American life, but equally of such urban problems as "the growth of slums, pollution, the loss of the tax base, a decent education for all, care for the elderly, the helpless, the unemployed."[71]

6 THE ALABAMA BUS

I'm a win-o, and I'm as high as I can be,
I've got a office in the White House, and all the laws are made by me.

I don't drink no good whiskey, and I can't stand beer or gin,
But I drink my good port and muscatel, until the bitter end.

I say I'm a great politician, and I make all the laws,
I've got a seat in Congress, right next to Santa Claus.[1]

Texas Blues guitarist Pee Wee Crayton (1914–1985) significantly picked political power as the topic of the drunkard's delusion when he recorded his "Win-O" in April 1954.

The 1954 recession forced the poor to visit the welfare stores, and comparisons were made with the Depression of the early 1930s. As usual, African Americans had a particularly hard time, but still only five songs from Eisenhower's first term deal explicitly with civil rights issues.

With the birth of the mass movement for civil rights in the US South in the mid-1950s, African-American "manhood" was increasingly defined in terms of racial pride and political activism, rather than simply in terms of the fabled sexual potency which the blues had long celebrated. Big Bill Broonzy (1898–1958) was

Pee Wee Crayton, The Netherlands, summer 1979. Photo by Diny van Rijn.

one blues singer who discussed notions of black manhood. While visiting London during October 1955, in the course of a concert tour, he recorded a song entitled "When Do I Get to Be Called a Man," which he was later to record again for American Folkways in the United States the following year. Whites routinely used the term "boy" for all African-American males, regardless of age, occupation or status, often as a means of demeaning and belittling them. In his 1955 autobiography *Big Bill Blues* Broonzy remembered the circumstances under which the song had been written:

> There was a man that I knew, when I was ten years old, that the white people called a boy. He was about thirty then. When I went to the army and came back in 1919, well he was an old man then and the white people was calling him Uncle Mackray. So he never got to be

called a man, from "boy" to "Uncle Mackray." And so it is still today. They call all Negro men "boys" and some of them is old enough to be their father. In fact I do think that some old men is glad to be called boys, but they call you so until you get to be fifty, and at the time you would appreciate to be called a boy they start to call you "uncle." That's the time when I would like to be called a boy, when I get to fifty or older. It's all right for my sister's kids to call me "uncle," but not by a man or a woman eighty years old.[2]

> When I was born into this world, this is what happened to me:
> I was never called a man and now I'm fifty-three.

chorus: I wonder when, yes, I wonder when,
> Yes, I wonder when will I get to be called a man, or do I have to wait to I get ninety-three?

> When Uncle Sam called me, I knowed I'd be called a real McCoy,
> But it wasn't no difference, they just called me soldier boy.

> When I got back from overseas, that night we had a ball,
> But I met the boss very next day, and he: "Get you some overalls!"

> I've worked on farms, levee camps and extra gangs too,
> But a black man's a boy, I don't care what he can do.

> I was called a plough boy on a farm and a soldier boy in Camp Hill,[3]
> Now I'm just old and grey and they just calls me "Uncle Bill."

> They said I was uneducated, my clothes was worn and torn,
> Now I've got a little education, but I'm a boy right on.[4]

In July 1955 female singer La Verne Holt signed a contract with New York record producer Joe Davis. Holt was to pay Davis $500, in return for which Davis would record two songs by her and distribute them throughout the South. A minimum of 500 78s and 500 45s were to be pressed. La Verne Holt, who was credited on disc as "Enyatta Holta," must have been very keen to get her ideas on disc.[5] The vaguely Afrocentric lyrics of "Mr. Black Man" were ahead of their time,

for 1955, long predating the "Say it loud, I'm black and I'm proud" vogue in the soul music of the late 1960s and early 1970s, and presaging some rappers' later concern to educate their audiences about African-American history. In 1974 Joe Davis reissued the song in the format of a 45-rpm single, clearly hoping that twenty years of change in African-American consciousness would generate sales that had not occurred in 1955.[6]

> Ooh, wee, Mr. Black Man, fine as you can be,
> But it's a real dirty shame, you don't know your history.
>
> When you talk about the Negro, where is Negro land?
> Black Man has been here, ever since the world began.
>
> Wake up, Mr. Black Man, please listen to my plea,
> You've been living in a dream, but you've got to face reality.
>
> Ooh-wee, Mr. Black Man, don't you love a gal like me?
> I'm a fine black beauty, proud of the fact you see.
>
> Ooh-wee, Mr. Black Man, please listen to my plea:
> Oh, a man without a root, is like a stump left from a tree.[7]

Gospel artist, promoter and composer Otis Jackson (1911–1962) produced a much-admired tribute to his beloved President Roosevelt in 1946 (analyzed in *Roosevelt's Blues*). In earlier chapters of this book we have seen that he also recorded notable songs on the war in Korea and on the NAACP in 1950. As well as performing and composing, Otis Jackson was a very popular gospel disc jockey at Radio Station WOKB in Orlando, Florida, and as a result he became quite well known in central Florida. For many years he traveled around to promote his gospel music by performing, selling his compositions and booking other singers. He worked in Jacksonville as a volunteer for the NAACP, not far from Daytona Beach, where Mme Mary McLeod Bethune, the great African-American educator and civil rights activist, lived.[8]

An admirer of FDR and an ardent New Dealer, it is perhaps not surprising that Dr. Bethune had not supported Eisenhower's candidacy in 1952, but had backed Stevenson instead. She said that Eisenhower had "compromised on basic issues, indulged in purely political maneuvers, played with out-and-out reactionaries and seemed, like many other politicians, willing to do almost anything to win."[9]

In 1955, when Mme Bethune died, Otis Jackson and the Dixie Hummingbirds recited her praises in a two-part recording entitled "The Life Story of Madame Bethune." Bethune had been one of the foremost advisers on African-American affairs to President Roosevelt,[10] had served as head of the Minority Affairs Office of the National Youth Administration, was a board member of both the NAACP and Urban League, and had been a founding member, and sometime president, of the National Council of Negro Women. Although she was revered in the black community as a resolute champion of black rights, her emphasis on educational initiatives and status as a companion of Presidents meant that she was not widely perceived as militant by whites. Consequently, African-American businessman Don Robey of Peacock Records in Houston probably felt little risk in issuing this gospel eulogy, which is unfortunately more notable for sincerity than poetry.

Part One

spoken: *I shall attempt to recite the life story of Madame Mary McLeod Bethune:*

spoken: *It was in the year of eighteen hundred and seventy-five,*
Another gift to America became alive.
Then I said to myself that it wasn't too soon,
Because we need more true Americans like Madame Mary McLeod Bethune.

spoken: *She was born in Mayesville, South Carolina, a little one horse town,*
I passed through there, and I just had to frown.
There she walked to school ten miles each day,
And her dear old mother would begin to pray,
For her precious little jewel child home to return,
To teach the rest of the family what she had learned.
Now, the seventeenth child lying cold in her grave,
The first member of her family that wasn't born a slave.
But I imagine seeing her rise to get up off-a her stools,
Determined to attend the very best of schools.
Some of the schools she could not reach,
But God Almighty helped her to major in the freedom of speech.
Now, all this was planned from a very small girl,
She said: "Fighting for my race with freedom of speech I shall tour the world."
She was educated at Scotia College in Concord, North Carolina,
> *graduated in eighteen ninety-three,*

And that's when she made up her mind just what she wanted to be.

She accepted a scholarship in Chicago to Moody Bible Institute,

Look out America, you may as well salute.

She said: "Fighting for my race I'll travel the north, east, west and south,

                       and even the great Equator,"

Now, her name is listed in the hall of fame as a great educator.

After being born in the midst of an old plantation,

She didn't own a cow and she didn't own a calf,

But she made her way to Florida with only a dollar and a half.

'T was in the year of nineteen hundred and four,

That's when she opened her own school, just for the Negro.

Now, her text for that day, she read the twenty-third psalm,

And on the opening day of her college she sang:

    "Lord, I'm leaning on your everlasting arm."

Part Two

spoken: *Now that you heard part one and this is part two,*
             And I hope that the whole story will be satisfactory to you.

spoken: *Madame Bethune's school merged with Cookman Institute in nineteen twenty-three,*
             And still she hadn't accomplished what she wanted to be.
             So she went to Washington, D.C., all by herself,
             Speaking of Bethune-Cookman College and all that she had left.
             But I imagine how this great educator felt,
             After giving counsel and advice beneficial to her race, to the late Franklin Delano Roosevelt.
             Now, her religious record you may also search,
             She never let her civic work interfere with the church.
             When time to go to church, you could always see,
             That she mostly pledged, and gave, to the AME.[11]
             Now, I think her race as a whole should mourn,
             To respect the battle she fought for us all, until Gabriel blows his horn.
             Now Madame Bethune has gone, she has gone to take her rest,
             We loved her, but God loved her best.
             Now, please don't take this story as just another tale,
             You just trust in God; Jesus, Jesus will never fail.

Jesus, never fails, heaven and earth shall pass away,
    But Jesus never fail, Lord.[12]

More than 5000 persons attended the funeral services and burial at Bethune Cookman College. Students at the college sang "Leaning on the Ever-lasting Arm," the gospel song she had sung the day she had opened the college.[13] The city of Daytona Beach had the slope where she was laid to rest landscaped as a monument to her.[14]

Gospel singer Brother Will Hairston (1919–1988) was a member of Love Tabernacle Church in Detroit. His recordings are characterized by the frequency of topical and political allusions in his songs. "I take to heart whatever happens to people, and then sing about it," he explained in a 1968 interview.[15] "Since it is history that he records, rather than emotions, controversy is almost nil," interviewer Rita Griffin explained, failing to note that black pride necessarily includes pride in African America's history of struggle and achievement in the face of racism. During one of his church services, the congregation was rallied in such a frenzy that someone mentioned afterwards that it looked as if a hurricane had been through the church. Ever since that moment Brother Will was known as the "Hurricane of the Motor City." The hit record that would have meant that he could leave the Chrysler plant on Eight Mile in Detroit never came about, but his recorded legacy affords some insight into a wide range of topics such as the gruesome fate of Emmett Till, his enthusiasm for Martin Luther King and President Kennedy, and his horror of the war in Vietnam.

The brutal murder of Emmett Till on 28 August 1955 formed a horrific landmark in the fight against Jim Crow. Till, a fourteen-year-old African-American boy, was slain on the pretext that he had said "Bye, baby" to a white woman in a shop in Money, Mississippi. A photograph of his cruelly mutilated body in *Jet* magazine aroused African-American anger. 250,000 people came to view the slain youth's body as it lay in state for four days.[16] The brave identification of the murderers by 64-year-old Mose Wright was a turning point in the history of the modern civil rights movement. In late 1955 Brother Will Hairston's two-part "My God Don't Like It" was released. The song, which was later reissued as " The Death of Emmet Till" [*sic*], presents an accurate account of the main events, and as such provides evidence of the profound effect Till's murder had on this black gospel artist:

Part One

chorus: *My God don't like it, I know,*
And it's a scandalous and a shame.

I want to tell you peoples just how I feel,
Out of Chicago came Emmett Till,
Down in Money, Mississippi, to visit a friend,
They tell me late one night, you know the mob tipped in,
He went to the store, just to buy some gum,
But they tell me that the woman began to run,
She said: "Looka here, people, don't you see?"
She said: "That little old boy, he whistled at me."

Well, I don't know, peoples, how mean they can be,
You know, they tell me that they killed Rev. George Lee,[17]
You know, they shot the poor man when it was dark,
You know, they killed a Negro out on the courthouse yard,
The poor man stood up in the court,
He said: "It's all as I wanna do is to vote."

Now at the home of Mr. Moses Wright,
You know, they taken little Emmett out late one night,
You know, they tied a rope around that poor boy's back,
You know, they told Uncle Mose: "You better get back,"
He said: "What y'all doing, you know it ain't no use,
Why don't you whip my little boy and turn him a-loose?"
You know, they tell me that the lamp it was very dim,
You know, it's a mob tipped in about two a.m.

You know, they tell me Mrs. Wright she began to cry,
Eh, then, eh, she began to bid little Emmett goodbye,
You know, they saw Brother Mose peepin' through the crack,
You know, they told Brother Mose that "We will be back,"
You know, they saw Mrs. Wright was standin' by his side,
Eh, then she began to hide the other child,
You know, they tell me Brother Mose he began to stop,
He said: "It's all as I wanna do is to finish my crop."

Part Two

You know, they taken little Emmett out to the barn,

You know, Willie Reed[18] *said he had a great big gun,*

You know, they shot little Emmett through the head,

You know, they want to make sure that he was dead,

Well, eh, they didn't know he was a fatherless child,

Now, so they taken his body to the riverside,

Now, well, eh, in that truck he began to jerk,

They had two hundred pounds tied around his neck,

Well, eh, on that bank they began to think,

They said that: "I am for sure he gonna sink."

You know, God is a God that we can trust,

It was three long days before Emmett come up,

You know, 'long come a man, comin' out of the field,

You know, he looked and he saw little Emmett Till,

You know, that poor man didn't know what to do,

You know, the man started to runnin', just tellin' the news.

You know, they called Mrs. Bradley[19] *on the phone,*

You know, they tell me that the woman weeped and moaned,

You know, they tell me that that woman began to walk,

You know, she called Mississippi and they wouldn't talk,

You know, it hurt Mrs. Bradley to her heart,

Now, when the woman looked around the world was dark,

Now, well, eh, in her heart she began to think,

Now, when the train stopped she began to faint,

You know, they taken little Emmett off the train,

You know, his mother only knew him by his ring.

Oh, well, I don't know peoples, but I feel very good,

Out of Detroit it came Charles C. Diggs,[20]

Charles C. Diggs, though I'm tryin' to relate,

He is a Negro leader in the United States,

They called Charles Diggs down Washington too,

And like zigzag lightning the call went through,

Diggs went down, he did what he could,

Because Emmett was a-lynched in a Mississippi wood.[21]

There was another contemporary recording entitled "The Death of Emmett Till, Parts 1 and 2." The artists were vocal group the Ramparts, and the November 1955 song was composed by Madame A. C. Bilbrew, a Los Angeles community leader and musician. The facts of the case are related uncompromisingly, and the two-part song is remarkable in its outspokenness. The chilling final stanza presents a horrifying picture of the failure to bring Till's killers to justice. Although the record was advertised in *Billboard*, nothing more was heard of it. It was probably killed off by lack of radio play in an era when stations did not want to offend sponsors and political bodies.

Part One

Folks, listen to this story, it's one the world should know,
Of a Negro boy of fourteen named Emmett Till,
From Chicago to Mississippi, to see his Uncle Mose,
But we won't see little Emmett anymore.

chorus: *Emmett Till, Emmett Till, his name will be a legend we all know,*
Tallahatchie, Mississippi, to see his Uncle Mose,
But we won't see little Emmett anymore.

When younger he had polio, his mother's only child,
She loved him as any mother would,
His daddy wore the khaki, fought bravely for Uncle Sam,
That his son might have the privilege that he should.

A few days in Tallahatchie, Emmett with his little pals,
To Money, Mississippi, grocery store to buy,
They bought bubble gum and candy from the woman at the store,
As they turned to leave little Emmett said: "Goodbye!"

His little pals said to him: "What you mean, saying goodbye,

To the woman in Money grocery store?" They said: "She is good looking,"

Emmett said: "(whistles), You're right,"

And that remark cost Emmett Till his life.

Part Two

'T was on the following Sunday, they say about 2 a.m.,

Two bad men came and knocked at Mose's door,

They said to Uncle Mose: "We've come to take the boy,

He whistled at that woman, and he must go."

He was taken to a stable, beat and shot right through the head,

All one could hear were blows and Emmett's cries,

Last words were: "Mama, save me, have mercy on me, Lord,"

The blows still fell, but little Emmett had died.

Weights were placed upon his body, in the river they did fling,

Believin' that fiendish crime they'd hide,

But in time the body came afloat, still wearing daddy's ring,

Ring and feet Uncle Mose identified.

The two men went to trial, sat and grinned and smoked and chewed,

As the fearful witnesses all did testify,

Jury's out sixty-five minutes, returned verdict in hand,

"Not guilty," was their very prompt reply.[22]

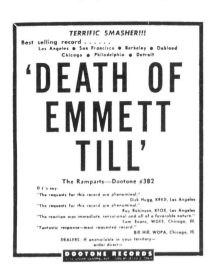

Advertisement for The Ramparts, "The Death of Emmett Till," Dootone 382. *First Pressings,* January 1956.

Despite the horrors of southern lynch law and white resistance to the deseg-regation decision of the Supreme Court in the *Brown* case, the fight against segregation continued to escalate. On 1 December 1955 Mrs. Rosa Parks, a seamstress and NAACP activist from Montgomery, Alabama, refused to give up her seat to a white man in a segregated bus. Her subsequent arrest led to the Montgomery bus boycott. The young Dr. Martin Luther King Jr. (1929–1968) led the campaign. Car-pooling was introduced and black boycotters drove "taxis." On 30 January 1956 King's house was bombed, and two days later an explosion took place at the home of E. D. Nixon, president of the Alabama branch of the NAACP, one of the foremost boycotters. On 21 February 89 blacks were indicted for conspiracy: Martin Luther King was fined $500. The boycott lasted from 5 December 1955 to 21 December 1956 and was called off only when a written mandate to integrate the buses from the Supreme Court arrived, follow-ing its decision to outlaw segregation on public transport.[23] The Montgomery bus boycott was a very significant event in the struggle for civil rights. It drew nation-wide attention, secured leadership for Martin Luther King and showed that his method of Gandhi-inspired non-violent protest paid off.

In 1956 Brother Will Hairston sang "The Alabama Bus – Parts 1 and 2" about the Alabama boycott, to the clattering accompaniment of Washboard Willie's makeshift percussion.[24]

Part One

chorus: *Stop that Alabama bus, I don't wanna ride (3×),*
          Lord, an Alabama boycott, I don't wanna ride.

          Lord, there come a bus, don't have no load,
          You know, they tell me that a human being stepped on board.
          You know, they tell me that the man sat on the bus,
          You know, they tell me that the driver began to fuss.

He said: "Looka here, man, you're from the Negro race,
And don't you know you're sitting in the wrong place?"
The driver told the man: "I know you paid your dime,
But if you don't move you gonna pay a fine."
The man told the driver: "My feets are hurtin',"
The driver told the man to move behind the curtain.

I wanna tell you 'bout the Reverend Martin Luther King,
You know, they tell me that the people began to sing.
You know, the man God sent out in the world,
You know, they tell me that the man had the mighty nerve.
You know, the poor man didn't have a bus to rent,
You know, they tell me, great God, he had the mighty strength.
And he reminded me of Moses in Israel land,
He said: "A man ain't nothing but a man."
He said: "Looka here, Alabama, don't you see?"
He says: "All of my people gonna follow me."
You know, they tell me Reverend King was very hurt,
He says: "All of my people gonna walk to work."

Part Two

They said: "Looka here, boy, you hadn't took a thought,
'Cause don't you know you broke the anti-boycott law?"
They tell me Reverend King said: "Treat us right,"
You know, in the Second World War my father lost his sight.
You know, they tell me Abraham signed the pledge one night,
He said that all of these men should have their equal rights.
You know, they had the trial and Clayton Powell was there,
You know, they tell me Clayton Powell asked the world for prayer.
You know, Diggs went down there to go his bail,
You know, they put Reverend King in a Alabama jail.

You know, they tell me Reverend King was a Bible inspired,
Uh, when all the buses was passin', nobody would ride.
You know, they tell me that the Negroes was ready to go,
They had-a-walked along the streets, until their feets were sore.
You know, they tell me Reverend King had spreaded the word,
At an Alabama bus stop, so I heard.

> *You know, they sent a lot of money, saying: "King go on,"*
> *You know, in nineteen and twenty-nine that man was born.*
> *You know, the five hundred dollar fine was very heavy,*
> *You know, the poor man was born the fifteenth of January.*[25]

Rosa Parks was replaced by "a man" for the sake of scansion, or sexism – as if such defiance was considered to be a male prerogative. Otherwise Hairston's account of events was generally accurate, and his evocation of the emotions they aroused, gripping. Moreover, the historical parallels with Moses, the hero of the Exodus story, and Lincoln, the Great Emancipator, are telling. The song was released on Joseph Von Battle's JVB Records, another of the relatively few black-owned labels in operation at this time. It was the first blues or gospel song to mention Dr. Martin Luther King. Hairston also mentions Harlem Congressman Adam Clayton Powell Jr. (1908–1972), who had compared President Eisenhower to "Pontius Pilate washing his hands of the race issue,"[26] and Charles C. Diggs (1922–1998) who was elected Congressman from Michigan in 1954 and had attended the trial of Emmett Till's murderers.[27]

The second Eisenhower term from 1957 to 1960 stands out for the virtual absence of blues and gospel songs with civil rights themes. These are the times of the Cold War, anti-Communism, political conformism and paranoia about radicals. This absence of records is not to be equated with acceptance of the status quo by African Americans, but rather reflects the conservatism and conformity of the record industry.

After the Supreme Court had ruled out school segregation in 1954, Eisenhower failed to act or even to offer verbal support for the measures. As a result, most southern school systems still refused to integrate their schools. In Little Rock, Arkansas, a token desegregation program was adopted that allowed only a limited number of black children to attend one of its schools: Little Rock Central High, which provided for 2000 white children from working-class backgrounds. When the new school year started on 2 September 1957, nine carefully selected black teenagers were to make their entry. Opposition to the integration was led by Governor Orval Faubus, who placed 250 National Guardsmen on the sidewalks. Intimidatingly, the troops obstructed the entry of the Little Rock Nine, who were severely abused by the racist crowd that had gathered. Eisenhower waited three weeks before he sent a thousand soldiers under federal authority to enforce admission.[28] Anxious to ease southern white fears of a second, federally imposed, Reconstruction, it was imperative for Eisenhower to erase the impression that he had sent troops to Little Rock to stimulate integration. Instead, the President made it known that he had merely acted to execute a federal court order and preserve order.[29]

Later that year Brother Will Hairston, the "Hurricane of the Motor City," chronicled the events in his "Shout School Children." It is the only blues or gospel song with a civil rights theme from Eisenhower's second term.

The song mentions Autherine Lucy (b. 1929), who was the first African American admitted to the University of Alabama, Tuscaloosa, in February 1956. Riots broke out, and she was expelled after three days. Thirty-two years later, the university wrote a letter notifying her that the expulsion had been revoked and she could re-enroll.

chorus: *Well, shout, school children,*
     Shout for joy.
  Well, shout, school children,
     Shout for joy.
  Why don't you shout, school children?
     Shout for joy.
  Shout, school children, shout for joy.

  Stop here, people, listen to my cry,
  I wanna tell you 'bout the Little Rock Central High,
  And if you read your newspapers and read them well,
  You oughta know about a story that I'm bound to tell.

  Well, nine colored kids, began to start,
  You know, Faubus he called out the National Guards,
  Well, he talked to the captain on the phone,
  He said: "Tell the National Guards to hurry on,
  Well, this is my word, don't pass it by,
  Don't let the colored school children into Central High,"
  Well, the colored school children, they tryin' to integrate,
  But the law of Arkansas, it just won't take.

Looka here, Faubus, Supreme Court Ruling,

Don't you see, they had to call the N-double A-C-P,

They tell me Roy Wilkins[30] began to walk,

Called Governor Faubus and he wouldn't talk,

Well, he called the Blair House,[31] the White House too,

Was askin' Eisenhower: "What you gonna do?"

Well, Eisenhower says: "There is no doubt,

Supreme Court order will be carried out."

Well, Eisenhower knew just what to do,

They tell me that he sent out the Federal troops,

Well, into Little Rock, about seven o' clock,

You know, they tell me Governor Faubus began to stop,

Well, the guards holdin' rifles, while they passed by,

The colored kids began to enter Central High,

Well, a great big crowd was looking very mad,

Taking our privilege with all we had,

Well, they had to stand guard all day long,

Because the colored kids had been treated wrong.

Oh, Autherine Lucy,

   Shout for joy!

Oh, Autherine Lucy,

    Shout for joy!

Oh, Autherine Lucy,

   Shout for joy!

Shout, school children, shout for joy!

I know you had a hard time,

   Shout for joy!

I know you had a hard time,

   Shout for joy!

I know you had a hard time,

   Shout for joy!

Shout, school children, shout for joy![32]

At my request, Brother Will Hairston's eldest daughter Sandranette interviewed her mother and kindly shared her memories of her father with me: "My
father always, even before retiring from the Chrysler plant in Detroit, read the

newspaper from cover to cover, followed by reading the Holy Bible and lastly he watched the 11:00 p.m. news. Dad would always tell me: 'You have to read the paper everyday, so you will know what's happening in the world.' Dad gathered information from the media, radio, television, and newspapers. He took factual information, rhymed the facts and put music with it. He was a rapper way ahead of his time. Dad had a lot of hobbies, which included writing and composing songs about current events that affected the African-American community during our many struggles."[33]

In an interview with blues writer Mike Rowe, Johnny Shines claimed to have recorded an as yet untraced "Eisenhower Blues," in the shape of a cynical parody of Psalm 23.

> Ike is my shepherd, I am in want,
> He makes me to lie down on park benches,
> I used to ride in a Cadillac, but now I don't.[34]

The first two lines also occur in an amazing extended parody of both Psalm 23 and the Lord's Prayer. The artist called himself "The Flock-Rocker" on his 1958 recording of "Political Prayer Blues." The real name of this blues-singing trumpet player and disc jockey from St. Louis, who later changed his recording pseudonym to Gabriel & His Trumpet, was Mitchell Hearns. Although he does not mention the President by name, the Flock-Rocker certainly pulls no punches in identifying Eisenhower as the target for his critique. Parodies of the Lord's Prayer may derive from a "toast" that was in general circulation. To an African American, ideally with a drink in his hand, a toast often provided a way to vent frustration by the use of abusive language in rhyme, more often than not loaded with sexual references.[35]

spoken: *I want all you peoples, to give a listen to what I'm gonna tell you:*
You know, since that last election,
I ain't had no protection.
So I want you to pay close attention to what I'm 'bout to tell you,
'Cause this is the natural born truth, I wanna thank you.

To our great leader who art in Washington,
(Yes, we all know who's to blame,)
When your job begun, our jobs was done.
Yes, give us this day,
Our starvation pay,
And forgive us for taking it,
As we forgive those who take it from us.
And lead us not into another depression,
For now I know this is a country of Ford and Packard and General Motors,
With Mark 2s, Eldorados and Mercuries and Lincolns for ever.
Yes, this holey shirt fits me well,
But these raggedy pants covereth me not.

Yes, he's my shepherd, but I am in want,
Yes, he maketh me to walk through the streets and alleys, but I am still hungry,
He maketh me to walk to the soup kitchen, but I am still in want,
Yes, he is my shepherd, and I am in want,
He maketh me to lie down upon the park benches,
And the police anoint my head with clubs,
Yes, and surely hard times follow me,
And bad luck will follow me all of the rest of the days of this present administration,
And I will dwell in a housing project for the rest of my life,
Amen! All right, Flock-Rocker![36]

Both in its blasphemous distortion of two of the most sacred of Christian prayers and in its outspoken criticism of the President of the United States, "Political Prayer Blues" is a remarkable composition for a black artist recording in 1958.

Robert Pete Williams (1914–1980) served time for murder at Angola State Prison Farm. While on parole, and working on a farm in conditions that amounted to servitude, he was recorded by folklorist Harry Oster in November 1960. The unissued talking blues, "Yassuh an' Nosuh Blues," laments traditional black subservience to white authority which was particularly vivid in the prison setting and which was maintained there, as in the wider southern society, by the ever-present threat of white violence. Fascinatingly, Williams does find one "white man" who breaks this pattern of abuse and brutalization to offer him succor, referring to God as "the white man on my side." Of course, religion and the formal black church constituted an important site of black solidarity and communal resistance throughout the Jim Crow era, and later as a vital vehicle for the mass mobilizations of the civil rights movement. Here, however, the invocation of a white God may suggest just how much men like Williams were still steeped in the racialized social relations of the time. In Williams' song power was equated with whites, and ultimate power with a white God.

> Well, on my way a-goin' along, I had no success at all,
> I go to my bossman's house, walk in, forgot to reach for my hat;
> When I forget, leave it on my head,
> 'Cause he liable now, get him a club, an' knock it off my head.
>
> Oh, if you forget, tells you: "Nigger, what's wrong with you?"
> "What you mean, boss?" "I want you to get that hat off yo' head!"
>
> Yassuh an' nosuh, all over this no good place,
> Oh, yassuh an' nosuh, all over this, eh, no good place;
> He may be young, he don't have to be no more than sixteen or seventeen,
> But you got to honor 'em as they grow.
>
> Well, they treat me so dirty, they jus' don't know how to treat no black man,
> Boy, if they let the Negro alone, everything gonna be all right.
> I heard the Governor man one day, if they let the Negro alone, everything gonna be all right,
> But all this politics is for the sake o' the black man.
>
> I know I'm black, walking 'round with a hung down head;
> I ain't got nowhere, God knows the way I try.
> Everybody but the white man that I got on my side;
> Wanta know who that? That the good Lord up above.[37]

There is one other song that briefly mentions the events at Little Rock, but it was recorded in October 1962, five years after the event, when the mass civil rights movement was well under way. It is entitled "Ride On Red, Ride On" and was recorded by Louisiana Red for single release. The song is about leaving the racist South, and refers to the Freedom Riders, civil rights activists who fought segregation in public transport, and to the White Citizens' Councils, racists who tried to intimidate African Americans by economic reprisals and occasional physical methods. One couplet refers to the events at Little Rock Central High School:

> We rolled into old Little Rock, had made another state,
> Where it took the whole US army to make one school integrate.[38]

In his second term blues and gospel singers ignored Eisenhower in the same way that he ignored the African-American community. There had been a "historic" first meeting of the President with four African-American leaders (Martin Luther King, A. Philip Randolph, Lester Granger and Roy Wilkins) on 23 June 1958, but afterwards King felt that the President failed to see the urgency of the situation. At a 27 August press conference Eisenhower admitted that he had told a friend in private that he thought integration should proceed more slowly.[39]

With no particular personal interest in civil rights and a steady belief in states' rights and voluntarism, as opposed to federal compulsion, in most areas of social life, Eisenhower offered little encouragement to African Americans. Ironically, it was partly because of this indifference that the freedom struggle gathered such great momentum during his two terms in office. Eisenhower failed publicly to endorse the Supreme Court's historic *Brown* decision of May 1954, which had declared segregated schooling in the South, and by implication segregation in general, unconstitutional. Indeed, he conspicuously failed to support genuine efforts to desegregate southern schools. His belated and reluctant intervention in the Little Rock school crisis of 1957 came only when civic order had broken down. True, the Civil Rights Acts of 1957 and 1960 carried great symbolic signifi- cance, being the first to pass for more than 80 years, but these were cosmetic gestures, for which Eisenhower had no enthusiasm, and which remained largely unenforced.

Given the under-representation of African-American label owners in the recording industry, a disproportionate number of these civil rights songs also appear to have been cut for black-owned labels. Maybe African-American owners, as those within the industry with the greatest personal stake in the Movement's success, were sometimes more willing to go out on a limb to record potentially controversial material. Yet, in truth, there was hardly a stampede to cut such songs from anyone, black or white. And there was no guarantee of a public airing for those which were recorded: fears of possible reprisals, doubts about their commercial appeal, and the certain knowledge that even if they avoided a formal ban, they would not get airplay on the radio, combined to ensure that many civil rights blues and gospel songs remained unissued.

All of this confirms how the racial situation provided a crucial context within which the artistry and commerce of African-American popular music took place. By the same token, however, it also illustrates how much the story of the creation, distribution and consumption of that music has to tell historians about the African-American community during years of great social upheaval and change.

The veterans of World War II had demanded social justice for the African-American population. African Americans began to speak out and discovered that major resistance by non-violence helped to bring about changes. In the 1960s this development would be speeded up by many black and white activists in the South who made Martin Luther King the center of the civil rights universe.

The 1960 campaign was between Eisenhower's Vice-President, Richard Nixon, and John F. Kennedy. When John Fitzgerald Kennedy was inaugurated on 17 January 1961, Eisenhower became just a retired five-star general again. Important decisions had been postponed under his presidency. The Communists reigned supreme in North Korea, North Vietnam and Cuba and race relations had hardly improved. But Ike had steered the States through the 1950s without going to war, in spite of the many crises.[40]

CONCLUSION

In undertaking this study my primary objective has been to shed new light on the question of how the presidencies of Harry S. Truman and Dwight D. Elsenhower were perceived and experienced by African Americans. With this aim in mind, I have carried out a thorough analysis of the blues and gospel lyrics of this period which contain explicit social and political comment. I believe that these lyrics, which no one has previously attempted to collate and transcribe in a systematic way, represent an important and hitherto untapped source.

In contrast to the Roosevelt era, when any such comment was for the most part restricted to describing the effects presidential decisions and policies may have had on individual singers and everyday life, the aftermath of World War II saw a gradual shift towards abstractions, generalizations and proposals for reform. One particularly noticeable innovation is the growth of interest in the political process itself.

Record sales showed a steady rise in the immediate post-war years as the shortage of materials was alleviated. However, the record companies faced opposition from James C. Petrillo, the president of the Musicians' Union, who adopted the position that the playing of records on vendors or "jukeboxes" and by disc jockeys in radio broadcasts was putting union members out of work. In an attempt to bring the record companies to terms, Petrillo, who had already proclaimed a ban on recording that lasted for thirteen months during 1942 and 1943,[1] issued a second ban in 1948. Since the record companies had built up an ample stock of recorded music in advance, his attempt to obtain better conditions for union members was unsuccessful.[2] The ban was short-lived, but its effects are evident in the following graph of US record sales (Figure 1).[3]

In the preceding chapters, 123 complete blues and gospel lyrics have been studied that contain references to the social and political situation of black people in the United States in the period from 1945 (when Truman succeeded Roosevelt) to 1961 (when Kennedy succeeded Eisenhower). Some of the other 185 recordings, which are referred to in the notes but have not been analyzed (in full) in this book, are unissued and unavailable (12 per cent), are alternative versions of the songs under discussion (43 per cent) or are instrumental (3 per cent). Others contained lyrics whose content was either duplicated by those quoted, or considered of less relevance to the present purpose (42 per cent). The following diagram (Figure 2) presents the relation between the total number of "political" blues and gospel songs (grey) and those selected for analysis (black).

The peaks in the diagram coincide with the end of World War II and the death of FDR (1945), the atomic bomb and inflation (1946), the resultant high prices (1947), the Korean War (1950–1953), and the beginning of the space race (1960). A comparison with Figure 1 shows a remarkable rise in political songs from 1950 to 1953 occasioned by the Korean War, in a period when the total record sales did not show a similar peak.

Twenty per cent of the songs in this book remained unissued at the time. This is about the same number as pre-war (22 per cent), but that high percentage was mainly caused by the field recordings of the Library of Congress. No field recordings of blues and gospel songs were made by the Library in the period from 1945 to 1960, so that this time one-fifth of the political recordings made for commercial record labels had to remain unissued. Obviously, the controversial nature of this group of lyrics is the likeliest explanation for the high percentage.

Of 79 per cent of the "political" lyrics from the period 1945–1960 referred to in this study the recording locations are known. At least 17 per cent were recorded in New York, 17 per cent in Chicago, 11 per cent in Los Angeles, 5 per cent in Detroit, 4 per cent in Memphis, 3 per cent in Houston, 3 per cent in New Orleans, 2 per cent in Cincinnati, 2 per cent in Atlanta and 1 per cent each in San Francisco, Crowley, Oakland, Hollywood, Dallas, St. Louis, Shreveport, Birmingham, Nashville, London (England) and Paris (France).

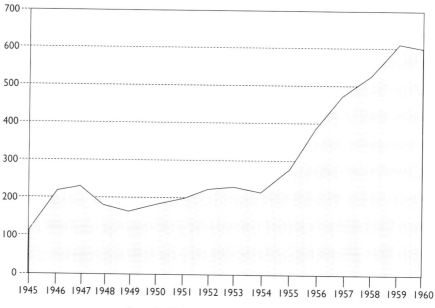

Figure 1. US record sales in millions.

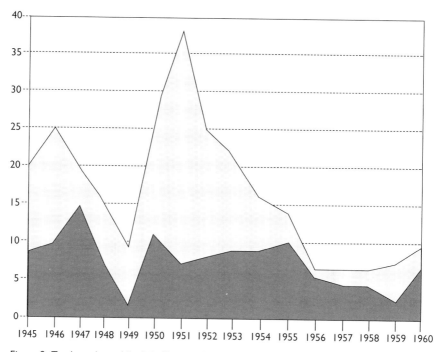

Figure 2. Total number of "political" songs (grey) and those selected for analysis (black).

This is not always a guide to the origins of the artists, who sometimes had to make extensive journeys to reach the recording studios of the big cities. However, this sort of travel is more true of the pre-war situation than of the post-war, as the small independent labels tended to record local talent, and were unable to perform long-distance talent searches or to pay travel expenses. It is clear, nevertheless, that the majority of the artists lived in the larger American cities, although they very often hailed from the country originally.

In comparison with pre-war recording locations, a lot of recording was now done in California (at least 19 per cent), reflecting the migration to the West. Fortunately the origins of most singers are known. Most of the 90 solo singers were born in the southern states: 22 came from Mississippi, fourteen from Texas, eleven from Louisiana, eight from Tennessee, six from Arkansas, five from Alabama, three from California, three from Missouri, three from Kentucky, two from Pennsylvania, two from South Carolina, two from North Carolina, two from Oklahoma and one each from Ohio, Virginia, Nebraska, Arizona, Georgia and Cuba. In comparison with the FDR era, there are fewer artists from Mississippi and Georgia and more from Texas, and in the earlier period there were no singers from California.

Some artists recorded more than one song with political comment. If we count different versions of the same song only once, the most important of these are J. B. Lenoir (six), Arthur "Big Boy" Crudup, Roosevelt Sykes, Huddie "Leadbelly" Ledbetter, John Lee Hooker, Smokey Hogg and Sam "Lightnin'" Hopkins (four different recordings each), William "Big Bill" Broonzy, the Golden Gate Quartet, Louis Jordan, the Pilgrim Travelers, the Sons of Jehovah, "Brother" Will Hairston and Josh White (each with three different songs). The political songs of these fourteen artists and groups constitute 25 per cent of the total in the period covered. Broonzy, Leadbelly, Jordan and White had also ranked high during the FDR era, and all had extensive recording careers, although many others with such careers recorded little political material.

Of the 308 "political" songs from this period fourteen (5 per cent) were sung by women. Some of these women commented on social conditions as they affected their men and in turn themselves. The women's lyrics are assertive in their outspokenness, and although they are even fewer in number than during the earlier period, they are certainly no less direct than the men's.

The sermon, with its impromptu exchanges between pulpit and pew, affords a unique view of political developments as they affected everyday life, and it is unfortunate that hardly any topical sermons were recorded in this period. This is in contrast to the situation both in the earlier period and during the late 1960s and the early 1970s, when dozens of political sermons would be recorded. The development of the long-play album was ideally suited to the recording of half-hour sermons.

In spite of the lack of recorded topical sermons, of the 308 songs selected for detailed analysis, 57 (= 19 per cent) were sung by gospel artists or groups, a far higher percentage than pre-war (6 per cent). To the gospel singers the atomic bomb was experienced as a fire from heaven (Pilgrim Travelers); poverty was fought by comparisons with the battle of Jericho (Richard Huey); prayers were said for the boys in Korea (Evening Star Quartet) and the major landmarks in the early history of the civil rights movement were carefully chronicled ("Brother" Will Hairston).

The relative scarcity of blues and gospel songs directly about Truman and Eisenhower is evidence of the fact that both Presidents had failed to inspire the African-American community. Of course, women like Rosa Parks and Mary McLeod Bethune and men like Adam Clayton Powell and Martin Luther King filled the void admirably. In the White House, however, Franklin Roosevelt was sorely missed and a new hero badly needed.

NOTES

Introduction
1. Gates (1987), p. xxxi.
2. Bell, p. 26.
3. Gates (1988), p. xii.
4. Charles Wolfe, "Where the Blues Is At: A Survey of Recent Research," *Popular Music and Society* 1 (1971–72), p. 153, as quoted in Barlow, p. 349. In spite of the note in Barlow's book this important statement is not to be found in the original article as published in *Popular Music and Society* 1, no. 3 (spring 1972).
5. Levine (1993), p. 36.
6. Evans (1982), pp. 27–30.

1. Those Reconversion Blues
1. Golden Gate Quartet, "The General Jumped at Dawn" (composer credit: "Neil–Mundy"), Chicago, 16 March 1945; issued on OKeh 6741; reissued on Document DOCD 5638.
   The original soundtrack from the 1944 Delmer Daves film *Hollywood Canteen* was issued on Document DOCD 5658.
2. "Induction Statistics" at: www.sss.gov/induct.htm
3. Flennoy Trio (vocal Jimmie Edwards), "The Induction Blues" (composer credit: "Carl 'Jeff' Jefferson"), Los Angeles, 1945; issued on Excelsior 117.
4. Josh White, "The Man Who Couldn't Walk Around," c. 1946; issued on Elektra EKLLP 203; reissued on Agram Blues ABCD 2018.
   Later versions of this song are:
   Josh White and His Guitar, New York City, 12 June 1947; issued on Apollo 157; reissued on DOCD 1013; and
   Royal Festival Hall, London, England, 1 April 1961; issued on ABC LP 407.
   Words by MacKinlay Kantor and music by Harry Rosenthal. Composed for the FDR Memorial Committee of the National Foundation for Infantile Paralysis.
5. Wald, p. 150.

6. "Café Society Downtown (Followup)," *Variety*, 26 February 1947.

7. For the circumstances see van Rijn (1997), pp. 194–204.

8. For the lyrics and a discussion see ibid., p. 195.

9. Bastin (1990), pp. 144–45 and 155.

10. Champion Jack Dupree, "God Bless Our New President!" (composer credit: "Joe Davis"), New York City, 18 April 1945; issued on Joe Davis 5102; reissued on Agram Blues ABCD 2018.

11. Walter (Confessin' the Blues) Brown, "I'm Glad to Be Back" (composer credit: "Walter Brown–Skip Hall"), New York City, 19 December 1945; issued on Queen 4106; reissued on Westside WESF CD 110.

12. Ottenheimer, p. 202.

13. "Cousin" Joe with Leonard Feather's Hiptet, "Post-War Future Blues" (composer credit: "Joseph"), New York City, 5 October 1945; issued on Philo/Aladdin 118; reissued on Agram Blues ABCD 2018.

14. "50,000 Lose Jobs Here!", *Chicago Defender*, 18 August 1945.

15. Louis Jordan and His Tympany Five, "Reconversion Blues" (composer credit "Fleecie Moore–Steve Graham"), New York City, 15 October 1945; issued on Decca 18762; reissued on MCA LP 510.183 and Charly CDX-7.

16. A reference to clarinetist Johnny Walker.

17. Roosevelt Sykes and His Piano, "High Price Blues" (composer credit: "Roosevelt Sykes"), Chicago, 9 October 1945; issued on BlueBird 34-0737; reissued on Blues Document BDCD 6048.

18. A reference to folklorist Frederic Ramsey Jr. (1915–1995), who was in the studio.

19. Huddie "Leadbelly" Ledbetter, "National Defense Blues," New York, c. early 1946; issued on Folkways LP 2488; reissued on Smithsonian Folkways SF CD 40010.
    Later versions of this song are:
    Leadbelly, "Defense Blues" (composer credit: "Huddie Ledbetter"), New York City, c. June 1946; issued on Disc 5085; reissued on Document DOCD 5311.
    "National Defense Blues," New York City, 15 October 1948; issued on Folkways LP 2(9)41.

20. Chafe, pp. 83–84.

21. Jay McShann's Sextet (vocalist Jimmy Witherspoon), "Shipyard Woman Blues" (composer credit: "Whitherspoon" [*sic*]), Dallas, 7 July 1945; issued on Premier 29011; reissued on Oldie Blues OLLP 8011.

22. According to Wentworth and Flexner, the slang word "hinkty" or "hincty" means "snobbish."

23. Jim Wynn's Bobalibans (vocalist Pee Wee Wiley), "Shipyard Woman" (composer credit: "Luper"), Los Angeles, late 1945 or early 1946; issued on Gilt-Edge 527; reissued on Whiskey, Women, And . . . KMLP 703.
    Other songs about the shipyards are:
    Wynonie "Blues" Harris, "Time to Change Your Town" (composer credit: "Wynonie Harris"), Los Angeles, September 1945; issued on Apollo 378; reissued on Route 66 KIXLP 20.

Frank Ervin, "Got My Shipyard Job Again" (composer credit: "Ervin–McCoy"), Los Angeles, 26 January 1951; issued on Mercury 8225.

24. Chafe, pp. 83–84.

25. "Wild" Bill Moore (vocal by Duke Henderson), "Home Coming Blues" (composer credit: "Moore"), Los Angeles, 4 December 1945; issued on Apollo 789; reissued on Delmark CD 668.

26. Arthur "Big Boy" Crudup, "Boy Friend Blues" (composer credit: "Arthur Crudup"), Chicago, 22 February 1946; issued on Victor 20-2989; reissued on Document DOCD 5201.

27. Lawyer Houston, "In the Army Since 1941" (composer credit: "Lawyer Houston"), Dallas, TX, 1950; Atlantic unissued; issued on Atlantic LP 7226.

28. "Big" Joe Turner, "I Got My Discharge Papers" (composer credit: "Joe Turner"), Los Angeles, 23 January 1946; Savoy unissued; issued on Savoy LP 2223.

29. Cousin Joe, "Desperate GI Blues" (composer credit: "T. Reig–P. Joseph"), New York City, 13 February 1946; issued on Savoy 5526; reissued on Blue Moon BMCD 6001.

30. Sonny Thompson (vocal by Jesse Edwards), "Uncle Sam Blues" (composer credit: "Glover–Mann–Bernard"), Cincinnati, 3 January 1951; issued on King 4431; reissued on Sequel NEMCD 900.

    Another song about the Jodie Man is:

    David Green with Melba Pope Trio, "Jodie-Jodie Blues" (composer credit: "Green"), Chicago, 1945; issued on Queen/King 4113.

31. See Jeff Hannusch, "The Legend of Jody: Ain't No Sense in Going Home, Jody's Got Your Girl and Gone," *Goldmine* 20, no. 8, issue 358 (15 April 1994): 68, 194.

32. "Duke" Henderson with Tiny Webb Trio, "GI Blues" (composer credit: "Duke Henderson"), Los Angeles, 1946; issued on Globe 108.

33. "Vout" is a word coined by jazz vocalist Slim Gaillard; in this context it means something like "excellent."

34. Shifty Henry and His "Flashes", "Hypin Women Blues" (composer credit: "Shifty Henry"), Los Angeles, c. 1945; issued on Enterprise 106.

35. Smokey Hogg, "Goin' Back to Texas," Los Angeles, 3 October 1949; issued on Specialty 342; reissued on Specialty SNTF LP 5018.

36. James (Beale Street) Clark, "Get Ready to Meet Your Man" (composer credit: "Clark"), Chicago, 24 October 1945; issued on Columbia 36948.

    This song became better known as "Look on Yonder Wall" and had a long history. Here are some examples:

    Jazz Gillum, "Look on Yonder Wall" (composer credit: "James Clark"), Chicago, 18 February 1946; issued on Victor 20-1974; reissued on Document DOCD 5200.

    Boyd Gilmore, "Just an Army Boy" (composer credit: "Gilmore"), Greenville, MS, 23 January 1952; issued on Modern 860; reissued on Kent KSTLP 9009.

    Elmore James, "Look on Yonder Wall" (composer credit: "Sehorn–James"), New Orleans, 1961; issued on Fire 504; reissued on Charly CD 180.

    Junior Parker, "Yonders Wall" (composer credit: "E. James"), New Orleans, 1961; issued on Duke 367; reissued on Duke LP 76/83.

Arthur "Big Boy" Crudup, "Look on Yonder Wall," New York City, late 1962; issued on Fire LP 103.

"Homesick" James Williamson, "Crutch and Cane" (composer credit: "James"), Chicago, August 1964; issued on Decca LP 4748.

37. Al (Stomp) Russell Trio, "World War 2 Blues" (composer credit: "Russell–Cowan"), Los Angeles, December 1946; issued on Queen 4162.

38. "COD" stands for "cash on delivery."

39. A "zombie" was a cocktail that was so strong that it was thought it could revive a corpse.

40. Ivory Joe Hunter and His Band, "Reconversion Blues" (composer credit: "Hunter"), San Francisco, 1945; issued on Pacific 601; reissued on Route 66 KIX LP 4.

41. Charles Gray and His Rhumboogie Five (= Buster Bennett disguising his identity while under contract to Columbia), "I'm a Bum Again" (composer credit: "C. Glenn–C. Gray"), Chicago, 1946; issued on Rhumboogie 5001; reissued on RST CD 91577-2.

The flipside of this record, "Crazy Woman Blues" (composer credit: "C. Glenn–C. Gray"), contains the line: *I ain't gonna shave, I ain't gonna wash my face, I guess you want me to look like one of Hitler's inhuman race.*

42. Roosevelt Sykes and His Original Honeydrippers, "Living in a Different World" (composer credit: "Roosevelt Sykes"), Chicago, 18 February 1946; issued on Victor 20-3315; reissued on Blues Document BDCD 6048.

43. Cf. van Rijn (1997), pp. 184–85, 189–90.

44. "Running the dark down" is "staying up all night."

45. Smokey Hogg, "Unemployment Blues" (composer credit: "Hogg"), Dallas, TX, 1947; issued on Modern 20-556; reissued on Ace CD CHD 780.

There is an alternative take of this song which was issued on Kent LP 9005. Contrary to the standard discography, Smokey here sings that it is 1948. The lyrics of this unissued take are totally different and far less important for our purpose.

46. For the NRA in blues and gospel lyrics, see van Rijn (1997), pp. 74–76.

47. For the OPA in blues and gospel lyrics, see van Rijn (1997), pp. 187–88.

48. Dossie "Georgia Boy" Terry, "The OPA Blues" (composer credit: "Dossie Terry"), New York City, 1946; issued on Chicago 117.

49. McCullough, p. 470.

50. *Chicago Defender*, 6 July 1946.

51. Brownie McGhee, "High Price Blues" (composer credit: "McGhee"), New York, late 1947; issued on Encore 102; reissued on Bear Family 10CD 15720.

52. George "Blues Man" Vann, "Can't Stretch It No More," Los Angeles, 1946; issued on Jewel 2005; reissued on Chicago Records CHLP 202. This song was issued on Savoy 811 under the title "Inflation Blues."

53. Ferrell (1994), pp. 229–30.

54. Ivory Joe Hunter and His Band, "High Cost, Low Pay Blues" (composer credit: "Hunter"), San Francisco, February 1947; issued on Pacific 630; reissued on Route 66 KIX LP 4.

55. Herbert Beard, "Luxury Tax Blues," Chicago, April 1953; issued on Cool 102 (I have not heard this song).

56. Eddie Vinson and His Orchestra, "Luxury Tax Blues" (composer credit: "Vinson–Robinson"), St. Louis, 29 April 1947; issued on Mercury 8051; reissued on Saxophonograph BPLP 507.

57. As quoted in Ferrell (1994), p. 230.

58. Smokey Hogg, "High Priced Meat," Los Angeles, 11 October 1947; issued on Modern 20-815; reissued on Agram Blues ABCD 2018.

59. Justin O'Brien, "The Dark Road of Floyd Jones," *Living Blues* 58 (winter 1983): 12.

60. This is addressed to harmonica blower Snooky Pryor (born in Mississippi in 1929).

61. Snooky & Moody (= Snooky Pryor and Moody Jones), "Stockyard Blues" (composer credit: "C. Scales"), Chicago, 1947; issued on Old-Swingmaster 22; reissued on Blues Classics LP 8. (The reference to "Buddy" was meant for Snooky's cousin Moody Jones (1908–1988), who was furious about it, as he wanted to be known by his real name on records.)

    Later versions of this song are:

    Floyd Jones, "Stockyard Blues" (composer credit: "Floyd Jones"), Chicago, June 1966; issued on Testament LP 2214.

    Floyd Jones, "Stockyard Blues," Chicago, November 1975; issued on Magnolia MLP 301.

    Floyd Jones, "Stockyard Blues," Chicago, June 1984; issued on Wolf CD 120863.

62. See www.workdayminnesota.org

63. This is a reference to pianist Sunnyland Slim.

64. Sunny Land Slim and His Sunnyland Boys (vocalist Floyd Jones), "Hard Times" (composer credit: "Floyd Jones"), Chicago, 1948; issued on Tempo-Tone 1001; reissued on Nighthawk LP 102.

    Later versions of this song are:

    Floyd Jones and Band, "Ain't Times Hard" (composer credit: "F. Jones"), Chicago, 3 February 1953; issued on VeeJay 111; reissued on Buddah LP 7511.

    Sunnyland Slim, "Recession Blues," Chicago, 1960; Atomic-H unissued; issued on Delmark LP 624.

    Floyd Jones, "Hard Times" (composer credit: "Floyd Jones"), Chicago, June 1966; issued on Testament LP 2214.

    Sunnyland Slim, "Depression Blues," Chicago, 10 June 1968; issued on Blue Horizon LP 7-63213; reissued on Airway LP 3220.

    Sunnyland Slim, "Depression Blues," Chicago, September 1971; issued on Jewel LP 5010.

    Sunnyland Slim, "Depression Blues" (composer credit: "Sunnyland Slim"), Paris, France, 1974; issued on Festival LP 648.

    Sunnyland Slim, "Depression Blues," Paris, France, 26 November 1974; issued on Black & Blue LP 33558.

    Sunnyland Slim, "Depression Blues," Chicago, 8 March 1977; issued on Red Lightnin' LP 0057; reissued on Delmark CD 735.

Sunnyland Slim, "Depression Blues," Chicago, 23 January 1980; issued on L+R LP 42015.

65. L. C. Williams, "Strike Blues," Houston, 1948; issued on Gold Star 667; reissued on Arhoolie LP 2006.

66. Cf. Jim Dawson, "Jessie Mae Robinson," *Juke Blues* 22 (winter/spring 1991): 8–12.

67. Jimmy Witherspoon, "Money Getting Cheaper" (composer credit: "Dootsie Williams–Jessie Mae Robinson"), Los Angeles, 15 November 1947; issued on Supreme 1501; reissued on Polydor LP 423241.

   Other versions of this song are:

   Charles Brown, "Money's Getting Cheaper" (composer credit: "Williams–Robinson"), Los Angeles, 1947; issued on Exclusive 257; reissued on Classics CD 1147.

   Chuck Norris, "Money's Getting Cheaper," Los Angeles, late 1947; issued on Coast 8044.

   Jimmy Witherspoon, "Time's Gettin' Tougher Than Tough," Los Angeles, 2 or 9 December 1959; issued on Hi Fi Jazz LP 426.

   Jimmy Witherspoon, "Money's Gettin' Cheaper" (composer credit: "Witherspoon"), Los Angeles, 15 August 1963; issued on Prestige 307; taken from Prestige LP 7300.

   Jimmy Witherspoon, "Times Are Getting Tougher Than Tough," London, 23 May 1966; issued on Fontana LP 5382.

68. "Consumer and Gross Domestic Price Indexes: 1913 to 1998." No. 1435 from "20th Century Statistics," US Census Bureau, *Statistical Abstract of the United States: 2001* 1st ed., Hoover's Business Press.

69. Louis Jordan and His Tympany Five, "Inflation Blues" (composer credit: "T. Southern–A. Alexander–L. Jordan"), Los Angeles, 1 December 1947; issued on Decca 24381; reissued on MCA LP 510.146.

   During the later era of Reaganomics, this song was recorded by B. B. King, whose lyrics are virtually the same. Considering the 35-year time gap, it is surprising that these lyrics about 1947 economics were still fully applicable in 1982:

   B.B. King, "Inflation Blues" (composer credit: "Louis Jordan–Tommy Southern–Alegretto Alexander"), New York, 15 September 1982; issued on MCA LP 5413.

70. "The Marshall Plan" at: www.nara.gov/exhall/featured-document/marshall/marshall.html

71. This phrase was first used by Blind Lemon Jefferson in his "Rabbit Foot Blues" (c. December 1926). Lemon sang about "those meatless and wheatless days" in a song with World War I references. On 26 January 1918, President Wilson had made a solemn proclamation establishing meatless, wheatless and porkless days. Americans were instructed to "hang this where you will see it every day" (February 1918, Index No. F. 4).

72. Jack McVea and His Orchestra (vocalist Rabon Tarrant), "Inflation Blues" (composer credit: "Southern–Alexander"), Los Angeles, December 1947; issued on Exclusive 260; reissued on Agram Blues ABCD 2018.

73. Cartoon by E. Simms Campbell, *Afro-American*, 23 August 1947.
74. Turner Willis, "Re-enlisted Blues," Oakland, CA, 1946; issued on Trilon/Big Town 1058.
75. Walter Davis, "Things Ain't Like They Use to Be" [*sic*] (composer credit: "Walter Davis"), Chicago, 5 February 1947; issued on Victor 20-2335; reissued on Document DOCD 5287.
76. The Eighteenth Amendment prohibited "the manufacturing, sale, or transportation of intoxicating liquors."
77. Sons of Heaven (= Selah Jubilee Singers), "The World Is in a Bad Condition," c. 1948, Raleigh, NC; issued on Cross 1004; reissued on P-Vine PCD-5547.

Relevant songs on the themes addressed in this chapter that for various reasons have not been used are:

Sonny Boy and Lonnie, "Big Moose Blues" (composer credit: "Bradley–Smith"), New York City, 1945; issued on Continental 6053; reissued on Document DOCD 5588.

Johnny Moore's Three Blazers (vocal Johnnie McNeil), "Axis Doom Blues" (composer credit: "Johnnie McNeil"), Los Angeles, c. March 1945; issued on Exclusive 204.

Roy Milton's Sextet, "Burma Road Blues, Parts 1 & 2" (composer credit: "Lionel Hampton"), Los Angeles, September 1945; issued on Hamp-Tone 104; reissued on Juke Box Lil JBLP 600.

Josh White, "Beloved Comrade," 25 October 1945; unissued Folkways acetate 3704; issued on DOCD 1018.

Joe Turner, "I'm Still in the Dark" (composer credit: "Joe Turner), Los Angeles, 23 January 1946; Savoy unissued; issued on Savoy LP 2223.

Roosevelt Sykes with His Original Honeydrippers, "Sunny Road" (composer credit: "Roosevelt Sykes"), Chicago, 18 February 1946; issued on Victor 20-1906; reissued on Blues Documents BDCD 6048.

Joe Turner, "I'm Still in the Dark," Chicago, 11 October 1946; issued on National 9106; reissued on Savoy LP 14012.

Johnny Moore's Three Blazers (vocal Charles Brown), "Sunny Road" (composer credit: "Roosevelt Sykes"), Los Angeles, late 1946; issued on Exclusive 233; reissued on Route 66 KIX LP 5.

Big Bill Broonzy, "Martha Blues," Chicago, 28 January 1947; Columbia unissued; issued on Document DOCD 5525.

Floyd Dixon Trio, "Drafting Blues" (composer credit: "Dixon"), Los Angeles, 1948; issued on Modern 20-700; reissued on P-Vine PCD 3064.

Pilgrim Travelers, "A Soldier's Plea," Hollywood, 22 July 1948; issued on Specialty 345; reissued on Specialty CD 7204.

Later versions of the same song are:

Mount Eagle Quartette, "A Soldier's Plea," November 1948; issued on Apex 1105.

Smokey Hogg, "Hard Time Blues" (composer credit: "Andrew Hogg"), Los Angeles, 1949; unissued; issued on Ace CD CHD 780.

Lightnin' Hopkins, "European Blues," Houston, TX, 1949; issued on Gold Star 665; reissued on Arhoolie CD 337.

Golden Crown Quartet, "A Soldier's Plea," New York City, 3 March 1949; issued on Score 5008.

Country Jim, "Philippine Blues" (alt. take) (composer credit: "James Bledsoe"), Shreveport, LA, c. April 1950; unissued; issued on Imperial LP 94000. The issued version, which has identical lyrics, is to be found on Imperial 5095.

John Lee Hooker, "Strike Blues" (composer credit: "John Lee Hooker–Bernard Besman"), Detroit, 28 April 1950; Modern unissued; issued on Specialty LP 2127.

John Lee Hooker, "Welfare Blues," Detroit, 28 April 1950; Modern unissued; issued on United Artists LP 5512.

Bulee Gaillard and His Southern Fried Orchestra (= Slim Gaillard), "Taxpayers' Blues," New York, 24 January 1952; issued on Mercury 8970; reissued on Metro LP 2356022.

St. Peter's Gospel Singers, "A Soldier's Plea," April 1952; issued on Calvary 304.

"Big Mama" Thornton, "Hard Times" (composer credit: "Robey–Thornton"), Los Angeles, 13 August 1952; issued on Ace LP 170; reissued on MCA CD 10668.

Pilgrim Travelers, "A Soldier's Plea," 1957; issued on Andex 5010; reissued on Andex LP 5001.

Pilgrim Travelers, "A Soldier's Plea," 1964; issued on Proverb 1020.

A relevant song that is unissued is:

Everett Johnson, "My Man's Gone to the Army," 1946; Disc unissued.

2. Atom and Evil

1. Ferrell (1994), p. 418, note 37.
2. Hamby, p. 289.
3. Ibid., p. 290.
4. Ibid., p. 205.
5. Pemberton, p. 51.
6. McCullough, p. 459.
7. Hamby, p. 337.
8. For the history of this Selah Jubilee composition see van Rijn (1997), pp. 155–59 and 234 notes 17 and 18.
9. Percy Wilborn Quartet, "Oh, What a Time (A History of World War II)," Retrieve State Farm, Snipe, TX, 12 March 1951; issued on 77 LA LP 12-3.
10. Samuel B. Charters, sleeve notes to *Introducing Memphis Willie B.*, Bluesville LP 1034.
11. "Memphis" Willie B. (Borum), "Overseas Blues" (composer credit: "Willie Borum"),

Memphis, TN, 12 August 1961; issued on Bluesville LP 1034; reissued on Agram Blues ABCD 2018.

12. Cf. Revelation 3, verse 12: "the name of the city of my God, which is New Jerusalem."

Cf. James "Peck" Curtis, "Jerusalem Blues," Helena, AR, 22 January 1952; issued on Kent LP 9007.

13. Olsson, p. 68.

14. Homer Harris, "Atomic Bomb Blues" (composer credit: "Homer Harris"), Chicago, 27 September 1946; Columbia unissued; issued on Testament LP 2207 and CBS CD 467249 2.

15. Three other examples of songs mentioning Tojo are "'41 Blues" by Doctor Clayton, "Soldier Man Blues" by Inez Washington and "End o'War Blues" by Charles Brown (cf. van Rijn (1997), pp. 151, 159–60, 190, 236).

One song that does mention Hirohito is Lucky Millinder's "We're Gonna Have to Slap the Dirty Little Jap" (ibid., pp. 154 and 262).

16. "Negro scientists help produce 1st atom bomb," *Chicago Defender*, 11 August 1945.

17. "7,000 employed at atomic bomb plant," *Afro-American*, 18 August 1945.

18. A reference to the 1929 pop song "I Faw Down an' Go 'Boom!'" which was successfully revived in the 1940s by Jerry Colonna for a pop hit.

19. Golden Gate Quartet, "Atom and Evil" (composer credit: "Zaret–Singer"), New York, 5 June 1946; unissued (?); issued on DOCD 5638; reissued on Agram Blues ABCD 2018. The original issue on Columbia 37236 is a different take.

20. Charles Wolfe, "Nuclear Country: The Atomic Bomb in Country Music," *The Journal of Country Music* VI, no. 4 (January 1978): 4–21.

21. Strangers Quartet, "This Atomic Age," c. June 1949; issued on Coleman 6010.

22. McCullough, p. 749.

23. The verse about the fire next time goes back to nineteenth-century spirituals.

One early recorded example is:

Rigoletto Quartet, "I've Got a Home in That Rock," New York, 18 August 1926; issued on Okeh 8386; reissued on Document DOCD 5541.

A related song about Noah and the flood is the famous Sally Martin recording "Didn't It Rain," which was immortalized by Mahalia Jackson for Apollo in 1954. See McCullough, pp. 443–44.

24. The Pilgrim Travelers, "Jesus Hits Like the Atom Bomb" (composer credit: "L. McCollum"), Hollywood, 30 January 1950; issued on Specialty 351; reissued on Agram Blues ABCD 2018.

25. The Charming Bells, "Jesus Hits Like the Atom Bomb" (composer credit: "Lee McCullom"), November 1949; issued on Selective 109; reissued on Folk Lyric LP 9045.

Melody Echoes, "Jesus Hit Like an Atom Bomb," late January 1950; issued on Regal 3253.

The Five Trumpets, "Jesus Hits Like the Atom Bomb" (composer credit: "John M. Blackburn"), 31 January 1950; issued on Coral 65027.

Soul Stirrers, "Jesus Hits Like the Atom Bomb," Hollywood, 24 February 1950; unissued; issued on Specialty CD 7013.

Famous Blue Jay Singers, "Jesus Hits Like the Atom Bomb," New York, 22 March 1950; issued on Decca 48150.

Silver Tones, "He'll Hit Like an Atom Bomb When He Comes," Memphis, c. 1951; Perkins disc 53-A-1.

26. Brother Will Hairston – The Hurricane of the Motor City, "The War in Vietnam," Detroit, c. 1968; issued on Knowles 106.

27. Sterling Jubilee Singers, "Atom Bomb," 22 November 1993; issued on Alabama Traditions cassette 105.

28. Some white versions are:

Red Pleasant and the Southern Serenaders (vocals by Milton Beasley and Miller Louther), "Jesus Hits Like the Atom Bomb" (composer credit: "L. V. McCullom"), 1949; issued on Selective 3.

Johnnie and Jack (= Johnny Wright and Jack Anglin), "Jesus Hits Like the Atom Bomb," 1949; issued on Victor 20-0314.

D. J. Lowell Blanchard with the Valley Trio, "Jesus Hits Like the Atom Bomb" (composer credit: "Lee V. McCullom"), c. April 1950; issued on Mercury 6260; reissued on Rounder LP 1034.

I have not been able to find any details about Lee V. McCullom. Another song by the Pilgrim Travelers that was written by the same composer is:

"The Life You Save May Be Your Own (The Safety Song)," 13 January 1955; unissued; issued on Specialty SPCD 7053.

29. Swan's Silvertone Singers, "Jesus Is God's Atomic Bomb" (composer credit: "Rev. Purcell L. Perkins"), Cincinnati, 23 June 1950; issued on King 4391; reissued on King LP 575.

30. Amos Milburn, "Atomic Baby" (composer credit: "Asser"), Los Angeles, 4 January 1950; Aladdin unissued; issued on Mosaic CD Box 155.

31. The Pilgrim Travelers, "Jesus Is the First Line of Defense" (composer credit: "J. W. Alexander"), Hollywood, 12 January 1951; issued on Specialty 800; reissued on Specialty CD 7030.

32. A later recording of this song is:

Sons of Jehovah, "Jesus Is the First Line of Defense," Memphis, late 1951; Perkins disc 52-A-2.

33. Frankie Ervin with Austin McCoy and His Combo, "I'd Rather Live Like a Hermit" (composer credit "R. Ellen" = Bob Shad), Los Angeles, 26 January 1951; Mercury unissued; issued on Mercury CD 9-528292.

34. "The Royal Telephone" was recorded by The Christian and Missionary Alliance Gospel Singers (1923), Rev. Sister Mary M. Nelson (1927), Blind Connie Rosemond (1927) and the Selah Jubilee Singers (1939).

35. Harlan County Four, "Atomic Telephone" (composer credit: "Smith–Glover–Mann"), October 1951; issued on King 1016.

36. The Spirit of Memphis Quartet, "The Atomic Telephone" (composer credit:

"Mann–Glover–Smith"), Cincinnati, 14 August 1951; issued on King 4521; reissued on Gospel Jubilee RFLP 1404.

37. Barry Lee Pearson, "One Day You're Gonna Hear About Me: The H-Bomb Ferguson Story," interview with H-Bomb Ferguson (21 September 1985), *Living Blues* 69 (1985): 17.

38. Little Ceasar [*sic*], "Atomic Love" (composer credit: "Jacques"), Los Angeles, 13 February 1953; issued on Recorded In Hollywood 239; reissued on Route 66 LP 24.

39. Fay Simmons, "You Hit Me Baby Like an Atomic Bomb," Philadelphia, 23 August 1954; Gotham unissued; issued on Flyright CD 37.

40. One of these later atomic lines is: *If you don't stop the war in Vietnam, I believe I'll drop that old atom bomb*: "Big" Joe Williams, "Army Man in Vietnam," Berkeley, CA, 14 December 1969; issued on Arhoolie LP 1053.

41. Ferrell (1994), p. 353.

42. *Gallup Poll*, 2:888.

Other blues and gospel songs about the atomic bomb which I have not heard are:
   Helen Humes, "Atomic Blues, Parts 1 & 2," Los Angeles, August 1950; issued on Discovery 529.
   The Travelers, "The Bomb" (instr.), c. 1961; issued on Image 5003.

3. The Freedom Choo Choo

1. *Chicago Defender*, 14 April 1945.

2. A. Harry McAlpin, White House correspondent, "President Truman Favors FEPC," *New York Amsterdam News*, 21 April 1945.

3. "FEPC Hope Grows," *Afro-American*, 8 September 1945.

4. Schainman Siegel, pp. 95–96.

5. These are references to people in China, Canada, the United States and Mali.

6. The Atlantic Charter was a joint declaration issued on 14 August 1941, during World War II, by the British Prime Minister, Winston Churchill, and President Franklin D. Roosevelt of the still non-belligerent United States, after five days of conferences aboard warships in the North Atlantic.

7. The San Francisco Conference, formally known as the United Nations Conference on International Organization (25 April–26 June 1945), was an international meeting that established the United Nations.

8. The Yalta Conference (4–11 February 1945), was a major World War II conference of the three chief Allied leaders, President Franklin D. Roosevelt, Prime Minister Winston Churchill, and Secretary General Joseph Stalin, who met at Yalta in the Crimea to plan the final defeat and occupation of Nazi Germany.

9. The Dumbarton Oaks Conference (21 August–7 October 1944) took place in a mansion in Georgetown, Washington, DC, where representatives of China, the Soviet Union, the United States, and the United Kingdom formulated proposals for a world organization that became the basis for the United Nations.

10. The Potsdam Conference (17 July–2 August 1945), was an Allied conference of

World War II held at a suburb of Berlin. The chief participants were President Harry S. Truman, Prime Minister Winston Churchill (or Clement Attlee, who became Prime Minister during the conference), and Secretary General Joseph Stalin.

11. Josh White, "Free and Equal Blues," New York City, 16 May 1946; Folkways unissued acetate 3653; issued on Document DOCD 1018; reissued on Agram Blues ABCD 2018.
    Later versions, entitled "Free and Equal Blues, Parts 1 & 2," are:
        London, 20 March 1951; unissued; and
        London, 19 November 1951; issued on London 1161.
    White omits the penultimate line, where the rhyme word might be "Litvinoff" (Russian Foreign Affairs Commissar Maxim Litvinoff).

12. Wald, p. 202.

13. Broonzy and Bruynoghe, p. 58.

14. In 1951 Broonzy recorded the song both in Europe and in the States, but significantly the American version remained unissued until after his death in 1958:
    Big Bill Broonzy, "Black, Brown and White" (composer credit: "Broonzy"), Paris, France, 20 September 1951; issued on Vogue 134; reissued on Vogue LP 512510.
    Big Bill Broonzy, "Get Back" (composer credit: "Big Bill Broonzy"), Chicago, 8 November 1951; Mercury unissued; issued on Mercury LP 20822.
    An unissued recording of "Black, Brown and White" was recorded for Alan Lomax on 2 March 1947. It was issued on Rounder CD 82161–1861 in 2002.

15. Brownie McGhee, "Black, Brown and White" (composer credit: "Big Bill Broonzy"), New York City, late 1947; issued on Encore 102; reissued on Bear Family 10CD 15720.

16. See "Hollywood and Vine," chapter 23 in Wolfe and Lornell.

17. Bunk Johnson (1890–1949), the legendary jazz trumpeter from New Orleans, worked with Huddie in New York for a time.

18. Huddie "Leadbelly" Ledbetter, "Jim Crow Blues" (composer credit: "Huddie Ledbetter"), c. 1946/47; issued on Folkways LP 2034; reissued on Smithsonian Folkways SF CD 40045 (with spoken intro) and Document DOCD 5310 (without the intro).

19. Huddie "Leadbelly" Ledbetter, "Jim Crow Blues #2," c. 1946/47; Folkways unissued; issued on Smithsonian Folkways SF CD 40045. The CD notes, which claim a recording date of February 1940, are almost certainly in error, as Leadbelly appears to refer to his Hollywood experiences in 1944/45.

20. Huddie "Leadbelly" Ledbetter, "Jim Crow Blues," Minneapolis, MN, 21 November 1948; unissued; issued on Document DOCD 5664.

21. See Sean Killeen, "A Union Man," *Lead Belly Letter* 5 #1/2 (Ithaca, NY: winter/spring 1995).

22. "Oh, hallelujah" is a substitute for "in hell."

23. Golden Gate Quartet, "No Restricted Signs (Up in Heaven)" (composer credit: "Drake"), New York, 5 June 1946; issued on Columbia 37832; reissued on Document DOCD 5638.

24. For a full account see Ray Astbury, "Bilbo Is Dead," *Juke Blues* 6 (autumn 1986): 23.

25. Tooze, p. 79.

26. Andrew Tibbs, "Bilbo Is Dead" (composer credit: "Chess–Aleta–Archia"), Chicago, September 1947; issued on The Aristocrat of Records 1101; reissued on Agram Blues ABCD 2018.

27. Cohodas, p. 39.

28. "Bilbo 'The Man' Dies; Mouth Proves Fatal," *Chicago Defender*, 23 August 1947.

29. "City Rededicated with Exhibits, Ceremonies, Awaits Freedom Train," *Chicago Defender*, 3 July 1948.

30. *Commercial Appeal*, 25 December 1947.

31. John White, "Civil Rights in Conflict: The 'Birmingham Plan' and the Freedom Train, 1947," *The Alabama Review* (April 1999): 129.

32. "Paul Robeson and 'Freedom Train'" at:
www.scc.rutgers.edu/njh/PaulRobeson/Activist/PRFreedom.htm

33. In 1775 the American Revolution had started. After a November 1775 proclamation by Lord Dunmore, the British Governor of Virginia, it had become possible for blacks to join His Majesty's troops. As a result, most states began to enlist African Americans in early 1776. On Christmas night 1776 two blacks, Prince Whipple and Oliver Cromwell, crossed the Delaware with General Washington in the freezing cold. The date 1776 also occurs in "Keep Still," where the Echoes of Zion sing: *We were there in seventeen seventy-six, in the streets of Boston our blood did mix.* Black blood had certainly been shed in Boston. In 1770 Crispus Attucks, a black laborer, was killed in the Boston Massacre and in 1775 blacks were killed in the Battle of Bunker Hill. The year 1776 is resonant above all because 4 July 1776 is the date of the Declaration of Independence.

34. Tommie Jenkins, "Freedom Choo Choo Blues" (composer credit: "Hunt"), Oakland, CA, 1948; issued on Olliet OTH-1; reissued on Agram Blues ABCD 2018.
Another song that alludes to the Freedom Train in a standard "leaving blues" is:
Lil Son Jackson, "Freedom Train Blues," Houston, 1948; issued on Gold Star 638.

35. Pemberton, p. 113.

36. Branch (1988), pp. 63-64. The account is based on the following newspaper reports: *New York Times* (27 July 1946): 1; *Atlanta Daily World* (17 July 1946): 1; *Atlanta Constitution* (28 July 1946): 1.

37. Dick Waterman, "Saying Goodbye to Four Beloved Musicians in a Sad Week for the Blues," *Blues Access* 9 (spring 1992): 26.

38. "Champion" Jack Dupree, "I'm Gonna Write the Governor of Georgia," c. August 1946; Folkways unissued (transcribed by Chris Smith).

39. For more on the growth and failures of southern racial liberalism at this time see Tony Badger, "Fatalism Not Gradualism: The Crisis of Southern Liberalism, 1945–1965," in Ward and Badger, eds, pp. 67–95.

40. "Harlem Rallies Protest Georgia Lynching of Four," *New York Amsterdam News*, 3 August 1946.

41. "Can't Hit Lynching: Truman to Robeson," *New York Amsterdam News*, 28 September 1946.

42. Memphis Slim ("Leroy"), Big Bill Broonzy ("Natchez") and Sonny Boy Williamson ("Sib"), "Blues in the Mississippi Night," New York City, 1 and 2 March 1947; issued on Nixa NJLLP 8; reissued on Sequel NEXCD 122.

43. McCullough, p. 570.

44. "15,000 hear HST's civil rights appeal," *Afro-American*, 5 July 1946.

45. Ferrell (1994), pp. 297–98.

46. "South in Revolt over Truman Rights Program," *Chicago Defender*, 7 February 1948.

47. John Cowley, Review of *The Life and Times of Leadbelly* by Charles Wolfe and Kip Lornell, *Blues & Rhythm* 78 (April 1993): 39.

48. Lord Invader, "God Made Us All," New York City, 21–22 December 1946; issued on Disc 5080. This song has six eight-line stanzas. Leadbelly sang the third, fourth and fifth ones.

49. Wolfe and Lornell, p. 244.

50. When the song was written by Lord Invader, Trinidad was a British colony.

51. Huddie "Leadbelly" Ledbetter, "Equality for Negroes," New York City, c. 15 June 1948; issued on BC 101 (first version) and BC 126 (second version). These recordings come from the Barnacle–Cadle Collection and were kindly supplied to the author by the ETSU Foundation/Archives of Appalachia Fund. There are no textual differences between the two versions of the song.

    On 21 November 1948 Leadbelly sang the song at a private party in Minneapolis, MN. A fragment of the recording was issued as "Nobody in the World Is Better Than Us" on Document DOCD 5664.

52. McCullough, p. 595.

53. Ibid., p. 645.

54. Ibid., pp. 540, 541 and 554.

55. "Restrictive covenants" were clauses in house purchase contracts making it obligatory that the house would not be resold to African Americans.

56. General Electric; Government Issue (= American soldier)

57. Richard Huey and Chorus, "Wallace Fit the Battle of America," unknown location, 1948; issued on Progressive Party WC-1948; reissued on Document DOCD 5628.

58. McCullough, p. 667.

59. Royal Harmonaires (= Dixieaires) (narrator: C. Ginyard), "Henry Wallace Is the Man," unknown location, 1948; issued on Progressive Party WC-1948; reissued on Agram Blues ABCD 2018.

60. Truman, p. 251.

61. Cf. Hamby, p. 437.

62. Ibid., p. 458.

63. Advertisement in the *Chicago Defender*, 2 November 1946: 16.

64. "Hail Negro Vote in Truman's Victory," *Chicago Defender*, 6 November 1948.

65. "Truman Stands Firm on Rights, Demands a 'Square Deal' for All," *Chicago Defender*, 22 January 1949.

66. Herman Ray (= Harmon Ray), "President's Blues" (composer credit: "J. Mayo Williams"), New York City, 20 May 1949; issued on Decca 48107; reissued on Agram Blues ABCD 2018.

67. See Tony Russell, "The Deputy High Sheriff from Hell, Harmon Ray," *Living Blues* 26 (March/April 1976): 14–15.

68. Van Rijn (1997), p. 143.

69. Hamby, p. 433.

70. For his biography see Guido van Rijn, "The Life Story of Otis Jackson," *Blues & Rhythm* 145 (Christmas 1999): 4–5.

71. The Gospel Pilgrims (in the Atlantic files called "The Otis Jackson Quartet"), "I'm So Grateful to the N.A.A.C.P." (composer credit: "Otis Jackson"), New York City, December 1950; issued on Atlantic 928; reissued on Agram Blues ABCD 2018.

72. Gillett (1988), pp. 19–27; Ward (1998), pp. 21–22.

73. Ertegun, p. 7.

74. Schulte Nordholt, p. 250; Steven F. Lawson, David R. Colburn and Darryl Paulson, "Groveland: Florida's Little Scottsboro," in Colburn and Landers, eds., pp. 298–325.

75. See "The 'Scottsboro Boys'," van Rijn (1997), chapter 11.

76. Lawson, Colburn and Paulson, p. 309.

77. For more on the movement's manipulation of American civic religion, see Keith Miller and Emily Lewis, "Touchstones, Authorities and Marian Anderson: The Making of 'I Have A Dream'", in Ward and Badger, eds, pp. 147–61.

78. Cf. note 33.

79. For Dorie Miller see van Rijn (1997), p. 200.

80. A reference to the Monroe lynching of July 1946, discussed earlier on (pp. 53–55).

81. A reference to the dynamite blast that struck the house of Harry T. Moore, the NAACP statewide coordinator, on Christmas Eve 1951. "Moore had been active in raising funds for the Groveland defendants, and following the shooting of Shepherd and Irvin, he had led a campaign urging Governor Warren to remove McCall from office" (Lawson, Colburn and Paulson, p. 315).

82. The Echoes of Zion, "Keep Still 'God Will Fight Your Battles'" (composer credit: "Harrison Smith"), Atlanta, GA, c. 1952; issued on Gerald 105; reissued on Agram Blues 2018.

83. Ferrell (1994), pp. 282–83.

84. Doug Seroff, sleeve notes to *Birmingham Quartet Anthology*, Clanka Lanka 2LP 144.001/2 (1980).

85. C.I.O. Singers, "The Spirit of Phil Murray," Birmingham, AL, 1952; issued on Tiger 100; reissued on Clanka Lanka 2LP 144.001/2.

86. C.I.O. Singers, "Satisfied," Birmingham, AL, 1952; issued on Tiger 100; reissued on Clanka Lanka 2LP 144.001/2.

87. Chafe, p. 90.

Civil rights songs from the Truman era that I have not yet heard are:
Jimmy Nelson, "My Civil Rights," 1948; issued on Olliet 1.
Traveling Echos, "Freedom Train" and "Freedom Song," May 1950; issued on Freedom 113.

4. Say a Prayer for the Boys in Korea

1. Ferrell (1994), p. 313.
2. Truman, p. 455.
3. Ferrell (1994), p. 324.
4. Cf. van Rijn (1997), pp. 163–64.
5. The Gospel Pilgrims (In the Atlantic files called the Otis Jackson Quartet), "Korea–Fightin' in the Foreign Land" (composer credit: "J. C. Ginyard"), New York City, December 1950; issued on Atlantic 928.

   This song was later recorded by:

   St. Peter's Gospel Singers, "The Battle Done Started Again," c. February 1953; issued on Apollo 271. The St. Peter's Gospel Singers added a new verse to the Otis Jackson original. It refers to J. A. Malik, the Soviet Deputy Foreign Minister, who was president of the UN Security Council for the month of August 1950. Malik called for a meeting on 1 August at the temporary headquarters at Lake Success. A vote was forced and it went against the Communists eight to three.

   Great God, then the American Council assembled, and they met up on Lake Success,
   Just to talk about trouble over in Korea, you know, Malik was president,
   Great God, then they tried to bar the Chinese Nationalists, vote the Reds into the UN,
   But all the nations, they said it wouldn't be, voted against it, eight to three;
   There's the Chinese, Britain, South Korea, Egypt and other lands,
   I declare, my Lord, that we got to win, because God's got us in His hand.

6. When this song was recorded on 30 November 1950 Clement Attlee was Prime Minister of Great Britain and Winston Churchill Leader of the Opposition.
7. Selah Jubilee Singers (as the Southern Harmonaires), "Who Will Your Captain Be," New York, 30 November 1950; issued on Apollo 237/529; reissued on Krazy Kat KKLP 7417.
8. Sam "Lightnin'" Hopkins, "War News Blues" (composer credit: "Lightnin' Hopkins"), Houston, 1951; RPM unissued; issued on Kent LP 9008.
9. Fats Domino, "Korea Blues" (composer credit: "A. Young–D. Bartholomew"), New Orleans, September 1950; issued on Imperial 5099; reissued on United Artists LP 29152.
10. These encouragements are addressed to harmonica player Snooky Pryor and guitarist Leroy Foster.
11. Sunnyland Slim, "Back to Korea Blues," Chicago, c. October 1950; issued on Sunny Records 101; reissued on Mamlish LPS 3799.
12. Smokey Hogg, "Classification Blues," Los Angeles, c. July 1950; issued on Modern 20-770; reissued on Ace CDCHD 866.
13. Sons of Jehovah, "Go and Tell the Reds We're Gonna Win," Memphis, c. 1951; Frank Perkins acetate 51-A-3.
14. Willie Mae Thornton, "No Jody for Me," Houston, 1951; issued on Peacock 1587; reissued on Ace LP 170.
15. J. B. and His Bayou Boys (= J. B. Lenoir), "Korea Blues" (composer credit: "J. B. Lenor"), Chicago, late 1950; issued on Chess 1449; reissued on Chess 2ACMBLP 208.

16. Transcription is phonetic; there is no certainty that this town was referred to.
17. J. B. Lenoir, "I'm in Korea" (composer credit: "Lenoir"), Chicago, 6 October 1954; issued on Parrot 802; reissued on Chess 2ACMBLP 208.
18. McCullough, p. 837.
19. Military Advisory Group, 01/0/2001 statistics.
20. L. B. Lawson, "Missing in Action," Memphis, January 1952; Sun unissued; issued on Sun LP 1060.   (ROK stands for "Republic of Korea.")
21. L. B. Lawson, "Got My Call Card" (composer credit: "Lawson"), Memphis, January 1952; Sun unissued; issued on Sun Box 107.
22. McCullough, pp. 820–22.
23. Ibid., p. 830.
24. Ferrell (1994), p. 330.
25. Ibid., p. 335.
26. René Hall Trio, "Old Soldiers Never Die (They Just Fade Away)" (composer credit: "Frank Westphal"), New York City, 26 April 1951; issued on Decca 48213.
27. Full desegregation came the moment MacArthur was fired, Marshall claims. In 1951 he had been asked by Truman to review the treatment of black soldiers under General MacArthur in the Far East. When asked why there were no blacks among the elite group guarding the general, MacArthur claimed that none were qualified. "I said, 'Well, I just talked to a Negro yesterday, a sergeant who has killed more people with a rifle than anybody in history. And he's not qualified? And he [MacArthur] said, 'No.' I said, 'Well, now, general, remember yesterday you had that big band playing at the ceremony over there?' He said, 'Yes, wasn't that wonderful?' I said, 'Yes, it's beautiful.' I said, 'Now, general, just between you and me: Goddammit, don't you tell me there's no Negro that can play a horn.' That's when he said for me to go." (Goldman, p. 150.)
28. "MacArthur Backer of JC," *Afro-American*, 21 April 1951.
29. Willie Brown, "Korea Blues" (composer credit: "Willie C. Brown"), Atlanta, GA, 30 August 1951; issued on Decca 48248; reissued on Ace LP 162.
30. Ryan, pp. 47–49.
31. Sherman "Blues" Johnson & His Clouds of Joy, "Lost in Korea" (composer credit: "S. Johnson"), Jackson, MS, 30 September 1952; issued on Trumpet 190; reissued on Alligator ALCD 2800.
32. Evening Star Quartet, "Say a Prayer for the Boys in Korea" (composer credit: "Cook"), c. 1952; issued on Gotham 732. Cf. Dan Kochakian. "Little Joe Cook: The Original Thriller," an Interview with the composer, *Whiskey, Women, And . . .* 15 (December 1985): 20–21.
33. Hamby, p. 605.
34. Estes Kefauver (Democrat, 1903–1963) was chairman of the Special Committee to Investigate Organized Crime in Interstate Commerce. He was an unsuccessful candidate for the presidential nomination in 1952 and for Vice President in 1956.
35. Robert A. Taft (Republican, 1889–1953) led the conservative Republican opposition against Roosevelt and Truman from his seat in the Senate. He unsuccessfully campaigned for the presidential nominations of 1940, 1948 and 1952.

36. Douglas MacArthur (Republican, 1880–1964) unsuccessfully bid for the presidential nomination of 1948. In 1952, after having been fired as general for insubordination, his electoral popularity was insufficient again and he was not a candidate.

37. Harold E. Stassen (Republican, 1907–2001) was Governor of Minnesota and vainly tried his luck at the presidential nomination in 1948, 1952, 1964, 1968, 1972, 1976 and 1980.

38. Dwight D. Eisenhower (Republican, 1890-1969) was the Allied supreme commander in Europe in World War II. He defeated the Democrat Adlai Stevenson (1900–1965), Governor of Illinois (who is not mentioned at all in this 8 May song as he became a candidate only on 24 July). Eisenhower became the 34th President of the United States in January 1953.

39. The symbolic animals for the Republican and the Democratic Parties are the elephant and the donkey.

40. Richard B. Russell (Democrat, 1897–1971) was United States Senator from Georgia from 1933 to 1971. Jordan's statement seems to be a disparaging dismissal of this southern segregationist.

41. Louis Jordan and His Tympany Five, "Jordan for President" (composer credit: "Louis Jordan"), New York City, 8 May 1952; issued on Decca 28225; reissued on Agram Blues ABCD 2018.

42. Ambrose, p. 285.

43. For details on Bob White see Mike Leadbitter, "Mike's Blues," *Blues Unlimited* 106 (February/March 1974): 18.

44. This reference in a 1953 song may point to Marilyn Monroe's daring walk in Henry Hathaway's film *Niagara* of the same year. "Rose Hathaway" may be a mix-up between the names of Henry Hathaway and Rose Loomis, the character Marilyn plays.

45. Emitt Slay Trio [sic], "Male Call" (composer credit: "Bob White"), New York City, 30 March 1953; issued on Savoy 1101.

46. Ambrose, p. 82.

47. Ibid., p. 203.

48. See van Rijn (1997), pp. 154–66, 233–34.

49. "Homesick" James Williamson, "Wartime," Chicago, 23 January 1953; Chance unissued; issued on P-Vine Special PLP 706; reissued on Agram Blues ABCD 2018.

50. Mike Leadbitter, Review of Spivey LP 1009, *Blues Unlimited* 53 (May 1968): 25.

51. Eddie King and the 3 Queens (= Eddie Milton), "Love You Baby" (composer credit: "Milton–Brown"), Chicago, 1960; issued on J.O.B. 1122.
    This may be the same artist as:
    "J. B. Lenoir," "Korea Blues," 1965; issued on Spivey LP 1009.

52. Red Callender and His Sextet (vocalist "Duke Upshaw"), "Soldiers' Blues" (composer credit: "D. Upshaw–R. Callender), Los Angeles, 1953; issued on Bay'ou 002.

53. Ambrose, p. 285.

54. For rationing see van Rijn (1997), pp. 158, 182–92, 207.

55. "Little Maxie" (= Maxie Bailey), "Drive Soldiers Drive," Nashville, first half of 1953; issued on Excello 2016; reissued on Agram Blues ABCD 2018.

An earlier unissued version of this song (probably with different verses) is "Ride Soldier Ride," New York City, 29 November 1950.

56. Sister Rosetta Tharpe, "There's Peace in Korea" (composer credit: "Rosetta Tharpe–M. Asher"), 27 July 1953; issued on Decca 48302; reissued on Agram Blues ABCD 2018.

57. Lightening Hopkins [sic], "The War Is Over" (composer credit: "Bob Shad"), Houston, 29 July 1953; issued on Decca 48842 and 28841; reissued on Blues Classics LP 30.

58. John Lee Hooker, "Build Myself a Cave" (composer credit: "James Lane" = Jimmy Rogers), 1949; unissued; issued on Ace CD CHD 799. An alternative unissued take was issued on Specialty LP 2125.

59. See beginning of this chapter, pp. 74–75.

60. Mr. Honey (= David Edwards), "Build a Cave," Houston, 1950; issued on ARC (Artist Record Co.) 102; reissued on Blues Classics BCLP 23.

61. Jimmy Rogers with His Rocking Four, "The World Is in a Tangle" (composer credit: "Jimmy Rogers"), Chicago, 23 January 1951; issued on Chess 1453; reissued on Chess 2ACMBLP 207.

62. Arthur Crudup, "I'm Gonna Dig Myself a Hole" (composer credit: "Arthur Crudup"), Chicago, 24 April 1951; issued on Victor 22/50-0141; reissued on Document DOCD 5203, which also reissues an alternative take from Victor LP 573.

63. Robert Lockwood, Jr., "I'm Gonna Dig Myself a Hole" (composer credit: "Lockwood, Jr."), Chicago, 15 November 1951; issued on Mercury 8260; reissued on Wolf WBCD 005.

64. Directed to tenor sax player J. J. Jones.

65. Big Boy Crudup, "The War Is Over" (composer credit: "Arthur Crudup"), Atlanta, GA, 9 November 1953; issued on Victor 47-5563; reissued on Document DOCD 5204.

66. King Perry and His Orchestra (with Dell St. John, vocal), "Welcome Home Baby" (composer credit: "Perry"), Los Angeles, CA, October 1953; issued on RPM 392. Label mistakenly says: "Vocal King Perry."

67. Keys of Heaven, "Let Your Light Shine on Ike," Miami, FL, August 1953; issued on Glory 4016.

68. Bastin (1990), p. 216.
Nat Foster, "Lonely Soldier Blues" (composer credit: "Foster"), Atlanta, GA, 20 January 1953; issued on M-G-M 11445; reissued on Krazy Kat KKLP 780.

69. Cf. Pete Lowry, sleeve notes to Texas Guitar: From Dallas to L.A., Atlantic ATL LP 40398.
Soldier Boy Houston, "Leavin' Korea," Hollywood, 1953/54; King unissued.

70. Cf. Living Blues 105 (September/October 1992): 39.

71. Cf. Blues & Rhythm 158 (April 2001): 25.

72. Living Blues 5 (January/February 1991): 47.

73. Blues Unlimited 114 (July/August 1975): 8.

74. Living Blues 57 (autumn 1983): 13.

75. *Living Blues* 101 (January/February 1992): 35.
76. *Living Blues* 157 (May/June 2001): 14–16. Page 14 presents a photo showing Moore entertaining the troops in Korea
77. E-mail letter from David Evans to the author, 11 September 2001.
78. Cf. *Blues Unlimited* 95 (October 1972): 8.
79. Louisiana Red, "Korea Blues," Greece, 1994; issued on Diastase SDCD 0007.
     Another blues singer who served in Korea was "Texas" Johnny Brown (b. 1928). He was a switchboard operator and mail clerk from 1951 to 1953. *Living Blues* 16 (March/April/May 2003): 50–51.
80. Korean Conflict Casualty File (KCCF), Center for Electronic Records, National Archives and Records Administration. Data supplied to the author by Bill Fischer, Reference Technician, 19 March 2001.
81. http://korea50.army.mil/history/factsheets/afroamer.html
82. Military Advisory Group, 01/0/2001 statistics.
83. Mullen, p. 61.
84. "Korea War Integrates U.S. Army," *Chicago Defender*, 30 July 1953.
85. "Korean Vets Find Jim Crow at Ft. Sill, Okla.," *Afro-American*, 8 November 1952.
86. Other Korea songs that have not been quoted in this chapter are:
     Clifford Blivens, "Korea Blues" (composer credit: "C. Blivens"), 1950; issued on Swingtime 236; reissued on Capricorn CD 9-42024.
     The Four Barons, "Got to Go Back Again" (composer credit: "Ruth–Bunn–Barfield"), December 1950; issued on Regent 1026.
     Macedonians, "Stop the War," 1951; issued on Octive 707.
     Johnny Williams (= John Lee Hooker), "Questionnaire Blues" (composer credit: "Williams"), Detroit, 1951; issued on Gotham 509; reissued on Krazy Kat KKLP 816.
     Five Blind Boys (= Five Blind Boys of Alabama), "All I have is Gone," 1951; issued on Gospel 138. (The label reads: "Dedicated to the Negro Servicemen in Korea".)
     Eddie Williams, "Your Papa Is a Soldier Again," c. 1951; issued on Crystal 303.
     Lightening Hopkins [sic], "Sad News from Korea" (composer credit "Morrie Price"), Houston, 1951; issued on Mercury 8274; reissued on Blues Classics BCLP 30.
     Johnny O'Neal, "War Bound Blues" (composer credit: "Johnny O'Neal"), Cincinnati, 23 January 1951; issued on King 4441.
     Max Bailey, "Sorry Girl Blues" (composer credit: "Max Bailey"), New York City, 15 May 1951; issued on Coral 65060; reissued on Blue Moon BMCD 6010.
     Rose Brown and Jimmie Harris with Bubbles and His Band, "Back from Korea" (composer credit: "Ulysses Smith"), 17 May 1951 (scratched in wax); issued on G S T 1001.
     Evangelist Gospel Singers of Alabama, "Lord Stop the War," June 1951; issued on Chess 1473.
     Robert Bland with Rosco Gordon's Band, "A Letter from a Trench in Korea," Memphis, August 1951; issued on Chess 1489.
     Doctor Isaiah Ross, "Little Soldier Boy" (composer credit: "Ross"), take 1, 29 November 1951; unissued; issued on Arhoolie LP 1065.
     Doctor Isaiah Ross, "Little Soldier Boy" (composer credit: "Ross"), take 2, 29 November 1951; unissued; issued on Sun Box 107.

Rosco Gordon, "Dream On Baby" (composer credit: "Gordon"), Memphis, December 1951; Phillips unissued; issued on Charly LP 30133.

Kalvin Brothers, "Somewhere in Korea," 1952; issued on Roost 549.

Bob Kent Band with King Curtiss [sic], "Korea, Korea" (composer credit: "Kent–Ousley"), New York City, 1952; issued on Par 1303.

Eddie (Guitar Slim) Jones, "Feelin' Sad" (composer credit: "Jones"), Nashville, 1952; issued on J-B (= Jim Bulleit) 603; reissued on Charly LP 30133.

Big Boy Crudup, "Mr. So and So" (composer credit: "Arthur Crudup"), Chicago, 15 January 1952; issued on Victor 20/47-4572; reissued on Document DOCD 5203.

Melvin Evans, "Draftin' Blues" (composer credit: "Melvin & Calvin Evans"), Atlanta, 25 January 1952; issued on Savoy 842. (This is a version of Roosevelt Sykes's "Sunny Road" from 1946.)

Dixie Humming Birds (lead: Ira Tucker), "Wading Through Blood and Water," February 1952; issued on Peacock 1594; reissued on Vogue EPL 7282.

Pine Bluff Pete (= pseudonym for unknown artist), "Uncle Sam Blues," Shreveport, LA, 12 March 1952; Specialty unissued; issued on Specialty LP 2149 and Sonet SNTFLP 5014.

Titus Turner, "Got So Much Trouble" (composer credit: "T. Turner"), New York City, 23 April 1952; issued on Okeh 6883; reissued on Epic CD 48912.

"Sleepy" John Estes, "Registration Day Blues," Memphis, 24 April 1952; Sun unissued; issued on Sun Blues Box 105.

"Bobby Blue" Bland, "Army Blues" (composer credit: "D. J. Mattis"), Memphis, 2 November 1952; issued on Duke 115; reissued on Ace CHLP 41.

Shirley Goodman, "Korea," New Orleans, 21 November 1952; Aladdin unissued; issued on United Artists LP 069.

The ? Marks, "Another Soldier Gone," c. 1953; issued on Swing Time 346; reissued (in two takes) on Night Train NTICD 7017.

Spirit of Memphis (lead: Little Ax), "God Save America" (composer credit: "Little Ax"), Memphis, c. January 1953; issued on Peacock 1710.

Handy Jackson, "Got My Application, Baby" (composer credit: "Phillips–Jackson"), Memphis, January 1953; issued on Sun 177; reissued on Redita LP 111.

Cumberland River Singers, "I Wonder Who Cares," Detroit, September 1953; issued on De Luxe 6008.

Charles Glass with Orchestra, "Left My Japanese Baby" (composer credit: "Maxine Cauble–C. Glass"), Charlotte, NC (?), c. October 1953; issued on Magnet 7011.

The Voilinaires [sic], "Another Soldier Gone" (composer credit: "DeShield"), Detroit, 1955; issued on Drummond 4000.

Mel Williams, "Soldier Boy" (composer credit: "Jones–Williams"), Los Angeles, July 1955; issued on Federal 12236.

Songs about Korea that were not used because the author was unable to hear them are:

Carolina Slim, "New Drafting Blues," New York City, 1 August 1950; Acorn unissued.

The Echoes of Zion, "Please Pray for South Korea," September 1950; issued on SIW/Castle 2018.

Five Voices, "Uproar About MacArthur," prob. c. 1951; issued on Five Voices 3500.

5. Things Are So Slow

1. "Space Cadet" refers to a popular "outer space" television show based on the novel *Space Cadet* by Robert A. Heinlein. The serial was broadcast by NBC-TV from 1950 to 1955.
2. Johnny Shines (as by Sunnyland Slim), "Livin' in the White House," Chicago, 12 January 1953; Chance unissued; issued on Flyright FLYLP 566.
3. Another blues artist who sang about a new President in 1953 was: Early Drane (= Earl Dranes), "A New President," Chicago, c. 1953; Parrot unissued.
4. Henry Lee Moon, "Election Post Mortem," *Crisis* 57 (December 1952): 616–17.
5. Bobo Jenkins, "Democrat Blues" (composer credit: "Jenkins"), Detroit, 1954; Chess 1565; reissued on Agram Blues ABCD 2018.
6. Bobo Jenkins interviewed by Bruce Iglauer, Jim O'Neal and Nigel Watson at the Detroit Free Blues Festival in August 1970, *Living Blues* 3 (autumn 1970): 9-10.
7. Eileen Orr, "Bobo Jenkins Obituary," *Living Blues* 63 (January/February 1985): 56.
8. Lawson, p. 81.
9. Memphis Slim and his House Rockers, "Four Years of Torment" (composer credit: "Fraser"), Chicago, 16 March 1954; issued on United U-182; reissued on Agram Blues ABCD 2018.
10. Schlesinger, Jr., ed., p. 3259.
11. Ibid., p. 3263.
12. See the chapter "Hard Time in Hooverville," in van Rijn (1997), pp. 16–29.
13. Eisenhower, p. 304.
14. J. B. Lenoir, "Eisenhower Blues" (composer credit: "Lenoir"), take 5, Chicago, 6 October 1954; issued on Parrot 802; reissued on Agram Blues ABCD 2018.
    The unissued take 1 of this song was issued on Relic LP 8017. Textual differences are minor.
15. Letter typed by J. B. Lenoir for John J. Broven, 28 October 1963. Courtesy John Broven and Mike Rowe. Cf. John Broven. "J. B. Lenoir," in Leadbitter, ed., p. 36.
16. J. B. Lenoir, "Tax Paying Blues" (composer credit: "Lenoir"), Chicago, 6 October 1954; issued on Parrot 802.
    Later version recorded on 2 September 1966; issued on Polydor LP 2482014; reissued on L+R LP 42012.
    Yet another version of this song is "Everybody Wants to Know" from 1955.
17. Cf. letters to the editor of *Living Blues* 3 (autumn 1970): 38; 8 (spring 1972): 5; 10 (autumn 1972): 4; 11 (winter 1972/73): 4; 13 (summer 1973): 4.
18. Chicago disc jockey Al Benson (1908–1978) was acclaimed as a community leader and civil rights advocate, attracting national attention in 1956 when he hired a plane to drop 5000 copies of the US Constitution over Mississippi. Jim O'Neal, Al Benson obituary, *Living Blues* 39 (July/August 1978): 57.

19. Ibid., same page.
20. E-mail from the artist to the author, 8 July 2001.
21. This is addressed to accompanying guitarist Eddie Taylor (1923–1985).
22. John Brim and His Stompers, "Tough Times" (composer credit: "J. Brim"), Chicago, March 1954; issued on Parrot 799; reissued on Chess LP 1537.
    Later versions of this song are:
      Alabama Watson (= Hilbert Watson) "Cost Time" (composer credit: "Hibert Watson" [sic]), Boston, 1964; issued on Bluestown 704; reissued on Wolf CD 013.
      John Brim, "Tough Times," 1994; issued on Tone-Cool TCCD 1150.
      John Brim, "Tougher Times," 2000; issued on Anna Bea ABCD 499.
23. Johnny Fuller, "Hard Times" (composer credit: "Josea"), San Francisco, March 1954; issued on Flair 1054; reissued on Kent KSTLP 9003.
24. For an analysis of the use of this term in blues music under Hoover see the section "The Panic Is On" in van Rijn (1997), pp. 27–29.
25. Jimmy McCracklin and His Blues Blasters, "The Panics On" (composer credit: "McCracklin"), Oakland, CA, 1954; issued on Modern 926; reissued on Ace CHCD 216.
26. Eisenhower, p. 305.
27. A "TV Mama" is a woman with a "big wide screen." Her praises had been sung in "Big" Joe Turner's "TV Mama" (composer credit: "Lou Willie Turner"), Chicago, 7 October 1953; issued on Atlantic 1016. Although Gatemouth no doubt borrowed the phrase from the Turner song, he here uses it for a woman who stays at home watching TV, rather than having to work.
28. Clarence "Gatemouth" Brown, "Depression Blues" (composer credit: "C. Brown"), Houston, 1954; issued on Peacock 1637; reissued on Python LP 26.
29. Dizzy Dixon (= Dave Dixon) with Al Smiths Combo, "Soup Line" (composer credit: "D. Dixon"), Chicago, November 1955; issued on Vee-Jay 174; reissued on Agram Blues ABCD 2018.
    Another song about the soup line was:
      Leon D. Tarver and the Chordones, "Soup Line," Chicago, 20 April 1954; Chess unissued; issued on Rarin' LP 777. A doctored version of this song was issued on P-Vine PCD 2130, where it was mistakenly credited to J. T. Brown.
30. Donovan, p. 219.
31. Eisenhower, p. 305.
32. J. B. Hutto and His Hawks, "Things Are So Slow" (composer credit: "Huzell"), Chicago, 19 October 1954; issued on Chance CH 1165; reissued on Charly CRBLP 1042.
33. Donovan, p. 221.
34. Ambrose, p. 347.
35. Ibid., p. 319.
36. Rowe, p. 123.
37. Although the standard discography lists Joe Montgomery (1909–unknown) as pianist on this song, Lenoir here addresses Joe's older brother Eurreal "Little Brother" Montgomery (1906–1985).

38. J. B. Lenoir, "Everybody Wants to Know (Laid Off Blues)" (composer credit: "J. B. Lenoir"), Chicago, 14 September 1955; issued on Chess LP 410; reissued on Chess 2ACMBLP 208.
39. Donovan, p. 212.
40. See the chapter "I Got to Go to That Red Cross Store" in van Rijn (1997), pp. 43–65.
41. Frigidaire (since 1916) is a brand of heating and cooling products. They were the inventors of the first home freezer.
42. One String Sam, "I Need a Hundred Dollars," Detroit, 1956; issued on JVB 40; reissued on Document DOCD 5223.
    One String Sam appeared at the 1973 Ann Arbor Blues Festival, whence the following remake of his song:
    One String Sam, "I Need $100," Ann Arbor, 8 September 1973; issued on Sequel NEXCD 274.
43. The Treniers (vocal Cliff Treniers), "(We Want a) Rock and Roll President" (composer credit: "Robert Colby–Jack Wolf"), 7 August 1956; issued on Vik 0227; reissued on Bear Family BCD 15418.
44. Candyman McGuirt and His Band (vocalist Geneva Vallier), "He's a Friend" (composer credit: "Wiltz" [James Wiltz, Rising Star Gospel Singer]), San Francisco, c. Sept 1956; issued on Irma 104.
    This song is an adaptation of the Sammy Gallop–Jerry Livingston composition "Wake the Town and Tell the People." Les Baxter had a hit with it in 1955 and Dinah Washington was to record it in 1961.
45. Burk, p. 170.
46. Ibid., p. 168.
47. Ambrose, p. 419.
48. Ibid., p. 452.
49. Roosevelt Sykes, "Sputnik" (composer credit: "Pickard–Buckalew"), Memphis, 1957; issued on House of Sound C&S 505; reissued on Blues Documents BDCD 6050.
    A later version of the same song is:
    Roosevelt Sykes, "Satellite Baby," Newark, NJ, 14 September 1960; issued on Bluesville 810; reissued on Bluesville LP 1014.
50. Eisenhower, p. 489.
51. Sons of Jehova [sic], "High Cost of Living" (composer credit: "F. Perkins"), 1957; issued on Nashboro 610.
52. B. B. King, "Recession Blues" (composer credit: "B. B. King"), Los Angeles, July 1958; Chess unissued; issued on Chess CAMCD 500.
53. "Consumer and Gross Domestic Price Indexes: 1913 to 1998." No. 1435 from "20th Century Statistics," US Census Bureau, *Statistical Abstract of the United States: 2001*.
54. WPA is the Works Progress Administration (cf. van Rijn (1997), chapter 6). PWA is the Public Works Administration (cf. van Rijn (1997), chapter 8). Triple A (= AAA) is the Agricultural Adjustment Administration. AID is the word "aid" spelled out. PDQ stands for "pretty damn/darn quick"!

55. Tommy Dean (vocalist Joe Buckner), "Recession," Chicago, 27 May 1958; VeeJay unissued; issued on VeeJay CD 718 and P-Vine CD 5271/4; reissued on Agram Blues ABCD 2018.

56. Mr. Bo (= Louis Collins), "Times Hard" (composer credit: "S. Willis–J. Matthews–J. Bennett"), Detroit, 1959/60; Northern 3731.

An unissued take, with minor textual differences, was issued under the title "Hard Times Once More" on Lupine CD 7110.

57. Ambrose, 453.

58. Harmonica George (Robinson), "Sputnik Music" (instrumental), Chicago, 1959; Atomic H unissued; issued on Delmark LP 624.

59. The Lawrence Roberts Singers, "If You Make It to the Moon" (composer credit: "Roberts"), New York City, 23 June 1958; issued on Savoy 4102.

60. Sister Dora Alexander, "Let God's Moon Alone," New Orleans, 8 March 1958; issued on Folkways LP 2461; reissued on Rhino R2 71135.

61. Chris Kenner, "Rocket to the Moon" (composer credit: "Kenner–Burmah"), New Orleans, 1960; issued on Ron 335; reissued on Agram Blues ABCD 2018.

The line about "Nero playing the fiddle while Rome burned" may have been borrowed from Louis Jordan's 23 January 1946 recording "Ain't That Just Like a Woman."

62. Eurreal "Little Brother" Montgomery, "Satellite Blues" (composer credit: "Eurreal Montgomery"), New York City, 1 July 1960; issued on Bluesville LP 1012; reissued on Prestige LP 7807.

Later versions of the same composition are:

Eurreal "Little Brother" Montgomery, "My Electronical Invention Blues," Chicago, 14 July 1960; issued on 77 LP12/21; reissued on Wolf CD 120.296.

Eurreal "Little Brother" Montgomery, "(New) Satellite Blues," Chicago, 6 September 1961; issued on Riverside LP 403; reissued on Original Blues Classics LP 508.

Eurreal "Little Brother" Montgomery, "Satellite Blues" (two versions), Chicago, 29 September 1968; Lakco unissued.

63. Joe Richardson (as "Bob Arnold & His Little Astronaut"), "Z Astronaut," New York City, 1960; issued on Enrica 1009.

64. Ambrose, p. 515.

65. Van Rijn (1997), p. 179.

66. Lightnin' Slim, "'GI' Slim" (composer credit: "J. West" = Jay Miller), Crowley, LA, September 1959; issued on Excello 2169; reissued on Excello LP 8000.

Two alternative takes of this song with similar lyrics remained unissued at the time. They were later issued on Flyright LP 607 ("GI Blues") and Flyright CD 47 ("I'm Goin' Join The Army").

67. John Lee Hooker, "Democrat Man," New York City, 9 February 1960; issued on Riverside LP 321; reissued on Battle LP 6113.

68. Evans (1982), pp. 139–40.

69. Pete Welding, "John Lee Hooker: Me and the Blues," *Down Beat* 35, no. 20 (3 October 1968): 17.

70. Chafe, p. 140.
71. Ambrose, p. 544.

Relevant songs from the Eisenhower era that have not been used are:

Bobby Sue and Her Freeloaders (possibly a pseudonym for Lucille Dalton, Jack Dupree's wife), "Relief Check" (composer credit: "Dalton"), New York City, 1955; issued on Harlem 2335; reissued on Moonshine blp 109.

Marie Taylor/Sleepy King's Orch., "Uncle Sam" (composer credit: "Parker–Daniels"), 1958; issued on Sue 705.

The Gospel Chordettes (lead: Lawrence Roberts), "I Can't Believe It" (composer credit: "Roberts"), New York City, 3 March 1958; issued on Savoy 4096.

Walter Rhodes, "Uncle Sam" (composer credit: "W. Rhodes"), New York City, 1959; issued on Mascot Records M-129.

Chris Kenner, "You Can't Beat Uncle Sam," New Orleans, 1960; issued on Pontchartrain 610.

Jerry McCain, "She's Tough" (composer credit: "Jerry McCain"), Birmingham, AL, 1960; issued on Rex 1014; reissued on Sundown CGLP 709-01

Songs about hard times and the space race in the Eisenhower era that I have not heard are:

Bob Geddins, "Space Moon," Oakland, CA, 1954; issued on Jumping 5001.

Preacher Stephens, "Unemployment Blues," Louisville, KY, 1957; issued on Fran 789.

Bill Parker, "Hard Times No. 2," Oklahoma City, 1960; issued on Showboat 501.

Willie Wright & the Sparklers, "Hard Times," Cincinnati, 27 May 1960; Federal unissued.

6. The Alabama Bus

1. Pee Wee Crayton, "Win-O" (composer credit: "Crayton"), New Orleans, 29 April 1954; issued on Imperial 5297; reissued on Liberty LLSLP 70052.
2. Broonzy and Bruynoghe, p. 71.
3. Army Camp #1615 in Tennessee was named after General Benjamin J. Hill (1825–1880).
4. "Big" Bill Broonzy, "When Do I Get to Be Called a Man," London, England, 27 October 1955; issued on Nixa 2012; reissued on Sequel CD 119.

A year later Bill also recorded the song in the States. The lyrics are similar although the interesting sixth verse is omitted:

"Big" Bill Broonzy, "I Wonder When I'll Get to Be Called a Man," New York City, 1956; issued on Folkways LP 2326.
5. Bastin (1990), pp. 238–40.
6. Ibid., pp. 278–79.
7. Enyatta Holta, "Mr. Black Man" (composer credit: "Enyatta Holta"), New York City, 7 July 1955; issued on Jay-Dee 123; reissued on Krazy Kat KKLP 796.

A demo of "Mr. Black Man" was recorded earlier that month as by "Laverne Holt." It was later issued on Krazy Kat KKLP 802.

8. Guido van Rijn, "The Life Story of Otis Jackson," *Blues & Rhythm* 145 (Christmas 1999): 145–46.

9. "Atty. Sampson and Dr. Bethune Explain Support of Stevenson," *Chicago Defender*, 25 October 1952.

10. Cf. van Rijn (1997), pp. 198, 200, 201 and 241.

11. The African Methodist Episcopal Church.

12. Otis Jackson, The Dixie Hummingbirds, Accomp., "The Life Story of Madame Bethune, Parts 1 and 2" (composer credit: "Otis Jackson"), August 1955; issued on Peacock 1753.

13. "Hundreds Pay Final Tribute to Mrs. Bethune," *Afro-American*, 28 May 1955.

14. "5,000 at Rites on Fla. Campus," *Chicago Defender*, 28 May 1955.

15. Rita Griffin, "Will Hairston Limits Performances to Church," *Michigan Chronicle*, 25 May 1968.

16. "250,000 View Slain Youth's Body," *Chicago Defender*, 10 September 1955.

17. Rev. George W. Lee was a black minister from Belzoni, Mississippi who had helped organize a branch of the NAACP and had also dared to register to vote. (Williams, p. 209.)

18. Willie Reed was the son of a black sharecropper. As a witness he testified that he had seen the accused J. W. Milam, armed with a gun, get water from a well to clean Emmett's blood from the back of the truck. (Williams, p. 48.)

19. Mrs. Mamie Bradley was Emmett Till's mother.

20. Charles C. Diggs (1922-1998) was elected Congressman from Michigan in 1954 and had attended the trial of Emmett Till's murderers.

21. Brother Will Hairston, Hurricane of the Motor City, "My God Don't Like It, Parts 1 & 2," Detroit, late 1955; issued on Church of Christ Recording 1/2; reissued as "The Death Of Emmet Till" [*sic*] (label reads "The Death of Emmet Teal"), on Knowles LP 1,000,000.

22. The Ramparts, "The Death of Emmett Till, Parts 1 & 2" (composer credit: "A. C. Bilbrew"), Los Angeles, c. November 1955; issued on DooTone 382.

23. "We're Not Moving to the Back, Mr. Blake: The Montgomery Bus Boycott," in Williams, pp. 58–89.

24. Bob Laughton and Cedric Hayes, "Post War Gospel Recordings of the 40's & 50's," *Blues Unlimited* 139 (autumn 1980): 37.

25. Brother Will Hairston, Hurricane Of The Motor City, "The Alabama Bus, Parts 1 and 2", Detroit, 1956; issued on J-V-B 44; reissued on Agram Blues ABCD 2018.

26. Brendon, p. 334.

27. Ploski and Kaiser, pp. 321–22.

28. Williams, chapter 4.

29. Lyon, p. 753.

30. Roy Wilkins (1901–1981) was executive director of the NAACP from 1955 to 1977.

31. Blair House, 1651–1653 Pennsylvania Avenue, is the President's Guest House. It was built in 1824 and was named after Francis Preston Blair, who acquired it in 1836. At present it has 112 rooms.

32. Bro. Will Hairston, Hurricane Of The Motor City, "Shout School Children," Detroit, late 1957; issued on Natural 111.
33. Taken from Guido van Rijn, "The Hurricane of the Motor City: The Life Story of Brother Will Hairston," *Blues & Rhythm* 167 (March 2002).
34. Rowe, p. 101.
35. Cf. David Evans, "The Toast in Context," *Journal of American Folklore* 90 (1997).
36. The Flock-Rocker, The Crown Prince of the Blues (= Mitchell Hearns), "Political Prayer Blues" (composer credit: "Mitchell Hearns"), East St. Louis, 1958; issued on Planet 100.
37. Robert Pete Williams, "Yassuh an' Nosuh Blues," Denham Springs, LA, 12 November 1960; unissued. (I have not heard the final seven lines of this song and had to rely on the transcription in Oster, p. 141.)
38. Louisiana Red, "Ride on Red, Ride On" (composer credit: "Glover–Levy–Reig"), New York City, c. October 1962; issued on Roulette 4469; reissued on Polydor LP 2941002.

    Two alternative takes were issued on Sequel CD 213, a slow version with harmonica and a fast one with guitar, both compositions credited to "H. Glover–M. Levy–T. Reig."
39. Lyon, p. 779.
40. Ambrose, p. 548.

Conclusion
1. Van Rijn (1997), p. 191.
2. Leiter, pp. 164–69.
3. Figures are from *Billboard* magazine, as published in Gillett (1971), p. 368.

BIBLIOGRAPHY AND FURTHER READING

Allen, Rick. *Singing in the Spirit: African-American Sacred Quartets in New York City*. Philadelphia: University of Pennsylvania Press, 1991.

Ambrose, Stephen E. *Eisenhower: Soldier and President*. New York: Simon & Schuster, 1990. Reprint, New York: Touchstone, 1991.

Bailey, Harry A., Jr. *Negro Politics in America*. Columbus, OH: Charles E. Merrill Books, 1967.

Barlow, William. *Looking Up at Down: The Emergence of Blues Culture*. Philadelphia: Temple University Press, 1989.

Bastin, Bruce. *Crying for the Carolines*. London: Studio Vista, 1971.

—. *Red River Blues: The Blues Tradition in the Southeast*. Basingstoke, Hampshire, England: Macmillan Press, 1986.

—. *Never Sell a Copyright: Joe Davis and His Role in the New York Music Scene 1916–1978*. Chigwell, Essex, England: Storyville Publications, 1990.

Bell, Bernard W. *The Afro-American Novel and Its Tradition*. Amherst, MA: University of Massachusetts Press, 1987.

Blum, John Morton. *V Was for Victory: Politics and American Culture During World War II*. San Diego, CA: Harcourt Brace Jovanovich, 1976.

Bradford, Perry. *Born with the Blues: His Own Story*. New York: Oak Publications, 1965.

Branch, Taylor. *Parting the Waters: America in the King Years, 1954–63*. New York: Simon & Schuster, 1988. Reprint, New York: Touchstone, 1989.

—. *Pillar of Fire: America in the King Years, 1963–65*. New York: Simon & Schuster, 1998.

Brendon, Piers. *Ike*. New York: Harper and Row, 1986.

Brinkley, Douglas. *Rosa Parks*. New York: Penguin Books, 2000.

Brogan, Hugh. *Longman History of the United States of America*. London: Longman, 1985. Reprint, London: Book Club Associates, 1993.

Broonzy, William, and Yannick Bruynoghe. *Big Bill Blues: Big Bill Broonzy's Story*. London: Cassell & Co., 1955. Reprint, New York: Oak Publications, 1964.

Broughton, Viv. *Black Gospel: An Illustrated History of the Gospel Sound*. Poole, Dorset, England: Blandford Press, 1985.

Bruin, Leo W. *Malvina My Sweet Woman: The Story of Big Joe Williams*. Utrecht, The Netherlands: Oldie Blues, 1974.

Burk, Robert Frederick. *The Eisenhower Administration and Black Civil Rights.* Knoxville, TN: University of Tennessee Press, 1984. Reprint, 1985.

Busch, Noel F. *Adlai E. Stevenson of Illinois.* New York: Farrar, Straus & Young, 1952.

Calt, Stephen. *I'd Rather Be the Devil: Skip James and the Blues.* New York: Da Capo Press, 1994.

Calt, Stephen, and Gayle Wardlow. *King of the Delta Blues: The Life and Music of Charlie Patton.* Newton, NJ: Rock Chapel Press, 1988.

Carawan, Guy and Candie. *Sing for Freedom: The Story of the Civil Rights Movement Through Its Songs.* Bethlehem, PA: Sing Out, 1990.

Chafe, William H. *The Unfinished Journey: America Since World War II.* Oxford: Oxford University Press, 1986. Reprint, New York, 1991.

Charters, Samuel B. *The Country Blues.* New York: Rinehart, 1959. Reprint, New York: Da Capo Press, 1977.

—. *The Poetry of the Blues.* New York: Oak Publications, 1963. Reprint, New York: Avon Books, 1970.

—. *The Bluesmen.* New York: Oak Publications, 1967.

—. *The Legacy of the Blues: A Glimpse into the Art and the Lives of Twelve Great Bluesmen.* New York: Da Capo Press, 1977.

—. *Sweet as the Showers of Rain: The Bluesmen,* Volume II. New York: Oak Publications, 1977.

Cheeseborough, Steve. *Blues Traveling: The Holy Sites of Delta Blues.* Jackson, MS: University Press of Mississippi, 2001.

Chilton, John. *Who's Who of Jazz: Storyville to Swingstreet.* London: Bloomsbury Bookshop, 1972. Reprint, London: Macmillan, 1985.

—. *Let The Good Times Roll: The Story of Louis Jordan and His Music.* London: Quartet Books, 1992.

Cohn, Lawrence, ed. *Nothing but the Blues: The Music and the Musicians.* New York: Abbeville Press, 1993.

Cohodas, Nadine. *Spinning Blues into Gold: The Chess Brothers and the Legendary Chess Records.* New York: St. Martin's Press, 2000.

Colburn, David R. and Jane L. Landers, eds. *The African American Heritage of Florida.* Gainesville: University Press of Florida, 1995.

Congress, Richard. *Blues Mandolin: The Life and Music of Yank Rachell.* Jackson, MS: University Press of Mississippi, 2001.

Courlander, Harold. *Negro Folk Music, USA.* New York: Columbia University Press, 1963.

Cowley, John. *Carnival, Canboulay and Calypso: Traditions in the Making.* Cambridge, England: Cambridge University Press, 1996.

Cowley, John and Paul Oliver. *The New Blackwell Guide to Recorded Blues.* Oxford: Blackwell, 1996.

Danchin, Sebastian. *Blues Boy: The Life and Music of B. B. King.* Jackson, MS: University Press of Mississippi, 1998.

—. *Earl Hooker: Blues Master.* Jackson, MS: University Press of Mississippi, 2001.

Davis, John P., ed. *The American Negro Reference Book.* Englewood Cliffs, NJ: Prentice Hall, 1966.

Dixon, R. M. W., and J. Godrich. *Recording the Blues*. London: Studio Vista, 1970.

Dixon, Robert M. W., John Godrich and Howard W. Rye. *Blues and Gospel Records 1890–1943*. 4th ed., Oxford: Oxford University Press, 1997.

Dixon, Willie, and Don Snowden. *I Am the Blues: The Willie Dixon Story*. London: Quartet Books, 1989.

Donovan, Robert J. *Eisenhower: The Inside Story*. New York: Harper & Brothers, 1956.

Edwards, David "Honeyboy." *The World Don't Owe Me Nothing: The Life and Times of Delta Bluesman Honeyboy Edwards*. Chicago: Chicago Review Press, 1997.

Eisenhower, Dwight D. *Mandate for Change: The White House Years*. London: Heinemann, 1963.

Ellison, Mary. *Extensions of the Blues*. New York: Riverrun Press, 1989.

—. *Lyrical Protest: Black Music's Struggle Against Discrimination*. New York: Praeger, 1989.

Ertegun, Ahmet. *What'd I Say: The Atlantic Story, 50 Years of Music*. New York: Welcome Rain Publishers, 2001.

Evans, David. *Tommy Johnson*. London: Studio Vista, 1971.

—. *Big Road Blues: Tradition and Creativity in the Folk Blues*. Berkeley, CA: University of California Press, 1982.

—. *The Coon in the Box: A Global Folktale in African-American Tradition*. Helsinki, Finland: Academia Scientiarum Fennica, 2001.

Fahey, John. *Charley Patton*. London: Studio Vista, 1970.

Ferrell, Robert H. *The Eisenhower Diaries*. New York: W. W. Norton, 1981.

—. *Harry S. Truman: A Life*. Columbia, MO: University of Missouri Press, 1994.

Ferris, William, Jr. *Blues from the Delta*. London: Studio Vista, 1970.

Ford, Robert. *A Blues Bibliography: The International Literature of an Afro-American Music Genre*. Bromley, Kent, England: Paul Pelletier, 1999.

Frazier, E. Franklin. *The Negro Church in America*. New York: Schocken Books, 1964.

Gallup, George, H. *The Gallup Poll: Public Opinion 1935–1971*, Volume One: *1935–1948*. New York: Random House, 1972.

Garon, Paul. *The Devil's Son-in-Law: The Story of Peetie Wheatstraw and His Songs*. London: Studio Vista, 1971.

—. *Blues and the Poetic Spirit*. London: Eddison Bluesbooks, 1975.

Garon, Paul, and Beth Garon. *Woman with Guitar: Memphis Minnie's Blues*. New York: Da Capo Press, 1992.

Gart, Galen. *First Pressings: The History of Rhythm & Blues* (in nine volumes from 1950 to 1958). Milford, NH: Big Nickel Publications, 1986–1995.

—. *ARLD: The American Record Label Directory and Dating Guide, 1940–1959*. Milford, NH: Big Nickel, 1989.

Gart, Galen and Roy C. Ames. *Duke/Peacock Records: An Illustrated History with Discography*. Milford, NH: Big Nickel, 1990.

Gates, Henry Louis, Jr. *Black Literature and Literary Theory*. New York: Methuen, 1984.

—. *Figures in Black: Words, Signs, and the "Racial" Self*. New York: Oxford University Press, 1987.

—. *The Signifying Monkey: A Theory of Afro-American Literary Criticism*. New York: Oxford University Press, 1988.

George, Nelson. *The Death of Rhythm & Blues*. New York: Random House, 1988.

Gillett, Charlie. *The Sound of the City*. London, England: Sphere Books, 1971.

—, *Making Tracks: The Story of Atlantic Records*, 2nd ed. London: W. H. Allen, 1988.

Glover, Tony, Scott Dirks and Ward Gaines. *Blues with a Feeling: The Little Walter Story*. New York: Routledge, 2002.

Goldman, Roger with David Gallen. *Thurgood Marshall: Justice for All*. New York: Carroll & Graf, 1992.

Gordon, Robert. *It Came from Memphis*. Winchester, MA: Faber and Faber, 1994. Reprint Boston, MA: Faber and Faber, 1995.

—. *Can't Be Satisfied: The Life and Times of Muddy Waters*. Boston, MA: 2002.

Goreau, Laurraine. *Just Mahalia, Baby: The Mahalia Jackson Story*. Waco, TX, 1975. Reprint, Gretna, LA: Pelican Publishing Company, 1984.

Govenar, Allan B., and Jay F. Brakefield. *Deep Ellum and Central Track: Where the Black and White Worlds of Dallas Converged*. Denton, TX: University of North Texas Press, 1998.

Green, Archie. *Only a Miner: Studies in Recorded Coal-Miner Songs*. Urbana, IL: University of Illinois Press, 1972.

Greensmith, Bill. *Henry Townsend: A Blues Life*. Urbana, IL: University of Illinois Press, 1999.

Groom, Bob. *The Blues Revival*. London: Studio Vista, 1971.

Hacker, Andrew. *Two Nations: Black and White, Separate, Hostile, Unequal*. New York: Charles Scribner's Sons, 1992.

Hamby, Alonzo L. *Man of the People: A Life of Harry S. Truman*. New York: Oxford University Press, 1995.

Hannusch, Jeff. *I Hear You Knockin': The Sound of New Orleans Rhythm and Blues*. Ville Platte, LA: Swallow, 1985.

Harris, Michael W. *The Rise of Gospel Blues: The Music of Thomas Andrew Dorsey in the Urban Church*. New York: Oxford University Press, 1992.

Harris, Sheldon. *Blues Who's Who: A Biographical Dictionary of Blues Singers*. New Rochelle, NY: Arlington House, 1979. Reprint, New York: Da Capo Press, 1989.

Harrison, Daphne Duval. *Black Pearls: Blues Queens of the 1920s*. New Brunswick, NJ: Rutgers University Press, 1988.

Haskins, Jim. *Nat King Cole: The Man and His Music*. London: Robson Books, 1986.

Hay, Fred J. *Goin' Back to Sweet Memphis: Conversations with the Blues*. Athens, GA: University of Georgia Press, 2001.

Heilbut, Anthony. *The Gospel Sound: Good News and Bad Times*. Garden City, NY: Anchor Press/Doubleday, 1971. Reprint, New York: Limelight Edition, 1985.

Jackson, Bruce. *Wake Up Dead Man: Afro-American Worksongs from Texas Prisons*. Cambridge, MA: Harvard University Press, 1972.

—. *Get Your Ass in the Water and Swim Like Me: Narrative Poetry from Black Oral Tradition*. Cambridge, MA: Harvard University Press, 1974.

Kirk, Elise K. *Music at the White House: A History of the American Spirit*. Urbana, IL: University of Illinois Press, 1986.

Kostelanetz, Richard, ed. *The B. B. King Companion: Five Decades of Commentary*. New York: Simon & Schuster Macmillan, 1997.

Kubik, Gerhard. *Africa and the Blues*. Jackson, MS: University Press of Mississippi, 1999.

Laughton, Robert, and Cedric J. Hayes. *Gospel Records, 1943 to 1969: A Black Music Discography*. London: Record Information Services, 1992.

Lawson, Steven F. *Running for Freedom: Civil Rights and Black Politics in America Since 1941*. New York: McGraw Hill, 1991, 2nd ed. 1997.

Leadbitter, Mike, ed. *Nothing but the Blues*. London: Hannover Books, 1971.

Leadbitter, Mike, and Neil Slaven. *Blues Records 1943–1970*, Volume One: *A to K*. London: Hannover Books, 1987.

Leadbitter, Mike, Neil Slaven, and Leslie Fancourt. *Blues Records 1943–1970*, Volume Two: *L to Z*. London: Record Information Services, 1994.

Leiter, Robert D. *The Musicians and Petrillo*. New York: Bookman Associates, 1953.

Lemann, Nicholas. *The Promised Land: The Great Black Migration and How It Changed America*. New York: Alfred A. Knopf, 1991.

Levine, Lawrence W. *Black Culture and Black Consciousness: Afro-American Folk Thought from Slavery to Freedom*. Oxford, England: Oxford University Press, 1977. Reprint, New York, 1980.

—. *The Unpredictable Past: Explorations in American Cultural History*. New York: Oxford University Press, 1993.

Lieb, Sandra. *Mother of the Blues: A Study of Ma Rainey*. Amherst, MA: University of Massachusetts Press, 1981.

Lomax, Alan. *The Land Where the Blues Began*. London: Methuen, 1993.

Lomax, John A., and Alan Lomax. *Our Singing Country: A Second Volume of American Ballads and Folk Songs*. New York: The Macmillan Company, 1949.

Lorenz, Wolfgang. *Bluebird Blues: The Blues of John Lee "Sonny Boy" Williamson*. Bonn, Germany: Moonshine Books, 1986.

Lornell, Kip. *Happy in the Service of the Lord: Afro-American Gospel Quartets in Memphis*. Chicago: University of Illinois Press, 1988.

—. *Virginia's Blues, Country & Gospel Records 1902–1943: An Annotated Discography*. Lexington, KY: University of Kentucky Press, 1989.

Lubin, Jacques and Danny Garçon. *Louis Jordan Discographie, 1929–1974*. Levallois-Perret, France: C.L.A.R.B., 1987.

Lyon, Peter. *Eisenhower: Portrait of the Hero*. Boston: Little, Brown and Company, 1974.

MacArthur, Douglas. *Reminiscences*. New York: McGraw-Hill, 1964.

McCullough, David. *Truman*. New York: Simon & Schuster, 1992.

McGrath, Bob. *The R&B Indies*, Volume One: *A–K*. West Vancouver, Canada: Eyeball Productions, 2000.

—. *The R&B Indies*, Volume Two: *L–Z*. West Vancouver, Canada: Eyeball Productions, 2000.

Macleod, R. R. *Yazoo 1-20*. Edinburgh, Scotland: Pat, 1988, 2nd ed. 2002.

—. *Yazoo 21-83*. Edinburgh: Pat, 1992.

—. *Document Blues – 1*. Edinburgh: Pat, 1994.

——. *Document Blues – 2*. Edinburgh: Pat, 1995.

——. *Document Blues – 3*. Edinburgh: Pat, 1996.

——. *Document Blues – 4*. Edinburgh: Pat, 1996.

——. *Document Blues – 5*. Edinburgh: Pat, 1998.

——. *Document Blues – 6*. Edinburgh: Pat, 1999.

——. *Document Blues – 7*. Edinburgh: Pat, 2000.

——. *Document Blues – 8*. Edinburgh: Pat, 2001.

——. *Document Blues – 9*. Edinburgh: Pat, 2002.

——. *Blues Document*. Edinburgh: Pat, 1997.

Mahony, Dan. *Columbia 13/14000-D Series: A Numerical Listing*. Highland Park, NJ: Walter C. Allen, 1961.

Malone, Bill C. *Country Music, USA*, 2nd ed. Austin: University of Texas Press, 1987.

McMillen, Neil R. *Dark Journey: Black Mississippians in the Age of Jim Crow*. Urbana, IL: University of Illinois Press, 1989. Reprint, 1990.

Meeker, David. *Jazz in the Movies*. New York: Da Capo, 1981.

Miller, Merle. *Plain Speaking: An Oral Biography of Harry S. Truman*. New York: Berkley Publishing Corporation, 1974.

Moore, Allan, ed. *The Cambridge Companion to Blues and Gospel Music*. Cambridge, England: Cambridge University Press, 2002

Moore, Dave. *Brown Skin Gal: The Story of Barbecue Bob*. Ter Aar, The Netherlands: Agram Blues, 1976.

Mullen, Robert W. *Blacks in America's Wars: The Shift in Attitudes from the Revolutionary War to Vietnam*. New York: Anchor Foundation, 1973. Reprint, 1990.

Murray, Albert. *Stomping the Blues*. London: Paladin, 1976.

Myrdal, Gunnar. *An American Dilemma: The Negro Problem and Modern Democracy*. New York: Harper and Row, 1944.

Napier, Simon, ed. *Backwoods Blues*. Bexhill on Sea, England: Blues Unlimited, 1968.

Oakley, Giles. *The Devil's Music: A History of the Blues*. London: BBC, 1976.

Obrecht, Jas, ed. *Rollin' and Tumblin': The Postwar Blues Guitarists*. San Francisco: Miller Freeman Books, 2000.

Odum, Howard W., and Guy B. Johnson. *The Negro and His Songs: A Study of Typical Negro Songs in the South*. Chapel Hill, NC: University of North Carolina Press, 1925. Reprint, Hatboro, PA: Folklore Associates, 1972.

——. *Negro Workaday Songs*. Chapel Hill, NC: University of North Carolina Press, 1926.

Oliver, Paul. *Bessie Smith*. London: Cassell, 1959.

——. *Blues Fell This Morning: Meaning in the Blues*. London: Cassell, 1960. Reprint, Cambridge, England: Cambridge University Press, 1991.

——. *Conversation with the Blues*. London: Cassell, 1967.

——. *Screening the Blues: Aspects of the Blues Tradition*. London: Cassell & Co., 1968. Reprint as *The Blues Tradition: A Fascinating Study of the Richest Vein of Black Folk Music in America*. New York: Oak Publications, 1970.

——. *The Story of the Blues*. London: Barrie and Jenkins, 1969.

——. *Savannah Syncopators: African Retentions in the Blues*. London: Studio Vista, 1970.

—. *Songsters & Saints: Vocal Traditions on Race Records.* Cambridge, England: Cambridge University Press, 1984.

—. *Blues off the Record: Thirty Years of Blues Commentary.* Tunbridge Wells, England: Baton Press, 1984. Reprint, New York: Da Capo Press, 1988.

—. ed. *The Blackwell Guide to Blues Records.* Cambridge, England: Blackwell, 1989.

Olsson, Bengt. *Memphis Blues.* London: Studio Vista, 1970.

O'Reilly, Kenneth. *Nixon's Piano: Presidents and Racial Politics from Washington to Clinton.* New York: The Free Press, 1995.

Oster, Harry. *Living Country Blues.* Detroit: Folklore Associates, 1969.

Ottenheimer, Harriet J. *Cousin Joe: Blues from New Orleans.* Chicago: University of Chicago Press, 1987.

Palmer, Robert. *Deep Blues.* New York: Viking Press, 1981.

Parmet, Herbert S. *Eisenhower and the American Crusades.* New York: Collier–Macmillan Ltd, 1972.

Pearson, Barry Lee. *Virginia Piedmont Blues: The Lives and Art of Two Virginia Bluesmen.* Philadelphia, PA: University of Philadelphia Press, 1990.

Pemberton, William E. *Harry S. Truman: Fair Dealer & Cold Warrior.* Boston: Twayne Publishers, 1989.

Ploski, Harry A., and Ernest Kaiser. *The Negro Almanac.* New York: Wiley, 1971.

Pratt, Ray. *Rhythm and Resistance: Explorations in the Political Uses of Popular Music.* New York: Praeger, 1990.

Price, Sammy. *What Do They Want? A Jazz Autobiography.* Wheatley, Oxford: Bayou Press, 1989.

Pusey, Merlo J. *Eisenhower the President.* New York: Macmillan, 1956.

Raben, Erik.

—. *Jazz Records 1942–80: A Discography*, Volume 1: *A–Ba.* Copenhagen, Denmark: JazzMedia Aps, 1989.

—. *Jazz Records 1942–80: A Discography*, Volume 2: *Bar–Br.* Copenhagen, Denmark: JazzMedia Aps, 1991.

—. *Jazz Records 1942–80: A Discography*, Volume 3: *Bro–Cl.* Copenhagen, Denmark: JazzMedia Aps, 1990.

—. *Jazz Records 1942–80: A Discography*, Volume 4: *Cla–Da.* Copenhagen, Denmark: JazzMedia Aps, 1993.

—. *Jazz Records 1942–80: A Discography*, Volume 5: *Dav–El.* Copenhagen, Denmark: JazzMedia Aps, 1995.

—. *Jazz Records 1942–80: A Discography*, Volume 6: *Duke Ellington.* Copenhagen, Denmark: JazzMedia Aps, 1992.

—. *Jazz Records 1942–80: A Discography*, Volume 7: *Ell–Fra.* Copenhagen, Denmark: JazzMedia Aps, 1999.

Ramsey, Frederic, Jr. *Been Here and Gone.* New Brunswick, NJ: Rutgers University Press, 1960. Reprint, 1969.

Raper, Arthur F. *Preface to Peasantry: A Tale of Two Black Belt Counties.* Chapel Hill, NC: University of North Carolina Press, 1936.

Ratner, Sidney. *Taxation and Democracy in America*. New York: Wiley, 1967. Reprint, New York: Octagon Books, 1980.

Rijn, Guido van. *Roosevelt's Blues: African-American Blues and Gospel Songs on FDR*. Jackson, MS: University Press of Mississippi, 1997.

Rookmaaker, H. R. *Jazz Blues Spirituals*. Wageningen, The Netherlands: Zomer & Keunings, 1960.

Rosenberg, Bruce. *The Art of the American Folk Preacher*. New York: Oxford University Press, 1970.

Rowe, Mike. *Chicago Breakdown*. London: Eddison Bluesbooks, 1973.

Russell, Tony. *Blacks, Whites and Blues*. London: Studio Vista, 1970.

Rust, Brian. *The Victor Master Book*, Volume 2: *(1925–1936)*. Hatch End, Middlesex, England: self-published. Reprint, Highland Park, NJ: Walter C. Allen, 1974.

—. *Jazz Records, 1897–1942*, Volume 1. New York: Arlington House, 1978.

—. *Jazz Records, 1897–1942*, Volume 2. New York: Arlington House, 1978.

—. *The American Record Label Book*. New Rochelle, NY, 1978. Reprint, New York: Da Capo, 1984.

Ryan, Marc. *Trumpet Records: An Illustrated History with Discography*. Milford, NH: Big Nickel, 1992.

Sackheim, Eric. *The Blues Line: A Collection of Blues Lyrics from Leadbelly to Muddy Waters*. Japan: Grossman Publishers, 1969. Reprint, New York: Schirmer Books, 1975.

Sacré, Robert, ed. *The Voice of the Delta: Charley Patton and the Mississippi Blues Traditions. Influences and Comparisons*. Liège, Belgium: Presses Universitaires de Liège, 1987.

—. *Les Negro Spirituals et les Gospel Songs*. Paris: Presses Universitaires de France, 1993.

—. *Saints and Sinners: Religion, Blues and (D)evil in African-American Music and Literature*. Liège, Belgium: Société Liégeoise de Musicologie, 1996.

Salem, James M. *The Late Great Johnny Ace and the Transition from R&B to Rock 'n' Roll*. Urbana and Chicago: University of Illinois Press, 1999.

Sanjek, Russell, and David Sanjek. *American Popular Music Business in the 20th Century*. Oxford, England: Oxford University Press, 1991.

Schainman Siegel, Dorothy. *The Glory Road: The Story of Josh White*. New York: Harcourt Brace Jovanovich, c. 1982. Reprint, White Hall, VA: Shoe Tree Press, an imprint of Betterway Publications, 1991.

Scheiber, Harry N., Harold G. Vatter and Harold Underwood Faulkner. *American Economic History*. New York: Harper & Row, 1976.

Scherman, Tony. *Backbeat: Earl Palmer's Story*. Washington, DC: Smithsonian Institution, 1999.

Schlesinger, Arthur M. Jr. *History of American Presidential Elections, 1789–1968*, Volume IV. New York: Chelsea House, 1971.

Schulte Nordholt, J. W. *Het Volk Dat in Duisternis Wandelt: De Geschiedenis van de Negers in Amerika*. Arnhem, The Netherlands: Van Loghum Slaterus, 1956. Reprint, 1957.

Seeger, Pete and Bob Reiser. *Everybody Says Freedom: A History of the Civil Rights Movement in Songs and Pictures*. New York: W. W. Norton, 1989.

Shaar Murray, Charles. *Boogie Man: The Adventures of John Lee Hooker in the American Twentieth Century*. London, England: Viking Press, 1999.

Shaw, Arnold. *Honkers and Shouters: The Golden Years of Rhythm and Blues*. New York: Collier Books, 1978. Reprint, New York: Macmillan, 1986.

Silvester, Peter. *A Left Hand Like God: A Study of Boogie-Woogie*. London: Quartet Books, 1988.

Smith, Chris. *Hit the Right Lick: The Recordings of Big Bill Broonzy*. Bromham, Bedford, England: *Blues & Rhythm* magazine, 1996.

—. *That's the Stuff: The Recordings of Brownie McGhee, Sonny Terry, Stick McGhee and J.C. Burris*. Shetland, Scotland: The Housay Press, 1999.

Southern, Eileen. *The Music of Black Americans: A History*. New York: W. W. Norton & Co., 1971, 3rd ed. 1997.

Spragens, William C. *Popular Images of American Presidents*. New York: Greenwood Press, 1988.

Springer, Robert. *Le Blues Authentique: Son Histoire et ses Thèmes*. France: Éditions Filipacchi, 1985.

—. *Fonctions Sociales du Blues*. Marseille, France: Éditions Parenthèses, 1999.

—. ed. *The Lyrics in African American Popular Music/Le Texte dans la Musique Populaire Afro-Américaine*. Bern and New York: Peter Lang, 2001.

Sterner, Richard. *The Negro's Share: A Study of Income, Consumption, Housing, and Public Assistance*. New York: Harper and Brothers, 1943.

Stewart-Baxter, Derrick. *Ma Rainey and the Classic Blues Singers*. London: Studio Vista, 1970.

Sullivan, Patricia. *Days of Hope: Race and Democracy in the New Deal Era*. Chapel Hill: University of North Carolina Press, 1996.

Taft, Michael. *Blues Lyric Poetry: A Concordance*. New York: Garland Publishing, 1983.

Taj Mahal with Stephen Foehr. *Taj Mahal: Autobiography of a Bluesman*. London: Sanctuary, 2002.

Tipaldi, Art. *Children of the Blues*. San Francisco, CA: Backbeat Books, 2002.

Titon, Jeff Todd. *Early Downhome Blues: A Musical and Cultural Analysis*. Urbana, IL: University of Illinois Press, 1977. Reprint, 1979.

Tooze, Sandra B. *Muddy Waters: The Mojo Man*. Toronto, Ontario, Canada: ECW Press, 1997.

Townley, Eric. *Tell Your Story: A Dictionary of Jazz and Blues Recordings 1917–1950*. Chigwell, Essex, England: Storyville Publications, 1976.

—. *Tell Your Story No. 2: A Dictionary of Mainstream Jazz and Blues Recordings 1951–1975*. Chigwell, Essex, England: Storyville Publications, 1987.

Tracy, Steven C. *Going to Cincinnati: A History of the Blues in the Queen City*. Chicago, IL: University of Illinois Press, 1993.

—. ed. *Write Me a Few of Your Lines: A Blues Reader*. Amherst: University of Massachusetts Press, 1999.

Traum, Happy. *Guitar Styles of Brownie McGhee*. New York: Oak Publications, 1971.

Truman, Margaret. *Harry S. Truman*. New York: William Morrow & Company, 1973.

Vreede, Max E. *Paramount 12000/13000 Series*. London: Storyville Publications, 1971.

Wald, Elijah. *Josh White: Society Blues*. Amherst: University of Massachusetts Press, 2000.

Ward, Andrew. *Dark Midnight When I Rise: How Black Music Changed America and the World.* New York: Farrar, Straus and Giroux, 2000. Reprint, New York: Amistad, an imprint of HarperCollins, 2001.

Ward, Brian. *Just My Soul Responding: Rhythm and Blues, Black Consciousness and Race Relations.* London: UCL Press, 1998.

—, ed. *Media, Culture, and the Modern African American Freedom Struggle.* Gainesville: University Press of Florida, 2001.

Ward, Brian and Tony Badger, eds. *The Making of Martin Luther King and the Civil Rights Movement.* New York: New York University Press: 1996.

Wardlow, Gayle Dean. *Chasin' that Devil Music: Searching for the Blues.* San Francisco: Miller Freeman, 1998.

Washington, Joseph R., Jr. *Black Sects and Cults.* New York: Anchor Press, Doubleday & Company, 1972.

Wentworth, Harold, and Stuart Berg Flexner. *Dictionary of American Slang.* New York: Simon & Schuster, 1960.

White, George R. *Bo Diddley: Living Legend.* Chessington, Surrey, England: Castle Communications, 1995.

Williams, Juan. *Eyes on the Prize: America's Civil Right Years, 1954–1965.* New York: Viking Penguin. Reprint, Harmondsworth, Middlesex, England: Penguin, 1988.

Wolfe, Charles, and Kip Lornell. *The Life and Legend of Leadbelly.* New York: HarperCollins, 1992.

Wright, Laurie. *Storyville 1996–7.* Chigwell, Essex, England: Storyville Club, 1997.

—. *Storyville 1998–9.* Chigwell, Essex, England: Storyville Club, 1999.

—. *Storyville 2000–1.* Chigwell, Essex, England: Storyville Club, 2001.

—. *OKeh Race Records: The 8000 "Race" Series.* Chigwell, Essex, England: L. Wright, 2001.

Young, Alan. *Woke Me Up This Morning: Black Gospel Singers and the Gospel Life.* Jackson, MS: University Press of Mississippi, 1997.

—. *The Pilgrim Jubilees.* Jackson, MS: University Press of Mississippi, 2002.

Zur Heide, Karl Gert. *Deep South Piano: The Story of Little Brother Montgomery.* London: Studio Vista, 1970.

Articles

Astbury, Ray. "Bilbo Is Dead." *Juke Blues* 6 (autumn 1986): 23.

Broven, John. "J. B. Lenoir." In Mike Leadbitter, ed. *Nothing but the Blues.* London: Hannover Books, 1971: 36.

Charters, Samuel B. Sleeve notes to *Introducing Memphis Willie B.* Bluesville LP 1034.

Cowley, John. Review of *The Life and Times of Leadbelly* by Charles Wolfe and Kip Lornell. *Blues & Rhythm* 78 (April 1993): 39.

Dawson, Jim. "Jessie Mae Robinson." *Juke Blues* 22 (winter/spring 1991): 8–12.

Evans, David. "The Toast in Context." *Journal of American Folklore* 90 (1997).

Griffin, Rita. "Will Hairston Limits Performances to Church." *Michigan Chronicle* (25 May 1968).

Hannusch, Jeff. "The Legend of Jody: Ain't No Sense in Going Home, Jody's Got Your Girl and Gone." *Goldmine* 20, no. 8, issue 358 (15 April 1994): 68, 194.

Iglauer, Bruce, Jim O'Neal and Nigel Watson. "Bobo Jenkins Interviewed at the Detroit Free Blues Festival in August 1970." *Living Blues* 3 (autumn 1970): 9–10.

Killeen, Sean. "A Union Man." *Lead Belly Letter* 5 #1/2 (Ithaca, NY, winter/spring 1995).

Kochakian, Dan. "Little Joe Cook: The Original Thriller, an Interview with the Composer." *Whiskey, Women, And . . .* 15 (December 1985): 20–21.

Korstadt, Robert and Nelson Lichtenstein. "Opportunities Found and Lost: Labor, Radicals, and the Early Civil Rights Movement." *Journal of American History* 75, issue 3 (1988): 786–811.

Laughton, Bob and Cedric Hayes. "Post War Gospel Recordings of the 40's & 50's." *Blues Unlimited* 139 (autumn 1980): 37.

Leadbitter, Mike. Review of Spivey LP 1009. *Blues Unlimited* 53 (May 1968): 25.

—. "Mike's Blues." *Blues Unlimited* 106 (February/March 1974): 18.

Lowry, Pete. Sleeve notes to *Texas Guitar: From Dallas to L.A.* Atlantic ATL LP 40398 (1972).

McAlpin, A. Harry, White House correspondent. "President Truman Favors FEPC." *New York Amsterdam News* (21 April 1945).

Melvin, Bob. "Big Bands Banned." Published on the Internet at www.recordfinders.com

Moon, Henry Lee. "Election Post Mortem." *Crisis* 57 (December 1952): 616–17.

O'Brien, Justin. "The Dark Road of Floyd Jones." *Living Blues* 58 (winter 1983): 12.

O'Neal, Jim. "Al Benson Obituary." *Living Blues* 39 (July/August 1978): 57.

Orr, Eileen. "Bobo Jenkins Obituary." *Living Blues* 63 (January/February 1985): 56.

Pearson, Barry Lee. "One Day You're Gonna Hear About Me: The H-Bomb Ferguson Story." Interview with H-Bomb Ferguson (21 September 1985). *Living Blues* 69 (1985): 17.

Rijn, Guido van. "Boogie Uproar. (The Life Story of Clarence 'Gatemouth' Brown)." *Blues Unlimited* 92 (June 1972): 8.

—. "The Guitar Junior/Lonnie Brooks Story." *Blues Unlimited* 117 (January/February 1976): 11.

—. "One Blues After Another Fell from My Pen: The Life Story of Thomas A. Dorsey." *Blues & Rhythm* 47 (October 1989): 4–6.

—. "The Apollo on Video." *Blues & Rhythm* 57 (Christmas 1990): 7.

—. "Mr Crump and the Memphis Jug Band." *Blues & Rhythm* 62 (July 1991): 4–6.

—. "Jim Jackson's Vaudeville Sketch." *Blues & Rhythm* 79 (May 1993): 21.

—. "Denomination Blues: Texas Gospel with Novelty Accompaniment by Washington Phillips." In Robert Sacré, ed. *Saints and Sinners: Religion, Blues and (D)evil in African-American Music and Literature.* Liège, Belgium: Société Liégeoise de Musicologie, 1996.

—. "The Life Story of Otis Jackson." *Blues & Rhythm* 145 (Christmas 1999): 4–5.

—. "Clara Smith Eyewitness Account 1926." *Juke Blues* 46 (spring 2000): 52–53.

—. "Praying for the Pastor: The Life of Rev. J. M. Gates." *Living Blues* 152 (July/August 2000): 48–51.

—. "Blues with Class: The Life Story of Joe Pullum." *Blues & Rhythm* 153 (October 2000): 153–54.

—. "The Dollar Has the Blues: Deflation and Inflation in African American Blues Songs." In Robert Springer, ed. *The Lyrics in African American Popular Music/Le Texte dans la Musique Populaire Afro-Américaine.* Bern and New York: Peter Lang, 2001.

—. "Climbing the Mountain Top: African-American Blues and Gospel Songs from the Civil Rights Years." In Brian Ward, ed. *Media, Culture, and the Modern African American Freedom Struggle.* Gainesville: University Press of Florida, 2001: chapter 6.

—. "From the Archives . . . Sunnyland Slim Interview." *Blues & Rhythm* 165 (Christmas 2001): 4–6.

—. "Expatriate Blues: Little Willie Littlefield." *Living Blues* 161 (February 2002): 30–36.

—. "The Hurricane of the Motor City: The Life Story of Brother Will Hairston." *Blues & Rhythm* 167 (March 2002): 14–17.

—. "Junior Wells: Another Vintage Interview from the Files of Guido van Rijn." *Blues & Rhythm* 174 (November 2002): 4–6.

—. "Imagery in the Lyrics." In Allan Moore, ed. *Cambridge Companion to Blues and Gospel Music.* Cambridge, England: Cambridge University Press, 2002: chapter 10.

—. "The Real Washington Phillips." *Blues & Rhythm* 177 (March 2003): 4–5.

—. "The Black Man the Father of Civilization: The Story of Rev. James Morris Webb, A.M.D.D." *Blues & Rhythm* 182 (September 2003): 16–19.

Rijn, Guido van, and Victor Pearlin. "Bobbin Records." *Blues & Rhythm* 152 (September 2000): 4–6.

Rijn, Guido van, and Chris Smith. "Jesse Thomas Live and Well in Utrecht." *Blues & Rhythm* 58 (February 1991): 16–17.

Rijn, Guido van and Max Vreede. "The Paramount L Master Series." *78 Quarterly* 9 (1996): 67–87.

Russell, Tony. "The Deputy High Sheriff from Hell, Harmon Ray." *Living Blues* 26 (March/April 1976): 14–15.

Seroff, Doug. Sleeve notes to *Birmingham Quartet Anthology.* Clanka Lanka 2LP 144.001/2 (1980).

Waterman, Dick. "Saying Goodbye to Four Beloved Musicians in a Sad Week for the Blues." *Blues Access* 9 (spring 1992): 26–27.

Welding, Pete. "John Lee Hooker: Me and the Blues." *Down Beat* 35, no. 20 (3 October 1968): 15–17, 38.

White, John. "Civil Rights in Conflict: The 'Birmingham Plan' and the Freedom Train, 1947." *The Alabama Review* (April 1999): 121–41.

Wolfe, Charles. "Nuclear Country: The Atomic Bomb in Country Music." *The Journal of Country Music* VI, no. 4 (January 1978): 4–21.

Newspapers

Afro-American
Atlanta Constitution
Atlanta Daily World
Chicago Defender
Commercial Appeal
Michigan Chronicle
New York Amsterdam News
New York Times

Magazines

Alabama Review
Block
Blues Access
Blues & Rhythm
Blues Revue
Blues Unlimited
Blues World
Crisis
Down Beat
Georgia Historical Quarterly
Goldmine
Jefferson
Journal of American Folklore
Journal of American History
Journal of Country Music
Juke Blues
Lead Belly Letter
Living Blues
Old Time Music
R&B Monthly
78 Quarterly
Soul Bag
Variety
Whiskey, Women, And . . .

SONG INDEX

ARTIST INDEX

GENERAL INDEX